Making Music

IN THE

Polish Tatras

Making Music
✦ IN THE ✦
Polish Tatras

Tourists, Ethnographers, and Mountain Musicians

Timothy J. Cooley

INDIANA UNIVERSITY PRESS

Bloomington and Indianapolis

This book is a publication of

Indiana University Press
601 North Morton Street
Bloomington, IN 47404-3797 USA

http://iupress.indiana.edu

Telephone orders   800-842-6796
Fax orders   812-855-7931
Orders by e-mail   iuporder@indiana.edu

© 2005 by Timothy J. Cooley

All rights reserved

The paper used in this publication meets the minimum
requirements of American National Standard for Information
Sciences—Permanence of Paper for Printed Library Materials,
ANSI Z39.48-1984.

MANUFACTURED IN THE UNITED STATES OF AMERICA

Library of Congress Cataloging-in-Publication Data

Cooley, Timothy J., 1962–
Making music in the Polish Tatras : tourists, ethnographers, and
mountain musicians / Timothy J. Cooley.
p. cm.
Includes bibliographical references (p.   ) and index.
ISBN 0-253-34489-1 (cloth : alk. paper)
1. Folk music—Tatra Mountains (Slovakia and Poland)—History and
criticism.   2. Tatra Mountains (Slovakia and Poland)—Social life and
customs.   3. Ethnomusicology.   I. Title.
ML3611.T38.C66 2005
781.62'9185043862—dc22
                                                          2004014534

1 2 3 4 5 10 09 08 07 06 05

For the people of Podhale

Górole, górole
góralsko muzyka
cały świat obyjdzies
nima takiej nika.

Contents

Preface and Acknowledgments

This book is a work of ethnography. Like all ethnographies it is a collaborative project relying on the generous contributions of many individuals and effectively having numerous co-authors. These contributors include the many musicians, dancers, and community members in the towns and villages in or near the Polish Tatras who endured my presence, questions, cameras, microphones, and so forth. Thank you. My gratitude and debt extends to individuals in Górale diaspora communities, especially in Chicago and Toronto. I also wish to express sincere gratitude to my teachers, to my students, and to my family and friends who have contributed in material, intellectual, and unfathomable ways to this book. You know who you are; thank you.

My fascination with the people and music identified with the Polish Tatras began in Chicago, Illinois, when in 1989 I first met individuals who identified themselves as Górale or Tatra Mountain Highlanders. At the time I was working for the Illinois Arts Council as a folklorist and ethnomusicologist researching what that state agency called "ethnic and folk arts." Meeting Poles in Chicago is not surprising—the windy city hosts a large population of Poles second only to Warsaw. What surprised me about the Polish Górale I met was their desire and ability to retain a distinct regional identity as Tatra mountaineers even when so far removed from their beloved mountains. One of the ways many Górale expressed their identity was through a vigorous music and dance quite distinct from any music that I was familiar with at the time. And yet the music resonated with another genre associated with mountains—American old-time stringband music with real and nostalgic links to the Appalachian Mountains. Górale violin styles featuring angular melodies that are pushed and pulled rhythmically within strongly articulated meters remind me of American old-time fiddle styles, a comparison first suggested by some of the Górale violinists I met in Chicago. Actively playing old-time music at the time on the banjo and guitar, perhaps I was aesthetically prepared to like Górale music, a music that seems either to attract or repulse listeners, leaving little room for ambivalence.

In Chicago the first Górale musicians I met included *prymista* (lead violinist) Władysław Styrczula-Maśniak and his student at the time, Andrzej Tokarz. A fine violinist, basy, bagpipe, and Górale flute player, Andrzej is a real mover and shaker in the Chicago Górale community. He keeps busy but has never refused me a request for information or assistance. It was Władysław's passionate and virtuosic violin playing that first inspired the wonder that would lead me to Poland. Władysław not only opened my ears, but he also opened the doors to his house in Chicago, as well as the doors to the homes of his large and exceptionally talented family in Poland. For these reasons, the Styrczula-Maśniak family name figures prominently in this book. Another family of musicians and dancers who hosted me on occasion when I needed a place to stay in Chicago was the Maciata-Lassak family: violinist Halina Maciata; her sister Janina, a dancer; and the brothers who became their husbands, respectively Tomasz and Janusz Lassak. Halina, who wrote a fine master's thesis on Górale flutes, was particularly helpful with a number of my projects by offering her language and music skills. In Chicago and in Poland I also benefited from the generosity and musicianship of Maria and Andrzej Krzeptowski-Bohac, their children, and their many students. The web of contacts among the Górale diaspora extended to Toronto, beginning with dancer and choreographer Tadeusz Zdybal. I am deeply grateful to all those in these communities, named here and left unnamed, who taught me so much. Thank you all.

In Poland, as in Chicago, I generally experienced individuals within their families. The first place I lived in the Tatra region was with Władysław Styrczula-Maśniak's father, Józef. At the time I was learning Polish and was far from conversant. For this reason I imagine I was not his easiest guest, but Józef, together with his warm and witty daughter Anna, were gracious hosts. Later I lived with Tadeusz Styrczula-Maśniak, Władysław's uncle and Józef's brother, for several extended periods. Tadeusz is a master dancer, singer, and basy player, as well as a Tatra Mountain wilderness ranger and an excellent skier. He taught me much about life in the Tatras. In his beautiful log house I enjoyed the hospitality and wisdom of his wife, Stanisława, and their son Edward. Edward is a true intellectual and an accomplished ethnographer who helped me both as a colleague and an adviser. Edward's brother Wojtek, together with his wife, Ewa, have also hosted me in their warm home, situated high in the hills of the village Kościelisko with an exceptional view of the Tatras.

I thank my mentor and friend, Józef Staszel, and his wife, Maria, son Paweł, and daughter-in-law Stanisława Trebunia-Staszel. This exceptional family of musicians and thinkers is a model of passionate and compassionate engaged living. A perfect winter day for me was when Józef would teach me to play a tune on the violin, take me to his favorite spot of wilderness for an hour or so of cross-country skiing, and then see how well I remembered the tune when we arrived home again. I hope to be such a fine teacher someday. An ethnographer in her own right (see references cited), Stanisława speaks English well and helped me out on many occasions when my Polish failed. Paweł, to his professional colleagues and students, is a professor of nuclear physics, but to me he is a fine violinist in the Górale tradition, and a kind and generous gentleman.

A third family, again of musicians and otherwise accomplished individuals, that was exceptionally helpful to me in Poland is the Trebunia-Tutka family. I have already mentioned Stanisława (Trebunia-Staszel), whom I met on the same day (my first ever in the Tatras) in 1992 that I met her cousin Krzysztof and her uncle Władysław. This father and son team of violinists, together with other family members, is quite well known throughout Poland and beyond. Yet both take hours each week to teach young children the very basics of the local music practices. I had the pleasure of rehearsing with one of Krzysztof's children's ensembles when living in Poland. Krzysztof and Władysław also welcomed me into their homes on several occasions to talk about music and culture in the Tatras. See especially chapters 4 and 5.

I wish to thank the Karpiel family, especially Zofia Karpiel (the "Queen of the Tatras"), Jan Karpiel-Bułecka, Anna Karpiel-Bułecka, Bolesław Karpiel-Bułecka, and others from this extended family. Each of these individuals welcomed me into their homes and shared with me something of their lives as old-family residents of Poland's Tatras. I also owe a great debt of gratitude to Marek Nowak and Katarzyna Krajewska, and their daughter Karolina, who opened their warm home to me whenever I was in Kraków. They were my friends and constant Polish language tutors, reminding me when I was speaking in the Górale manner and perhaps not as they do in Kraków. In Vienna, not far from the Tatras, ethnomusicologist Rudolph Pietsch and his wife and violist Francisca were my frequent hosts. They introduced me to ethnomusicologist Emil Lubej, who, together with his son, documented for me the wedding of Stanisława Trebunia-Tutka and Paweł Staszel when I was unable to attend.

In Poland I also had the honor and pleasure of working with

a community of scholars whom I hope I may call colleagues. Before traveling to Poland, I was introduced to the fine tradition of scholarship there by these individuals' published articles and books. In particular, I thank Anna Czekanowska at Warsaw University who generously opened her home to me and provided advice from her extensive experience in Polish ethnomusicology and anthropology. Professor Czekanowska also wrote letters on my behalf before I ever met her in person. Thank you. Also exceptionally helpful were Professor Ludwik Bielawski, head of the ethnomusicology program of the Institute of Art, Polish Academy of Sciences, in Warsaw, and his colleagues Piotr Dahlig, Zbigniew Jerzy Przerembski, and Ewa Dahlig. Professor Bielawski's generosity extended beyond the professional when he and his wife, Krystyna, welcomed me into their home as a guest on numerous occasions. Also combining hospitality with intellectual companionship in Warsaw was ethnomusicologist Anna Gruszczyńska-Ziółkowska and her anthropologist husband, Mariusz Ziółkowski.

Moving out of Warsaw and toward the Tatras, I benefited greatly from my consultations with acknowledged independent scholar of Górale music Aleksandra Szurmiak-Bogucka. Familiar with Szurmiak-Bogucka's books and articles (see references cited) before I ever traveled to Poland, I was honored by her sustained generosity toward me during our many meetings, both in Tatra villages and in her Kraków apartment. Another scholar I wish to thank is Jan Gutt-Mostowy who selflessly shared his wisdom both when we would meet in the Tatras and later, when I was back in America, via letters. I also warmly thank Teresa Jabłońska, the director of the Muzeum Tatrzańskie in Zakopane, whose office door was always open to me. She and her dedicated staff spent many hours helping me access valuable information from the museum's collections and library. I am grateful also to Witold Henryk Paryski, renowned historian of the Tatra region, who carefully reviewed and critiqued an earlier version of chapter 2.

Others read portions or even the entire manuscript of what became this book, and I owe them my gratitude. As my dissertation at Brown University was effectively the first version of this book, I begin with my dissertation committee: Paul Austerlitz, Carol Babiracki, William Beeman, Mark Slobin, and Jeff Titon. I am particularly grateful to Jeff, my committee chair. Thank you for your gentle and insightful encouragement. In Poland, professors Ludwik Bielawski and Włodzimierz Kotoński gave this first manuscript very close readings, as did Tadeusz Zdybal and Louise Wrazen, both from Toronto. Thank you for the many corrections and suggestions you made. Rob Hodges, Gibb S. Schreffler, and several other students at the University of California, Santa Barbara, read early versions of the book and provided very helpful comments. Michael Beckerman and Nancy Currey read and provided valuable critiques on earlier versions of the introduction. Thank you, Sonia Seeman, for your careful review of chapter 2 and Veit Erlmann for critiquing chapter 5. Philip V. Bohlman, Rebecca Tolen, and an anonymous reader at the bidding of Indiana University Press all reviewed and made very helpful comments on the manuscript. Finally, Eve McPhearson and my good friend Cathy Oliverson carefully read the entire book shortly before I made the final revisions.

For me, learning the Polish language and the beautiful Górale dialect is a lifelong endeavor, and I am grateful to the many individuals who have helped and continue to help me along the way. I begin with my Polish language teachers Anna Barańczak at Harvard and Wiesława Stolarczyk at the Jagiellonian University in Kraków. In Poland, Canada, and the United States I have relied on the language skills of Andrzej Tokarz, Halina Maciata, Jakub Omsky, Stanisława Trebunia-Staszel, Paweł Staszel, Maria Trochimczyk, Maciej Mrugała, Jack Mrugała, Monika White, Diana Makowska, Tadeusz Zdybal, Dorota Dutsch, and Anna Gąsienica-Byrcyn. I am especially grateful to Dorota Dutsch, who reviewed every use of a Polish word in the entire book, and Anna Gąsienica-Byrcyn, who checked all the Górale dialect portions—major undertakings performed for the love of language and with selfless generosity. Still, I am sure I have managed to insert mistakes. These errors are mine and not those of my language consultants.

Finally, I thank Andrzej Stopka for driving me through the snow from village to village in his fine Volkswagen van to help me locate people from whom I sought permission to publish photos, audio recordings, and so forth. I thank Gretchen Longwell for intellectual, moral, and material support during the first decade of this project. And now I thank Janet Rabinowitch and her colleagues and staff at Indiana University Press for taking this project on and for working so diligently to bring the book to fruition. If there is anything good in the pages that follow, it is a result of the assistance I received from the individuals listed above, other individuals unnamed, and the support of the organizations listed below. All mistakes and misunderstandings contained in the book, however, are mine alone.

Financial support for my studies in Poland came from a number of sources. I traveled to Poland for a total of five months during the summers of 1992 and 1993 for intensive language study and lecture courses on Polish history and culture at Kraków's Jagiellonian University. During those summer trips I also spent time in Warsaw, primarily at the Institute of Art, the Polish Academy of Sciences, and in the Tatras conducting preliminary research. For these summer research trips I am very grateful for financial support from the American Council of Learned Societies, the Kosciuszko Foundation, and the Polish American Teachers Association. From September 1994 to August 1995 I conducted fieldwork and archival research in Poland (with research trips to the Slovak Republic and Rumania). This dissertation research year was funded by an International Research and Exchanges Board fellowship, and by stipends from the Kosciuszko Foundation and the Polish Ministry of Education, all generous support for which I am very grateful. In the summer of 1997 I returned to Slovakia and Poland briefly for a conference and to conduct follow-up fieldwork with the support of a Graduate Fellowship from Brown University. I was able to return to Poland during the summer of 2000 with the generous support of an International Research and Exchanges Board Short-Term Travel Grant, and again in the winter of 2002–2003 with the support of the University of California, Santa Barbara.

*   *   *

This book is dedicated to the memory of four individuals. I gratefully remember Stanisława (Gąsienica) Styrczula-Maśniak (1934–1995), the mother and wife of the family with whom I lived in the village of Kościelisko, Poland, from September 1994 to August 1995. I sat in her kitchen for many hours learning more than I have in any college class. Her death in May 1995 left a void in many people's lives, including my own. I express gratitude and fondly remember Józef Styrczula-Maśniak (1922–1998), the father of Władysław, whose violin playing fired my curiosity in Chicago, and my host during my first residence in the Tatras in 1992. Józef was a virtuoso violinist in the Górale tradition, an artisan furniture maker and carpenter (see fig. 4.7), and a conscientious farmer. Tadeusz Gąsienica-Giewont (1915–1999) was a formidable character who embodied the qualities of his namesake, Giewont Mountain, which rises behind Zakopane, his hometown. Frequently introduced as the oldest living Górale musician, Giewont was respected for his knowledge of tradition and history, as well as for his facility

with a violin (see fig. 2.1). We spent many hours in his home recording tunes and stories, generally followed by a walk to the Sopa
bar for a pint of Polish beer. Finally, I wish to thank and remember
Marek Łabunowicz (1972–2001), who died as he lived, helping others. I enjoyed his violin and cimbalum playing, to be sure, but I
remember best his ready smile and his passion to share ideas about
music. Both Józef Styrczula-Maśniak and Marek Łabunowicz can
be heard contributing their talents to help mourn the passing of
another on tracks 4, 46, and 47—sounds from the Tatras that I
hope will be heard as a fitting memorial to these four exceptional
individuals.

* * *

The maps and the diagram of the interior of a festival tent
were created by Kirk Goldsberry. Unless otherwise indicated, photographs and music transcriptions are by the author. The music
notations were prepared by Matthew Dorman using *Sibelius* com-
puter notation software, and reformatted with the generous assistance of Leslie Hogan.

Note on Citations of Fieldwork Media

References such as ac19.vii.92.1 direct the reader toward fieldwork documentation. The numbering system indicates media (ac = audio cassette, v = Hi8 video, Dv = mini digital video, and VHS = VHS video cassette). The first Arabic numeral refers to the day the documentation was collected, the roman numeral refers to the month, and the next Arabic numeral is the year (two digits for the twentieth century, four for the twenty-first century). If more than one cassette was used on that date, a digit is added after the year to indicate each cassette sequentially. All fieldwork documentation is housed at the University of California, Santa Barbara, and copies of the audio recordings can be found at the Muzeum Tatrzańskie in Zakopane, Poland.

Making Music
IN THE
Polish Tatras

Introduction

Approaching the Tatra Mountain town of Zakopane from the southeast along a street named T. Chałubińskiego, one encounters a monument to the street's namesake, Dr. Tytus Chałubiński (1820–1889) (fig. 0.1). The monument features a pedestal topped with a larger-than-life bust of the renowned physician from Warsaw who, in the late nineteenth century, set up a sanatorium in Zakopane and actively promoted tourism to the Tatras. His promotion involved not only touting the clean mountain air and healing hot springs but also championing the folkways of the villagers called "Górale" (mountaineers or highlanders).[1] He was famous for arranging excursions into the high Tatras for which he employed local Górale who acted as guides and porters, and who provided music and dance around the evening campfires as depicted in a woodcut from the late nineteenth century (fig. 0.2). The physician's preferred mountain guide was Jan Krzeptowski-Sabała (1810–1894), who is also featured in the monument. Sabała is seated at the base of the pedestal, represented in full body but in smaller scale than the bust of Chałubiński. He is in traditional Górale cos-

Figure 0.1. Monument to Chałubiński on T. Chałubińskiego Street, Zakopane.

tume and holds a small boat-shaped folk-violin in his left hand while gesturing with a bow (now broken off) in his right hand. Legendary for his storytelling and fiddling, and for his friendship with Chałubiński, today Sabała is celebrated as a prototypical old-world Górale.

The monument to Chałubiński and Sabała was a keen statement in 1903 when it was erected to honor two influential individuals in the Tatra region's recent history.[2] A century later the monument stands as a symbol of forces that continue to shape present-day cultural practices and society in the Tatras, forces that are the subjects of this book: Górale, or the "indigenous" residents

Figure 0.2. "W Tatrach" by E. Gorazdowski, drawn by W. Eljasz. Chałubiński is standing to the right, facing forward. Reproduced from the Polish magazine *Kłosy* 30, no. 781 (1880): 392. Courtesy of the Tatrzański Park Narodowy, Zakopane.

of the Tatras, and "outsiders," particularly tourists who were also the first ethnographers of the region. Established theories that social reality is the product of human imagination (Anderson 1991 [1983]) and invention (Hobsbawm and Ranger 1983) suggest that the whole notion of "indigenous" people contrasting with "outsiders" fosters an imagining of difference and here the invention of Górale ethnicity. The representations of Chałubiński and Sabała on the monument capture the essence of imagined differences at a crucial moment in the inventing of that ethnicity. The good physician from the city was a thinking man, the gifted doctor who used his knowledge to ease the pain of the unlettered Górale, so only his head is represented, larger than life, on the monument. In contrast, Sabała is represented in full body caught mid-gesture. A symbol of place, he is in regional costume with his feet planted on the earth. He is of the soil, of the Tatras, and is so marked with his distinctive dress and peculiar regional violin. Chałubiński is a "normal" if laudable man, unmarked by symbolic clothing and musical props. Although social and political status of the time were complicated by the fact that Poland was partitioned between Prussia, Russia, and the Austro-Hungarian Empire, relative to Górale, Chałubiński could have been considered to be in a dominant position. In the politics of relationships, "dominant groups are never ethnicities" (Wilmsen 1996, 4). Sabała, on the other hand, is marked as "ethnic," a distinction he gains in relation to his unmarked companion above him on the pedestal. Górale are both possessors of and marked by a unique folk culture, while the tourist/ethnographer *inteligencja* are unmarked thinkers free to interpret the world they survey. Górale do culture; inteligencja interpret and explain culture. In the monument on T. Chałubińskiego Street, the two legendary historical figures are joined in a permanent symbolic representation of the dynamic relationship between all that these individuals represent, a relationship I seek to understand and describe in the following chapters.

This book is a musical ethnography of a specific Tatra Mountain region called "Skalne Podhale" (Rocky piedmont), here referred to simply as Podhale. It is about making mountain music, making both the idea of mountain music as well as making the sounds, dancing the dances, and singing the songs that have come to identify Górale of Podhale. It is also about the making of mountaineers, Górale, as a distinct ethnic group. The current volume is distinguished from other ethnographies of the region in that it does not accept the proposition noted above that Górale do culture while inteligencja (including ethnographers) simply interpret and explain culture. Central to this study is the recognition that over a period of two centuries, tourists and ethnographers (the core of the inteligencja represented by Dr. Chałubiński in the monument) have joined with the long-time residents of Podhale in imagining and inventing Górale and the music-culture associated with them. As an ethnographer, tourist, and musician, I find myself implicated in the symbolism of the Chałubiński monument, and it is with a sometimes uncomfortable reflexive twitch that I join those who would interpret Górale cultural practices, especially music-culture. How have my actions as a tourist, researcher, fieldworker, musician, and writer contributed to the ongoing imagining and inventing of Górale and their cultural practices? Answers to this question are sought here by observing how past ethnographers were complicit in creating the very cultural practices about which they wrote.

This book is also about a place and the people who inhabit that place. People invent and continually reinvent the cultural practices of Podhale, giving human meaning to geography and creating locality.[3] The Tatra Mountains are a geological fact that attracted migrants for certain reasons at one time, and for different reasons at other times. Dr. Chałubiński, for example, was attracted to the Tatra Mountains by the same myths that attracted tourists before and since: the Tatras are isolated, untouched, pure. But the earliest settlers of the Tatras were not drawn there by ideas about mountain purity; rather, they fled to the mountains to avoid social, economic, and political oppression, as I discuss in chapter 2. For these early settlers, the mountains were a refuge of last resort. The Tatras are the tallest mountains of the Carpathian chain which arcs up from the Balkans and runs along the border between Poland and Slovakia before descending toward Vienna. The villages considered in this study are located in the northern shadows of the Tatras, the least hospitable terrain in Central Europe. The alpine Tatras are a defining feature of Podhale and an influential force on local cultural practices, contributing to the political, social, and economic conditions that resulted in Podhale becoming a classic region for the study of folklore in Europe by the end of the nineteenth century. The powerful myth of isolation, purity, and authentic folklore survives to this day. Whereas other classic locations of folkloristic imagination in Europe and North America—the Austrian Steiermark, the Swiss Alps, the islands off the Scottish and Irish coasts, and the Appalachians—succumbed to modernity, the Tatras remained apart, veiled by the Iron Curtain, preserved in the imagined past.[4] The myth of Tatra Mountain isolation is paired with the myth of unique, authentic folklore and folk music. In chapter 1 I introduce the people and the folk music–culture associated with the place Podhale. The chapters that follow show the many ways in which the place, the people, and their music have been imagined for nearly two centuries up to the present.

Like Chałubiński, I, too, was attracted to the Tatras by the myth of isolated purity and authenticity, and by the sound of the music from these mountains. I first traveled to Podhale in 1992 in search of the source of the "authentic" folk music that had captured my attention a few years earlier when I met Górale musicians in

Chicago, Illinois. Once in Podhale, I began to realize that there is a different story to be told about the Tatras, a story not about isolation and purity but about contact, transregional and eventually transnational networks, and shared and contested histories. Ironically it was an individual I imagined as embodying authenticity and purity who first led me to the realization that ethnographers of music (ethnomusicologists and musical folklorists) were an active force shaping Górale music-culture. Józef Styrczula-Maśniak (1922–1998) was the father of the first immigrant Górale violinist I met in Chicago, and a respected elder musician himself. I lived with him in his log house in a Tatra village the first summer I traveled to Podhale and, to my surprise, during one of our extended conversations about his music, he began critiquing the work of musical ethnographers who came before me. So much for purity and isolation. So much for my own nostalgic longings for an idyllic mountain preserve of untouched European folk music.

Józef Styrczula-Maśniak's comments about musical ethnographers (a category in which I was clearly included) launched me on an excursion into the history of ethnography in Podhale, and into the theories of cultural invention and imagination that are at the core of this study. Especially important is the imagination of Podhalan locality and Górale ethnicity, and the invention of a music-culture which symbolizes that locality and ethnicity. The history of ethnography is also the history of tourism in the Tatras. The first tourists were the first ethnographers, and the two industries are deeply implicated in the making of Górale ethnicity and music-culture. Chapter 2, "Making History," is an interpretation of the settlement history of Podhale, the final settlement wave resulting from what I call the "new migration" of tourists. Differing fundamentally from previous forms of migration, tourist migration established in Podhale what John Comaroff calls "relations of inequality." As he theorizes, it is such relations that often stimulate the creation of an ethnic group (Comaroff 1987; 1996, 166). Relations resulting in group identities of various sorts did not begin and end with tourism in Podhale. One presumes that identities were being negotiated in Podhale, never truly isolated or primordial, for as long as people inhabited its valleys. But I suggest that tourism established new types of group relations which set in motion the imagination of a Górale ethnicity, and that tourism is one of the leading causes for the maintenance of that ethnicity, though always imagined anew. The relations of inequality between the indigenous people of Podhale and elite Polish tourists are symbolized in the T. Chałubińskiego Street monument. Historically Podhale's first ethnographers were among these early tourists. Since Chałubiński's time, academic disciplines defined by ethnography have changed and developed, and the relationship between the tourist and ethnographer has become more complex. However, my research shows that the relationship remains important and effective in Podhale. Chapter 3 is an interpretation of the related histories of tourism, ethnography, and music making in Podhale.

Social scientists began critical analysis of tourism in the 1960s and 1970s (Nuñez 1963; MacCannell 1989 [1976]; Smith 1977). In the 1970s and 1980s the uncomfortable similarities between ethnographers and tourists were noted (MacCannell 1989 [1976], 5, 173–179; Errington and Gewertz 1989; Kaeppler and Lewin 1988; Kirshenblatt-Gimblett 1988). The links between tourism and ethnography are most thoroughly demonstrated by folklorist Regina Bendix in her work on the concept of "authenticity" (1989, 1997). In the 1980s and 1990s ethnomusicologists began to take stock of their association with tourists and tourism, as seen, for example, in a collection of essays published following the International Colloquium of the International Council for Traditional Music held in Jamaica in 1986 (Kaeppler and Lewin 1988), in Wolfgang Suppan's 1991 collection of essays *Musik und Tourismus*, and in a special issue of *The World of Music* edited by Mark DeWitt (1999). The present book joins recent musical ethnographies by Margaret Sarkissian (2000) and Katherine Hagedorn (2001) that recognize the study of tourism as essential for understanding certain music-cultural practices.

The integration of tourism and ethnography in Podhale is a historic fact, but the way I conceptually link the two requires an explanation of what I am calling "ethnography." Included are all varieties of writings about people and their ways of life based on firsthand observation and experience. In Podhale, for example, the first tourists wrote pseudo-scientific descriptions of the villagers they encountered. These are often in the form of travelogues—a genre with a long history in anthropology—and, in the case of music, song text collections. Thus my relating of tourists and ethnographers reflects not only an interpretation of history in Podhale, but it is also a rhetorical device designed to broaden the conception of ethnography in order to understand certain aspects of Podhalan society. Polish inteligencja were attracted by the distinct cultural practices and mountain scenery found in this region, and they began to frequent Podhale in the nineteenth century (Dahlig 1991, 84; Gromada 1975, 6). In what I define as the beginning of the region's tourist industry, Górale musicians and dancers performed for these early visitors, who then represented Górale to others in the form of ethnographies, including travelogues. Starting in the 1870s ethnographic activities intensified (and became institutionalized) along with the rise of the deliberate development of Podhale as a tourist destination. Although the motivations, actions, and influences of tourism and ethnography can be conceptually separated, I argue that what connects them calls for interpreting them as related phenomena. Separating them would absolve ethnographers from the cultural impact often attributed, with derision, to tourists. Recognizing the relations between tourism and ethnography, and showing how historically and socially situated fieldwork, writing, and cultural intervention in Podhale affected the people and the cultural practices studied, provides a model for ethnomusicologists and other ethnographers to better understand the impact of their actions on those they study.

As first revealed to me by Józef Styrczula-Maśniak, ethnographic descriptions of Górale cultural practices are known to many Górale musicians today, and the actions of past ethnographers are held in living memory and preserved in oral histories. Tourism, the sister of ethnography, is an important source of employment for regional musicians. An irony exists in modern Podhalan society: outside interest (ethnographic and touristic) has negated the most frequently cited reason for Górale's distinct cultural identity—isolation. Here I argue that outside interest also stimulated the very invention of Górale ethnicity and that it now provides, through the tourist industry, an important motivation for maintaining this ethnicity. At the same time, outside interest in Górale cultural practices has created multiple layers of representation evident in Podhale today, where Górale self-representations are in continual dialogue, and sometimes dispute, with representations of Górale ethnicity by others.

The ethnic distinction maintained by Górale, and the long history of tourism and ethnography in Podhale, make it an ideal location for the study of multilayered representations of ethnicity. I am especially interested in how tourists and ethnographers interact with Górale in the cultural realm of musical behavior to create Górale ethnicity. Scholars of expressive culture effectively demonstrate how groups represent themselves, but less is known about how groups are constructed and represented by others (Wolf 1994, 6; Comaroff 1996). In the humanities we know that a people's music not only reflects society but also helps to shape that society, including the ethnic identity and borders of that society (Stokes 1994). Relevant case studies by ethnomusicologists are many, and issues of music and identity verge on the axiomatic in ethnomusicology. A few studies that are particularly influential in this book include Mark Slobin's work treating Jews in Europe and America as ethnic groups with sometimes eclectic interethnic musical connections (Slobin 1982, 3; 1984); Jocelyne Guilbault's consideration of the individual, age, national, and super-ethnic identity implications of *zouk*, another eclectic music, this time from the Caribbean (Guilbault 1993, 200–203); and a collection of essays in the volume *Ethnicity, Identity, and Music* edited by Martin Stokes (1994). Ethnicity and nationality are inseparable concepts and are at the root of music scholars' interest in music and identity. Recent ethnomusicological statements about nationalism that have helped to shape my approach include Austerlitz (2000), Guy (1999), Marošević (1998), Moore (1997), Remes (1999), Scruggs (1999), Sugarman (1999), Turino (2000), and Wade (2000).

That we often help invent the objects of our observation is now an established tenet of ethnography. Drawing on Said's theories (1978) of "essentializing form" and "Orientalism," Gewertz and Errington (1991, 80) have asked in distant but analogous situations if both tourists and ethnographers have vested interests in constructing ethnic "others." The question extends to individuals within the constructed ethnic group: Is it to their advantage to maintain ethnic distinction? In Podhale the question is one of distinction between groups who share nationality. Most studies of tourism involve international contact, and these studies are often prefaced with well-established theories of layered interaction beginning with explorers, conquerors, colonialists, and so on. Eastern European area studies provide an often more subtle field for observing group construction—the interaction and reconfiguration of ethnic boundaries within single nation-states (see Nagengast 1991; Wedel 1992). More recent theories of transnationalism and globalization work well in this setting, since they de-emphasize nation-states and stress instead unequal power relations within any given locality (see Pieterse 1996; Comaroff 1996; Appadurai 1996). Globalization theories also acknowledge subaltern agency (here Górale agency) even within global information networks, an idea considered in chapters 4 and 5.

The later chapters of the book illustrate how the ideas presented in chapter 3 are worked out in Podhale. With chapter 4 I start in the most obvious locus of touristic and ethnographic intervention: the folkloric festival. This chapter includes two case studies. The first is a symbolic interpretation of festival performances as modern ritual. The second presents a debate between some ethnographers and individual Górale musicians about the "authenticity" of a particular music style. This debate brings to the foreground ideological differences between musical ethnographers and Górale musicians, and goes to the heart of the issue of who has the power to represent Górale ethnicity with music.

One way to interpret folklore festivals is to view them as the opposite of "authentic" folklore: they take what was in-group, local, circumscribed, and place it on a stage, making it public, open for potentially global consumption, and for external interpretation. Festivals are a classic example of touristic commoditization (Cohen 1988; Greenwood 1977). As a researcher, my initial impulse was to devalue festival performances and to seek out more private performances by Górale for Górale. The importance of festival performances, however, is evident in the energy and care many Górale musicians give them. It eventually became clear to me that what made tourist festivals interesting and meaningful was not how well they represented village life onstage but rather how the festivals themselves were a phenomenon. I now interpret these festivals as present-day rituals that replace other more traditionally recognized rituals, yet, like the rituals they replace, festivals also serve to define a people's relationship to their universe, and to ensure their continued livelihood.

The interpretation of festivals as vital rituals is consistent with the two most prominent uses of the term "ritual" in the social sciences and humanities. First, rituals are symbolic representations of objects, beliefs, or truths of special significance to a group (Connerton 1989, 44; Durkheim 1915; Lukes 1975, 291). Second, they are transformative or effective (Schechner 1983, 131–158; Turner 1984, 21). As transformative symbolic practice, these festival rituals are no longer performed to insure successful crops, as were some more traditional calendric rituals, for example, but instead they are used to define a place for Górale ethnicity in a changing world. They are what Arjun Appadurai calls "cultural" performances that express "the mobilization of group identities" (1996, 13). The conscious development of tourism in Podhale was historically the primary means by which Górale experienced globalization. The highly controlled and symbolic interaction among the increasingly international and transnational audience members and participants at folklore festivals provides an opportunity for Górale to respond to social, political, demographic, and economic changes experienced in the past century (for examples in other parts of Europe, see Baumann 1996, 2001; Bendix 1985, 1989, 1997; and Ronström 1996). I interpret performances within the tourist folklore frame as local responses by individuals, in relatively clearly defined culture groups, to their own life experiences with, ultimately, globalizing forces.

Both case studies in chapter 4 address the issue of "authenticity," a subject that also links the industries of tourism and ethnography. Music folklore studies in Europe, folklore studies in Europe and America, and, in some cases, European ethnomusicology today all show the influence of a quest for national authenticity in the language of folk poetry, a quest that is often mistakenly attributed to Johann Gottfried Herder (see Bendix 1997, 16–17; Bohlman 2002a, 38–41; and Suppan 1976, 117–120). The dichotomous view of cultural practice as either authentic or spurious has been challenged in academic ethnography in recent decades (Bendix 1997, 13), although it is still found in both scholarly and lay people's discussions of Górale music-culture. Here I use the term "authenticity" as a concept rather than as something out there to be discovered. Authenticity is a human construct, created in a process of "authentication." Like ethnicity and music, it is an invention imbued with cultural meaning. The questions become, as Bendix put it in her definitive study on authenticity (1997, 21), "not 'What is authenticity?' but 'Who needs authenticity and why?' and 'How has authenticity been used?' " Authenticity, then, becomes a field for playing out the other issues addressed in this book, and a theme that resonates throughout the remaining chapters.

In chapter 5 I explore the extreme limits of what might be considered Górale music as this category relates to the canonized repertoire introduced in chapter 1. In 1991 a radio producer from Warsaw decided to try to create a "world beat" fusion of Górale music and reggae. He succeeded in bringing together a Jamaican reggae band and a Górale family band, each recording separate raw tracks in a Warsaw studio. These tracks were then mixed together in London and released on three commercial recordings in 1992 and 1994. Several of the fusion tracks were commercial successes, reaching the top ten on European worldbeat charts as well as gaining an audience of young people in Poland, and among Górale diaspora groups in Western Europe and North America.

Sonically these fusion experiments are different from anything else considered in this book, but ideologically they tell a similar story. The story is about music associated with a particular locality and ethnicity being used by individuals who come from different places and express diverse ethnicities. The Polish inteligencja from lowland cities of the late nineteenth century is replaced by a Polish radio producer from a lowland city in the late twentieth century. Illustrating Appadurai's theories of modernity and globalization, this mix of migration (Jamaicans to Poland, Górale to Warsaw and eventually to Jamaica) and transnational media impels individuals to imagine themselves globally. For the Polish producer and the Górale musicians involved in this project, the heart of this global imagination was a fusion of *ideas*—the fusion of musical *sounds* came later and was more labor-intensive. The radio producer fused the bands ideologically around notions of authenticity (both the Jamaican band and the Górale family band were verifiable "roots" [read "authentic"] musicians) and of independence (reggae being associated with black Jamaicans' struggle for freedom, Górale embodying the myth of isolated independence). At least one of the individual Górale musicians, Krzysztof Trebunia-Tutka, involved in this fusion project used the experience as a platform to express his own ideas about what is at the heart of Górale music, and to express his own agency as a musician with a long family tradition. In interviews with me, and in a song text he wrote for a later CD release, he names some of the individual ethnographers surveyed in chapter 3. Trebunia-Tutka knows what others have said and written about Górale music-culture, and in a deliberate move to reverse the power imbalances inherent in the relations of those who would represent Górale, he has made use of his new access to media and "world beat" music to broadcast his ideas.

The final two chapters return to a discussion of music practice, considered to be at the core of Górale music, first music played for tourists at restaurants (chapter 6) and then music played for weddings and funerals (chapter 7). The key tourist town of Zakopane has a growing number of restaurants that advertise themselves as "regional." Several are rustic log structures, while others have false rustic interiors. All offer regional fare, are staffed by individuals wearing Górale costumes, and hire Górale musicians, and sometimes dancers, to provide entertainment. The restaurants considered here are also owned and managed by individuals who describe themselves as old-family Górale. Tourist restaurant performances may be the most common, most pervasive, and most lucrative places for Górale musicians and dancers to perform. Priced beyond the means of the majority of local residents, the restaurants serve tourists from lowland Poland and frequently from other European countries, America, and Japan. Restaurants, then, are places where Górale are in direct contact with international tourists, often literally while dancing together. They are also places where Górale attract tourists with the promise of a regional experience—with the experience of locality represented with cultural markers: food, costume, music, and dance. Restaurants offer Górale the opportunity to invent representations of themselves that, unlike festivals and commercial recordings, are unmediated by ethnographers or record producers, on the one hand, but heavily influenced by capitalism on the other. An analysis of the repertoire performed in these settings suggests two interpretations. The first interprets a canonized Górale music as ritually separated in the restaurant performances from an extended repertoire of popular international dance styles (polkas, waltzes, etc.). A second understanding includes all the music performed in the restaurants in a new, expanded canon. Broadening the canon opens up a new musical representation of Górale ethnicity that harkens back to pre-canon representations discussed in chapter 3.

When asked where one might experience "real" Górale music, Górale musicians often recommend weddings. Not surprisingly, weddings are a locus of conservative traditions in many ways. In the weddings visited here, the participants present in stylized form their "Góraleness" for wedding guests who are for the most part also Górale. These enactments of self-identity revolve around local costumes worn by the bride and groom, and their attendants, as well as many family members and guests; ritual acts deemed local and Górale; and a Górale band that plays almost constantly for the celebrations which can last several days. Chapter 7 draws from several weddings documented in Podhale and among Górale in Chicago but focuses on one particular wedding as a case study. My description of the wedding highlights significant moments of ritual activity accompanied by music believed to be specifically Górale.

Yet the repertoire on the whole has much in common with tourist restaurant performances and challenges the recognized canon of Górale music.

The second part of chapter 7 turns to the music at funerals, the least talked about and studied aspect of music-culture in Podhale. Yet funerals are poignant moments of community reflection with no mediation from outside influence, with the exception of the Catholic Church to the extent that one considers the Church "outside" Górale society. There are no ethnographers or festival directors suggesting repertoire. There is no need to attract and accommodate tourists. No specific ensemble is engaged for the occasion, and musicians are not paid to play at funerals. They simply show up at the funeral with instruments in hand to join others in paying homage. The semipublic music making at funerals in Podhale may be the least affected by outside pressures. Interestingly Górale cultivate no special lament genre as is done in many world music-cultures, including other regions of Poland. Instead, the repertoire performed at funerals is the same repertoire played at other events. What seems to make the music at these funerals ritually appropriate is the style of playing: all the music, with the exception of Catholic chants and songs, is played on instruments, not sung. The repertoire remains within the canon of Górale music as described by Górale musicians, although the style of playing and some of the repertoire itself is at odds with musical ethnographers' descriptions of the canon. Perhaps the ultimate return to the village, funerals are a context for reflective ritualized music making that gives voice to some of the conflicted processes of imagining and representing identity considered throughout this book.

This book is a work of ethnomusicology. Ethnomusicologists do perhaps a little more than their share of self-defining, but this obsession might be blamed on their object of study: music or, even more troubling, music-culture. Attempts to create definitions of music that apply worldwide are necessarily vague, and definitions of culture fare even worse. Although probably not intended as a field-defining statement, Jeff Todd Titon (1996, xxii) has suggested that ethnomusicology is the "study of people making music." By placing the emphasis on the study of people—people engaged in an activity generally considered highly symbolic—this definition moves away from music sound itself as object or text. But what is so special about the human activity of music making? Many ethnomusicologists believe that people may be at their best when making music. Music behavior, however defined, throughout the world seems to be a locus of people's most deeply held beliefs, motivations, and meanings. Music is especially useful for expressing the unquantifiable and intangible such as religious belief, historical narrative, profound emotion, and ideas about identity. A basic tenet of ethnomusicology is that music function is reflected in music form, the music sound itself. Many ethnomusicologists begin as musicians trained to recognize and analyze music forms, and then go on to study sociology, anthropology, folklore, and so forth, in their effort to better understand how these music forms express essential qualities of human existence. By straddling the institutional divide between the humanities and social sciences, ethnomusicologists develop the tools for working with music sound and with music-culture, tools that distinguish them from most scholars in anthropology, folklore, history, sociology, and so on.

Ethnomusicologists also draw from and contribute to these sister disciplines. It may be evident from the above that anthropology and folklore are especially influential in my work. Most American ethnomusicology, and to some extent Western European ethnomusicology, is aligned closely with cultural anthropology by the methodology of fieldwork and by the descriptive/interpretive act of ethnography. The disciplines, however, have separate histories and tend to interpret ethnography differently. Because elsewhere I have considered these histories in greater length (Cooley 1997, 2003), here I only summarize and reinterpret a few points. Alan Merriam (1960, 1964) championed the mid-twentieth-century rise of anthropological ethnomusicology emphasizing the interpretation of music as culture and as human behavior. This challenged a musicological approach that focused on music sound itself. One contemporary musicological approach was Mantle Hood's "bimusicality" method that encouraged ethnomusicologists to learn to perform the music they studied (1960; 1982 [1971], 25–40). The opposition between these various methods has since been mediated by scholars who have shown that learning to play music in the communities they study is a way to gain insight not only into the music system but also into the society and cultural practices as a whole. Especially influential on my own approach is the work of Timothy Rice (1994, 1997) and Jeff Todd Titon (1997), who have theorized epistemologies for participant-observation and knowing music-cultures by becoming involved as a musician. Some ethnomusicologists have come to believe that their deep participation in music-culture offers them unique insights not available through other forms of participant-observation (i.e., Shelemay 1997; Hagedorn 2001). Of course, many anthropologists include music in their studies but generally as one among many other social behaviors. Folklorists also contribute to our understanding of music, but their tradition is to treat music as text—song texts or melodic texts. American folklorists have, however, helped to develop performance studies, an approach important in this present work. As musicians who typically are active participants in the music making of the societies they study, ethnomusicologists are best equipped to interpret this aspect of expressive cultures.

This book is also an example of a particular style of ethnomusicology usually identified with North America. For example, American ethnomusicology, and to some extent recent European ethnomusicology, tends to focus on issues of identity, change, and new music forms, and often employs a synchronic approach based on extensive and intensive fieldwork. Eastern European ethnomusicology highly values tradition, history, taxonomies of melodic types, and the origins of music forms—goals more consistent with folklore and philology paradigms, and a science paradigm discussed below. In general, American ethnomusicologists are interested in the social and cultural contexts of music; Eastern Europeans are more concerned with the music itself. My project is a conscious attempt to address the issues and concerns of both European and American scholarship, but the approach is clearly American.

Key in Western European and American ethnomusicological works from the past three decades is a reinterpretation of—and sometimes move away from—an earlier science paradigm. In the science paradigm of ethnomusicology, music is an objectively observable fact to be collected and later manipulated in the laboratory using methods such as transcription and analysis (Cooley 1997, 5). This approach is clearly important in the pages that follow, but it alone cannot answer the questions about human relations, and the negotiation and representation of identities at the center of this book. For this reason I engage in musical participant-observation methods with the epistemological goal of understanding rather than explaining music-culture (Titon 1997, 89–90). These methods emphasize reflexive ethnography that includes the fieldworker in the representation, and narrative approaches that do not try to eliminate all ambiguities and contradictions. Renato Rosaldo

(1989, 93) called this "processual analysis," one that stresses cultural study from different perspectives that do not necessarily add up to a unified summation. For these reasons I employ narrative in many of the following chapters that places me as a fieldworker among my Górale consultants. Narrative is also useful for conveying a sense of place and locality that is so important to Górale both for their self-conceptions and their conceptions of music. I also use transcriptions of recorded conversations, with minimal interpretation, to incorporate the voices of those who shared so much with me. This effort continues with the audio examples on the accompanying compact disk. Although the selection and editing of these examples bear the heavy hand of my ethnographic mediation, they stand alone as examples of the beauty and complexity of human invention and imagination explored in the chapters that follow.

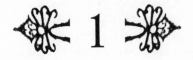

Podhale

Place and People

Only one major player in this book is not human-made and that is the place itself—the Tatra Mountains. And even this is dramatically altered by human activity. The other topics of interest here are all human-made; they are human inventions. The danger of ethnographic descriptions (including what follows) is that they tend to reify the thing described; they create the culture they purport to analyze and explain. Scholars in the social sciences have long recognized this tendency to invent the traditions they present as ethnographic discoveries (Fabian 1983), and it is with circumspection that I propose to describe Podhale, the people of Podhale, and the music they call their own. Though the mountains—the Tatra, Gorce, and Pieniny mountains—that hem in the small region called Podhale are not human inventions, what it *means* to be a mountaineer, to be Górale, is a human social, historical, and cultural construct.

Podhale is on the southern border of Poland, one hundred

kilometers below the ancient city of Kraków, which was the royal seat of Poland until 1611 when the government was moved to Warsaw, in part to remove it from attacks and threats of attacks from Tartar invaders. Kraków remains, however, a cultural and administrative capital for southern Poland, and for more than a century it has been the most common staging point for recreational and short-term business travel (tourism) to Podhale. Leaving the Gothic and Renaissance splendor of Kraków by horse-drawn wagon (in the nineteenth century), by train (around the turn of the twentieth century), or by bus or automobile today, one traverses increasingly hilly terrain as one moves south to the town of Nowy Targ (New Market). The largest and one of the oldest towns in Podhale, Nowy Targ is on the edge of the Gorce Mountains and overlooks a moderate-sized valley containing the most agriculturally viable land of the region. The Gorce Mountains (part of the Beskid Mountains) define the northern border of Podhale; the southern border is formed by the Tatra Mountains, the tallest peaks of the Carpathian range and the largest mountains in Central Europe. The Polish/Slovak border runs through the Tatras, dividing the mountains in such a way that only about 20 percent of the High Tatras lie within the political borders of Poland. The Białka River marks the eastern boundary of Podhale, and the western boundary runs just outside the Czarny Dunajec River, incorporating the villages of Podczerwone and Czarny Dunajec (fig. 1.1). The entire region is only about thirty-four kilometers north to south and twenty-four kilometers east to west.

The alpine Tatras are the defining geographic characteristic of the region with implications for the history and culture of the area. They are dramatic, jagged mountains cloaked in snow early in autumn until late in the spring when the fields burst alive with flowers and the creeks run clear with frigid snow-melt. The foothills are scattered with houses topped with steep-pitched roofs effective in snowy areas. The traditional and still preferred building material is native spruce logs left unpainted on both interior and exterior sides. The exteriors of the log homes are ideally scrubbed every other year and acquire a rich blond color. The wooden structures mimic the angular beauty of the Tatra peaks, the highest of which is Mount Gerlach on the Slovak side at 2,655 meters above sea level. The highest peak in the Polish portion of the Tatras is Mount Rysy at 2,499 meters. Most of the villages lie in the foothills between 600 and 1,000 meters above sea level. With the exception

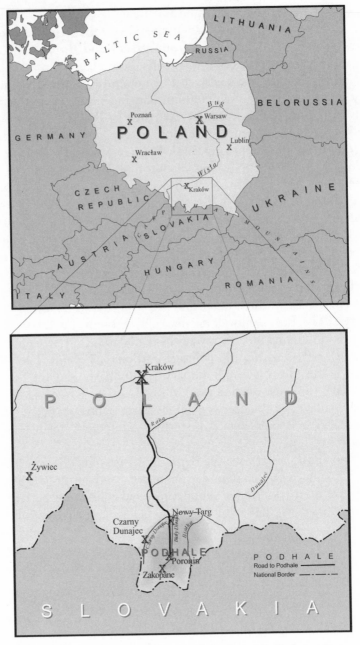

Figure 1.1. Map of Central Europe, Poland, and Podhale.

of the relatively broad and flat fields of the Nowy Targ Valley on the northern edge of Podhale, the land is rugged and hilly—generally less hospitable on the northern Polish side of the Tatras than the more gently sloping and relatively sunny southern Slovak side. "Life is easy on the Slovak side," I am told by more than one Górale. "There they grow grapes and make wine." Lying just above the forty-ninth latitude (roughly equivalent to Vancouver but without the moderating influence of the ocean), Podhale has a cold climate with a short summer suitable for growing oats, potatoes, and wildflowers, but little else (fig. 1.2).

The name "Podhale" is derived from the Górale dialect word *hala* meaning mountain pasture or mountains generally. *Pod* means below, thus "Podhale" (sometimes *Podhole* in Górale dialect) means "piedmont" or below the mountains. More specifically, the area in which I concentrate my research is called *Skalne* Podhale, or "rocky" Podhale, referring to the southern areas of the region closest to the Tatras. According to Włodzimierz Kotoński, who researched Górale music in the early 1950s, the terms "Podhale" and "Podhalanie" (nominative plural form used to refer to the people from Podhale) were used by inteligencja but were not prevalent among local residents. The more commonly used term was *góral*, the masculine-singular noun meaning "mountaineer" (Kotoński 1956, 13). The root word is *góra* (mountain); the adjective form is *góralski*. Here I follow Louise Wrazen's lead (1991, 175) and use "Górale" (the Polish plural noun form) as both noun and adjective, singular and plural, rather than declining the word in the Polish manner. "Górale" refers to all who hail from mountainous areas, but I use the word specifically for people of the Polish Tatra region. Since I am using the term as the name of a group of people I use a capital "G," although the word is not capitalized in Polish. In my conversations with individuals in Podhale, the term "Podhale" is used by local people (Górale) as are the terms *góral* and *góralski*, suggesting that the vocabulary has expanded to include all these words since the time when Kotoński did his research.

Music-Culture

Here I adopt the term "muzyka Podhala" (music of Podhale) to refer specifically to a bounded repertoire that was canonized by musical folklorists in the late nineteenth and early twentieth centuries. "Góralska muzyka" (Górale's music) is also used by musi-

Figure 1.2. Mountains surrounding Dolina Kościelisko, winter 1995.

cians and scholars to describe this repertoire and style of playing, but my choice of "muzyka Podhala" is in homage to composer and musical folklorist Stanisław Mierczyński, who published 101 tunes collected in Podhale in a book he titled *Muzyka Podhala* (1930). In chapters 2 and 3 I show that Mierczyński's book represents a crucial moment in the making of this musical canon that I am calling "muzyka Podhala," and I also demonstrate how this moment is reflected in the simultaneous creation of a Górale ethnicity. In this current chapter my objective is to familiarize readers with the music and dance recognized at the time of my research by scholars and Górale themselves as music-culture uniquely connected with Podhale.

The main genres of this music, described below, are *pasterskie, wierchowe, ozwodne, Sabałowe, Janosikowe, krzesane, drobne, juhaskie, zbójnickie, zielone*, marches, and *nuty cepowiny*.[1] Most of these genre names are derived from Górale dialect taxonomy. I also describe the related dance genres *góralski, juhaski*, and *zbójnicki*.[2] Although I provide representative examples of most genres, the border between genres is blurry and many tunes can be classified in several ways. Vocal music can also be played on instruments, and all instrumental music is rooted in song, including instrumental dance music. In vocal and instrumental music, dotted rhythms are frequent ($\flat$ $\flat$.), often relaxed into triplets ($\flat^3\flat$), and, when metered, muzyka Podhala is almost invariably in duple meter, although different genres do have distinct rhythmic characteristics. In general, muzyka Podhala is characterized by short descending melodic phrases, often with a prominent augmented fourth above the tonic. Many melodies have a narrow range of about a sixth, although certain genres extend to at least an octave (e.g., *Sabałowa* genre below). A tune is not conceived of as fixed but rather as a melodic idea called *nuta* that is given new life with each performance. Jan Stęszewski (1980, 31) equates *nuta* with melody, but Włodzimierz Kotoński concludes that very different melodies may be considered the same *nuta* by Górale. He wrote that the concept of *nuta* is based on a harmonic foundation (*basy* and *sekund* patterns), and that melody line and rhythm are just manifestations of that harmony (Kotoński 1953a, 6–7). I have noticed that the idea of *nuta* as a broad melodic category is most appropriate for dance tunes and unaccompanied *pasterska*-style singing. On the other hand, certain popular songs have immediately recognizable melodies that are varied less dramatically. "Mój Janicku" (see fig. 1.30, below) is such a song, as is a subcategory of songs called *Duchowe*, also described below.

Much muzyka Podhala is ensemble music—either groups of singers or small ensembles of bowed instruments—and the vocal and instrumental traditions are closely linked. A woman or man may sing alone, but if other Górale are present they will likely join in the singing. Solo instrumental performances are most often associated with shepherding or otherwise being alone in the mountains and playing bagpipes or one of several varieties of wooden flutes or whistles. The most common instrumental ensemble includes three violins and a *basy*, a three-stringed cello-sized bowed lute. The violins are tuned in standard European tuning (GDAE), although they may be pitched higher than standard. The three strings of the *basy* are tuned D, D an octave higher, and A pitched between the two Ds. The two D strings are usually bowed together and the A string alone. Most frequently there is one lead violinist, called the *prymista* or *prym*, and each accompanying violinist (there may be several) is called a *sekundzista* or *sekund* (plural, *sekundy*). Just one *sekund* is acceptable and some believe traditional. Today two *sekundy* are more common, and often there are many more. The *basy* plays in tandem with the *sekundy* and is occasionally supported with a double bass, all sounding on the quarter-note beat (as most typically transcribed and as can be seen in the following figures), changing bow direction with each beat. Together the *basy* and *sekundy* produce harmonic ostinatos (repeated bass lines and "chords"), although what they play should not be considered "functional harmony" in the sense of European common practice tonal harmony. While musical practices among Górale are influenced by European "classical" music, they are governed by different aesthetics.

Vocal ensembles similarly recognize a leader. The lead singer is usually an individual with a particularly strong voice but in some cases may simply be the one who initiated a song, is in a position of power or responsibility, or perhaps knows a lot of songs. The lead singer begins a song and other singers join in after a few notes, harmonizing below the lead singer, but invariably cadencing in unison with the singer. The overall structure featuring parallel harmonies, including parallel fifths but ending in unison, reminds some musicians of medieval organum, but the prominent melodic tritone suggests otherwise. Polyphonic a cappella singing is a valued social and aesthetic practice, but singing may also be accompanied by instruments. As we will see below, solo singing accompanied by string ensembles is the most traditional way to start a dance.

Vocal and Instrumental Genres

Two characteristic and related vocal genres are *pasterska* (pastoral) and *wierchowa* (mountain peak song/tune). Both usually contain two

Pijes gorzałecke	Drink moonshine
Pij do mnie, pij do mnie.	Drink to me, drink to me.
Jak cie nocka zajdzie	If night overtakes you
Przydź do mnie, przydź do mnie.	Come to me, come to me.

Figure 1.3. *Pasterska*, singing led by Stanisława Szostak (ac19.vii.92.1).[3] *CD track 21*

lines of text (A and B lines), each line set to a different melodic phrase (A and B musical phrases), but sometimes both lines are sung to the same melodic material (AB text, AA music). Usually the second line of music and text is repeated, forming an ABB or AAA musical structure. If more than one singer is available, the lead singer begins alone and the accompanying singers join in after a few beats, harmonizing at the interval of a third or a fifth below. Figure 1.3 is a *pasterska* that illustrates this practice (CD track 21). Note also that it uses only one melodic line, repeated twice to form an AAA melodic structure fitted with the ABB poetic structure. Figure 1.4 is a *wierchowa* with a different melodic line accompanying the second line of text (ABB poetic and melodic structure). The border between the two genres is blurred, but *pasterskie* are usually rhythmically free (unmetered or performed with extreme rubato), and *wierchowe* are typically in duple meter, although they may also be rhythmically free.

One very distinctive feature of singing in Podhale is that men and women sing in the same octave: men in a high register, women in a low register. My transcriptions are represented at pitch.[4] To sing from my transcriptions, men must sing at pitch, not down an octave as is the convention when men read music in the treble clef.

A *wierchowa* is structurally similar or even identical to the *oz-*

Sk⁰o-da Boze ciebie
sk⁰oda Boze i mnie
ze my sie k⁰ochali
syćk⁰o nadarémnie.

God, it's unfortunate for you
God it's unfortunate for me
that we loved each other
in vain.

Figure 1.4. *Wierchowa*, sung by Władysław Pieróg (from Sadownik 1971 [1957], 271, no. 31).

wodna, also called *rozwodna*. Outside the context of music, the meaning of the dialect term *ozwodna* is unclear, but "slowly" or "in a circle, turning" have been suggested. Although there are exceptions, both *wierchowe* and *ozwodne* have ten-beat phrase structures, a feature that sets them apart from most Polish folk genres. A slow, rhythmically free *wierchowa* played more rapidly in 2/4 meter by instruments is often referred to as an *ozwodna*. This would seem to negate the interpretation of the word *ozwodna* as meaning "slowly" except that an *ozwodna* is generally danced much slower than a *krzesana* or *drobna*, described below. A *wierchowa* is usually considered to be music for listening, and an *ozwodna* music for dancing, but I have heard Górale refer to some instrumental tunes as "*wierchowe* for dancing." The distinction between *pasterskie*, *wierchowe*, and *ozwodne* is best thought of as a continuum from unmetered music for listening to metered music for dancing (see fig. 1.5). Figures 1.6, 1.7, and 1.8 are versions of the same *nuta*: 1.6 is a rhythmically free *pasterska* (CD track 1), 1.7 a metered *wierchowa* (CD track 2), and 1.8 an *ozwodna* for dancing (CD track 3).

The next genre of tunes considered here bears the name of Jan Krzeptowski-Sabała, the violinist, storyteller, and mountain guide memorialized in the monument to Chałubiński. These tunes, called

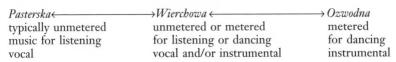

Figure 1.5. *Pasterska, wierchowa, ozwodna* continuum.

Hej, juhasicek biedny,
nie obłapi nigdy.
Hej, owiecki paść musi
choc go dziewce kusi.

Hey, poor shepherd boy,
he never hugs (cuddles).
Hey, sheep he must pasture
while a girl seduces him.

Figure 1.6. *Pasterska*, performed by the troupe *Skalni* (ac19.viii.92.4). *CD track 1*

Ej, śpiewam jo se śpiewam ciese (?__)
Ej, ło dam nie Janicku (?__)

Hey, I sing, I sing (?__)
Hey, (?__) Jack (?__)

Figure 1.7. *Wierchowa*, sung by Bogusława Łowisz, 2003 (compare to Szurmiak-Bogucka 1959, 35). *CD track 2*

Hej, ani jo nie juhas,   Hey, I am not a shepherd (apprentice),
ani jo nie baca.   Nor am I a chief shepherd.
Hej, sama mi ciupaska   Hey, my hatchet by itself
owiecki nawraco.   takes care of the sheep.

Figure 1.8. *Ozwodna*, performed by the troupe *Skalni* (ac19.viii.92.4). *CD track 3*

Sabałowe (of Sabała), were probably not composed by Sabała but may have been favored by him. They are considered an older layer of tunes and are sometimes called *staroświeckie*, meaning "of the old world" (Wrazen 1988, 97–99). My interpretation is that they probably were not composed by Sabała; composition does not seem to be an important practice in Górale musical aesthetics. Instead, they are linked with Sabała as symbols of an earlier, definitive period. The tunes in this genre are distinguished by harmonic shifts to G (most tunes center around D) and an extended melodic range cadencing down on an A or G, the G cadences requiring the use of the D string of the violin (see fig. 1.9, CD track 4). Most other genres can be played by the *prym* using only the A and E strings. Usually *Sabałowe* are performed slowly for listening, but they may

Modulate up 5th to D, then back to G

Variant, Part B

Figure 1.9. Instrumental *Sabałowa*, Stanisław Michałczek, *prym. CD track 4*

also be used for dancing. Figure 1.9 is an instrumental *Sabałowa* recorded at a funeral in 1995, and figure 1.10 is a sung *Sabałowa* transcribed in the 1950s.

Other family names are associated with certain tunes, but none suggests a stylistic genre like the *Sabałowa/staroświecka* tunes. For example, Stanisław Mierczyński, the composer and musical folk-lorist mentioned above, transcribed a tune called *Ozwodna Bartusiowa* after violinist Bartuś Obrochta, and another called *Ozwodna Zakopiańska Gąsienicowa* after the family name "Gąsienica" common in Zakopane (Mierczyński 1930, nos. 28, 49). I have documented tunes bearing the Maśniak family name, for example, *Wierchowa Maśniakowa* (v11.xii.94). Similar to the *Sabałowa* tunes, these are not believed to have been composed by the individuals or families for whom they are named but are associated with them because they were known to have liked playing the tunes.

An exception are songs for listening, called *Duchowe*, believed to have been composed by Andrzej Knapczyk-Duch (1866–1946) from the Podhalan village Ciche (literally meaning "quiet"). Aleksandra Szurmiak-Bogucka challenges this, however. She believes that only one melody among those called *Duchowa* may have actually been composed by him (personal communication, fieldnotes,

Ej, na ᵘorawskiej pyrci
kᵘozicka sie kryńci
ej, kᵘozicka nie kryńć sa
strzelem ci do sérca.

Hey, on the path to Orawa
a mountain goat is moving
hey, mountain goat don't move
for I'll shoot into your heart.

Figure 1.10. Vocal *Sabałowa*, sung by Bronisława Konieczna
(from Sadownik 1971 [1957], 259, no. 1).

7 February 1995). An educated man trained in music, Knapczyk-Duch was able to notate melodies, and the tunes he wrote down may have been transcriptions of what he heard others play and not his own compositions. In fact, some pieces attributed to Knapczyk-Duch are similar to *Janosikowe* (considered next). What I find significant is that he is considered a composer by Górale, and this distinguishes Knapczyk-Duch from all other renowned Górale musicians. In general, Górale musicians place little value on the composition of new tunes but value, instead, knowledge of and ability to improvise on and give life to existing *nuty*. Knapczyk-Duch's songs have relatively fixed wedded tunes and texts, departing from the spirit of the *nuta* concept and the usual promiscuity between texts and tunes. Perhaps for these reasons his music is not considered traditional by some musical folklorists, yet Górale musicians like his songs and accept them as part of their tradition (K. Trebunia-Tutka ac20.xi.94.1).

Musically *Duchowe* have much in common with an additional tune/song genre also named after an individual. *Janosikowe* are ballads named after Janosik (Juraj Jánošík), a historical figure who was born in Terchowa, Slovakia, in 1688, and who led a band of robbers called *zbójniki* (brigands or highway robbers) in the mountains until he was captured and executed in 1713. Compared by Górale to

Figure 1.11. Instrumental *Duchowa*, Jan Karpiel-Bułecka, *prym. CD track 5*

Robin Hood, Janosik and his band of *zbójniki* ostensibly stole from the rich (Hungarian, Polish, and Slovak nobility, traveling merchants) to provide for the poor (Górale). Although Slovak, Janosik and the *zbójnik* legends are central to the Polish Górale sense of identity, and *Janosikowe*, as well as a dance genre called *zbójnicki* (see below), are very popular and important in Górale music-culture (Wrazen 1988, 107–108). A distinctive feature of many *Janosikowe* and of Knapczyk-Duch's songs is an odd number of beats per phrase. Sometimes these are transcribed in 3/4 time (see Mierczyński 1930, no. 24), but based on the way Górale musician Krzysztof Trebunia-Tutka taught me to play the accompanying violin parts for these songs, I transcribe them 2/4 but with a single 3/4 measure at the end of some phrases, as represented in figure 1.11 (CD track 5).

Music for Dancing

Much of the music discussed above is considered music for listening, with the exception of the *ozwodna* which is music for dancing.

Figure 1.12. *Drobna* (from Mierczyński 1930, no. 64).

Other genres of music for dancing include *krzesana* and *drobna*. The tunes and dance types *krzesany* and *drobny*[5] are similar, and the terms are sometimes used interchangeably. If anything distinguishes them, some *drobne* are characterized by harmonic accompaniments that are more complex than the typically two-chord *krzesane* accompaniments (fig. 1.12), although some *krzesane* also have relatively complex harmonic structures. Perhaps the two were more distinct genres at one time, and this distinction has since faded. Both genres feature duple-meter tunes that are used in the dance called *góralski*, described below. *Krzesane* and *drobne* are usually played fast with virtuosic improvisation by the lead violinist. Most have short eight-beat phrase structures, but there are many different and sometimes unusual phrase structures that are the defining characteristics of distinct *krzesane* or *drobne*. For example, a *krzesana* called "wiecno" (also spelled *wiecna*, dialect form of Polish *wieczny*, meaning eternal, perpetual) has two different phrases, each of which can be extended in length by the lead violin, even "eternally." For the first phrase of the song, the *basy* and *sekundy* play only a D chord until the final beat of the phrase at which time they change to an A chord; the A chord then is repeated throughout the second phrase until the final two beats which cadence back on D (see fig. 1.13, and CD track 6, noting the variable phrase lengths). Like "wiecno," many *krzesane* are named after their accompaniment patterns: "Po dwa" (in two) for which the *basy* and *sekundy* play each chord for two beats (fig. 1.14, CD track 7); "Po śtyry" (in four) (also spelled *po cztery*) with four beats on each chord (fig. 1.15, CD track 8); "Trzy a roz" (three and one) with an ostinato of three Ds and one A arranged as follows: DDAD, repeat (fig. 1.16, CD track 9).

Górale also play a number of marches, some as part of the *zbójnicki* dance cycle discussed below, and others as processionals. One in particular, called "Hej Madziar Pije" (Hey the Hungarian drinks) or simply "Marsz Madziarski" (Hungarian march) is played to welcome and honor guests as they enter a room on festive occasions. As the name implies, the tune is believed to have originated in Hungary, probably referring to the Kingdom of Hungary that included the south side of the Tatras before World War I (fig. 1.17, CD track 10).[6]

In the instrumental versions of all the genres discussed above, the accompanying violins and *basy* mark the duple-meter rhythm in a similar manner: bowing together on the quarter note beats in

Figure 1.13. *Krzesana* "wiecno," played by Marion Styrczula-Maśniak (v10.i.2003). *CD track 6*

2/4 time with a down-bow on the first beat and an up-bow on the second (e.g., figs. 1.12 and 1.17). Although the accompanying violinists (the *sekundy*) may play eighth notes, they are slurred, and the violinist continues to change bow direction only on the quarter note beat. This straightforward rhythmic punctuation is a characteristic of muzyka Podhala and differs from other duple-meter music genres played in Poland, including krakowiaks and polkas, that usually feature the *basy* marking the quarter note beat and the violins marking the offbeat, and also differs from Slovak and Hungarian styles with a double-pulse bowing technique called *düvö*[7] (for example, see fig. 1.33 below and CD track 20).

Several tunes for the *zbójnicki* dance cycle employ an accom-

Figure 1.14. *Krzesana* "po dwa" (in two) (from Kotoński 1956, no. 2). *CD track 7, variant*

paniment pattern that distinguishes them from the rest of the mu-zyka Podhala repertoire. Figure 1.18, "Marsz Chałubińskiego," a favorite of Dr. Chałubiński, illustrates this accompaniment (CD track 11).[8] Rather than bowing only on the quarter notes, as in other Górale music, the accompanying violins add an eighth note staccato A on the offbeat. This is accomplished with a down-bow on the beat, chording (double-stopping) on the low G and D strings, and rocking the bow to the open A string with an offbeat up-bow, giving this "Marsz Chałubińskiego," as well as several other tunes in the *zbójnicki* sequence, a distinctive immediately rec-ognizable lilting quality. Not all the tunes to the *zbójnicki* cycle use

Figure 1.15. *Krzesana* "po śtyry" (in four), played by Marion
Styrczula-Maśniak, *prym* (v10.i.2003). *CD track 8*

this same accompaniment, but of the eight tunes that I have documented being used in the cycle, half of them employ this distinctive accompaniment.

Like the Janosik ballads (*Janosikowe*) and the *zbójnik* legend,
the *zbójnicki* tunes are recognized as being from outside Podhale
on the southern, Slovak side of the Tatras (Brzozowska 1965, 464–
465). One *zbójnicki* tune was collected among Romanian Wallachians and published in 1782 by Franz Joseph Sulzer, suggesting that
the historical origins extend south and east along the Carpathian
mountain range (Chybiński 1961, 167; Kotoński 1953b, 51–52; and
Wrazen 1988, 105–107). Similarly, related *zbójnicki* cycles are
danced in neighboring regions of Poland and Slovakia, reinforcing

Figure 1.16. *Krzesana* "trzy a roz" (three and one), played by Paweł Staszel, *prym* (VHS19.viii.92). *CD track 9*

shared aspects of music-culture in the wider Tatra area. The Gó-rale musicians I worked with were very aware of what types of music and what specific songs or tunes are accepted as being from Pod-hale, and which are from outside. Music from neighboring regions is considered kin, related mountain music, if not technically mu-zyka Podhala. Although the region of Podhale has traditionally remained within the lands of the Polish kingdom and nation-state, the political borders in the broader area have been malleable. The current border dividing Poland and Slovakia was established after World War I and redrawn after World War II. For more than a century prior to World War I, both sides of the Tatras were part of the Austro-Hungarian Empire, with the south side falling within Hungary and the north side in Austrian Galicia. Some older Górale talk about the time of the empire as when "there was no border" (Gąscienica-Giewont ac1.vi.95). Certainly cultural affinity knows no borders in the Tatras.

The final genre of muzyka Podhala that I will consider, and which points musically beyond the confines of Podhale, is a group of *nuty* used in weddings. Of concern here are a series of four tunes

Figure 1.17. "Hej Madziar Pije" (from Mierczyński 1930, no. 94).
CD track 10, variant

Figure 1.18. "Marsz Chałubińskiego" (from Mierczyński 1930, no. 92). Bowings added. *CD track 11, variant*

associated with a ritual called *cepowiny* during which the bride's wreath (head-dress) is replaced with a scarf. This ceremony includes a sequence of ritual exchanging and bargaining between men, married women, the joining families, and the community at large (fig. 1.19). The entire event, which generally lasts well over an hour, is danced and sung to music consisting almost exclusively of four distinct tunes. These tunes and their ritual function are considered in detail in chapter 6, but I mention them briefly here. All four tunes are what Tadeusz Styrczula-Maśniak described to me as krakowiak-like; that is, they each have an offbeat accompaniment pattern similar to polkas but more likely related to the much older krakowiak dance form from the Kraków region north of Podhale. Figure 1.20 illustrates this offbeat accompaniment. Figure 1.21 is a version of the same *nuta* as published by Mierczyński but transcribed in 3/4 time. Szurmiak-Bogucka (1974, 97) also represents this same *nuta* in 3/4 time. Yet I hear the tune in 2/4 as I have transcribed it in figure 1.20, and the dance steps used with this tune also suggest duple meter (CD track 12).

Figure 1.19. Bride Wioleta Karpiel-Replon dancing with her
bridesmaids during a *cepowiny* ritual, Olcza, 1995.

Figure 1.20. *Cepowiny* (Chicago ac25.ix.93.2). *CD track 12*

Figure 1.21. *Cepowiny* (from Mierczyński 1930, no. 65).

Figure 1.22. Adam Karpiel, the first *drużba* (first groomsman or "best man"), calling a dance before the band at a wedding (the backs of the violinists' heads and bows are visible), Olcza, 1995.

Dance Genres

Though all the genres of muzyka Podhala are song-based, most are also used for one of several dance cycles: the *góralski, juhaski,* and *zbójnicki.* The *góralski* is the only indigenous dance for a male/female couple in Podhale. Although the start of each individual dance within a *góralski* sequence may involve several additional dancers, the *góralski* is danced primarily by one couple while others observe. The *góralski* is a sequence of different dance genres manipulated on the spot by the male dancer. Many of the genre types introduced above refer to their function in the *góralski* dance sequence: *drobny* (small [dance steps]), *krzesany* (striking [dance steps]), *ozwodny* (slowly, drawn out, or circling [dance steps]).

The *góralski* sequence of tune/dance types is improvised by the solo male dancer within a basic framework. The sequence is initiated by the dancer who approaches the band and requests a dance by slipping money into the f-hole of the *basy* and singing a *przyśpiewka* (pre-song/introduction) for an *ozwodna* (fig. 1.22). The band

Figure 1.23. Adam Karpiel, best man, dancing with the bride, Wioleta Karpiel-Replon, Olcza, 1995.

then picks up the tune and plays it while the man dances a triple pattern against the duple-meter tune and waits for the female dancer to be introduced to the dance floor. The lead male dancer has previously asked one of his friends to introduce the girl or woman of his choice to the dance area with a special step called *zwyrtanie*. After the lead man and woman are united in the dance area, they dance the *ozwodny* together, the man controlling the dance and the woman responding to the man's gestures, although they do not actually touch each other (fig. 1.23).

When the man has danced to the first tune as long as he wishes, he dances up to the band and requests another dance by singing another *przyśpiewka*, or by simply calling out the name of a particular dance or tune. This second dance may be another *ozwodny* or a *krzesany/drobny*. Subsequent to being introduced to the dance floor by a man or boy, the female dancer is re-introduced to the dance area by a female friend or a small group of women using the *zwyrtanie* turning dance step. After dancing as many *ozwodne* and *krzesane* as the male dancer wishes, he calls for or sings one of two *nuty* called "zielona" (literally, meaning "green") (figs. 1.24 and 1.25, CD tracks 13 and 14). The band switches into "zielona" with-

Zie - lo - na lip - ka, i ja - wor, cy - jes to dziyw - ce? Bo - ze mój!

Typical text:

Zielona lipka, i jawor,   Green linden and sycamore,
cyjes to dziywce? Boze mój!   whose girl is this? My God!

Figure 1.24. "Zielona" *nuta* 1. *CD track 13, variant*

Zbo - la - ły mnie no - ski mu - se cho - dzić pred - cki ja - ze ku Koś - cie - lis - ku

Ni mom jo se ni mom, ni mom jo se ni mom ko - cha - ne - cki po blis - ku

Sample words, many other texts are used:

Zbolały mnie noski,   My legs ache,
muse chodzić predcki   I must walk far
jaze ku Kościelisku.   up to Kościelisko.

Ni mom jo se ni mom,   I don't have, I don't have,
ni mom jo se ni mom   I don't have, I don't have
kochanecki po blisku.   a lover who is closer.

Figure 1.25. "Zielona" *nuta* 2. *CD track 14, variant*

out pausing, and the male dancer ends the dance by spinning the female with the *zwyrtanie* step, touching her for the first time in the dance sequence. The name "zielona" comes from the most typical text for one of the two special tunes (fig. 1.24).

Related to the *góralski* is a dance performed by men or boys together when no women or girls are available (Kotoński 1956, 123). Named after a young apprentice shepherd, the *juhaski* features dance steps similar to the *góralski* and uses the same tune repertoire. Górale women do not have a corresponding all-female dance tradition. However, all-female dance arrangements have been developed for the stage in the last twenty to thirty years (Paweł Staszel, personal communication).

Figure 1.26. *Zbójnicki* dance with *ciupagi*. Bukowina Tatrzańska, 1995.

A different genre wildly popular in Podhale but probably originating from the Slovak side of the Tatras is the *zbójnicki* dance. The adjective *zbójnicki* is derived from the noun *zbójnik*, which refers to the legendary robbers associated with Janosik, introduced above. The *zbójnicki* is danced by a group of men or boys or both in a circle, wielding *ciupagi* (fig. 1.26). The dance is related to military recruiting dances, especially the Hungarian *verbunkos*, and is also similar to Slovak and Hungarian folk dances, as well as to men's dances from farther east in Ukraine. Although at least one early source suggests that this dance was semi-choreographed (Goszczyński 1853) in the mid-nineteenth century, some twentieth-century ethnographers assume that the dance was previously more spontaneous, with each dancer performing different steps (Zborowski 1972 [1930], 331). Song and dance troupes today combine some elements of spontaneity with rehearsed choreographed steps. In performances I have seen, the circle of dancers will have a leader who calls out different changes such as: "Hej siad!" (squat), "Hej bok!" (squat while turning to one side), "Hej puść!" (release [toss] the *ciupagi*), "Hey bier!" (grab the *ciupagi*), and "Hej zbyrk!" (turn and strike the *ciupagi* with the dancer next to you to make a ringing or clanking sound) (Tadeusz Zdybal, e-mail communication, 5 June 1998).

Song Texts

Improvisation is a valued skill in all aspects of Górale music-culture, including the ability to improvise topical song texts to fit a situation. Singers also draw from a large storehouse of texts preserved in oral tradition. With the exception of ballads, the poetry has two rhymed lines per verse, each line typically has twelve syllables, and the second line is usually repeated when sung (ABB):

Górol jo se Górol, zyjem w Zokopanem.	Górale, I am a Górale, I live in Zakopane.
Choć ta na mnie biyda, to se jestem panem,	Although I am poor, I am a lord,
Choć ta na mnie biyda, to se jestem panem.	Although I am poor, I am a lord.

Alternatively the poetry can be conceived of as having four lines of six syllables each:

Dziywcyno cyjasi,	Somebody's girl,
lubiom cie Juhasi.	shepherd boys like you.
Lubi cie Baca nas.	Our head shepherd likes you.
Podź z nami na sałas.	Go with us to our hut.

The most comprehensive collection of traditional texts from Podhale is Jan Sadownik's 1971 (1957) *Pieśni Podhala: Antologi* (Songs of Podhale: Anthology). A second collection, the largest compilation of texts with English translations, accompanies the compact disk recordings *Fire in the Mountains*, volumes 1 and 2 (Cooley and Spottswood 1997a, 1997b). These CDs are re-releases of recordings by Górale immigrants in Chicago from 1927 to the 1950s and are the earliest commercial recordings of Górale music (CD tracks 10 and 13 are from these re-releases).

The texts are typically short, emblematic verses that stand alone, the exceptions being *Janosikowa* ballads and a few other songs that are separate from the dance genres. Single short verses are especially prevalent when rendered in *przyśpiewka* form to call a particular dance tune. Like the tunes themselves, they are brief gestures expressing a single thought, and in this sense are not unlike Japanese haiku. The poetry is often loosely organized around themes of love, sex, courtship, and marriage; place, especially the

Tatra Mountains; legendary robbers; and even on the theme of Górale music itself. The advent of audio recordings encouraged stringing together several verses to create longer poems, a trend illustrated on the *Fire in the Mountain* recordings cited above. An additional influential trend comprises several waves of Górale literary movements that promote dialect poetry (Kolbuszewski 1982; Majda 1991). Recent compact disk recordings by the Trebunia-Tutka family are manifestations of this dialect literary movement by including new poetry in Górale dialect reflecting modern social issues (see chapter 5).

Muzyka Podhala in Context

On any day in Podhale one will have the opportunity to experience a much greater variety of music than muzyka Podhala. Although cultural practices are always changing and the situation may be different now, during the 1990s in Nowy Targ and Zakopane, discos played the latest dance music; classical chamber music concerts were held in museums and other small venues; specific clubs featured jazz; and others employed Roma bands. In Zakopane alone I documented three active Roma ensembles that played music often considered the purview of Roma, including csárdáses and verbunkoses, and they also played popular songs, polkas, tangos, and other ballroom dances. Górale musicians also played polkas, waltzes, csárdáses, tangos, and other music that suited their typical string ensembles, as well as their fancy, and was popular among the groups that hired them to play. In this sense the Górale bands were similar to the Roma bands: they specialized in a repertoire identified with their ethnic group, and they expanded their repertoire to increase their marketability and personal enjoyment of music making.

An experience during the very first day I spent in Podhale illustrates some of the context of muzyka Podhala and helps to convey the idea that, like all music traditions, muzyka Podhala is a constructed tradition that some Górale consciously maintain as a separate repertoire, distinct from other music that they also perform. During the summer of 1992 I was enrolled in a Polish language and culture program at Jagiellonian University in Kraków. On Sunday, 19 July, I boarded a bus for the two hour trip south into Podhale to attend *Poroniańskie Lato* (Poronin Summer), a folk

Figure 1.27. Festival in Poronin, 1992. Photographed from behind
the stage looking toward the audience. Photograph by Angi
Bezeredi.

music and dance festival in the village of Poronin (fig. 1.27). I was
invited to the festival by Aleksandra Szurmiak-Bogucka, an ethnomusicologist specializing in Górale music with whom I had been
in communication but had yet to meet. Thus I was traveling to
Podhale with the objective of meeting a senior Polish colleague,
and of experiencing, in the place of its origin, the music that fascinated me.

Once in the village the site of the festival was obvious, and I
had little trouble locating and meeting Szurmiak-Bogucka, who,
almost immediately, began giving me a tutorial on the festival stage
performances by song and dance troupes from Podhale and neighboring regions. Onstage the Podhalan groups performed repertoire
strictly within the genres described above, with the exception of a
polka at the end of most performances. I often hear such a polka
referred to as a "góralska polka," suggesting that it was composed
by a Górale, although the genre is not considered muzyka Podhala
or indigenous. Perhaps these polkas are best considered local versions of an imported genre. During the festival stage shows I took

notes but did not brandish my field audio recorder. At the time I viewed the shows as instructional but geared toward tourists and of secondary interest for my ethnographic goals. I had yet to theorize the centrality of tourism in music-culture, the historic role of tourism as it relates to Podhale, or my own role as an ethnographic tourist. I longed to experience muzyka Podhala in a more "authentic" or "natural" setting.

In the early afternoon the festival stage shows paused for dinner. Szurmiak-Bogucka invited me to join her and others officially associated with the festival for dinner in the basement level of a large home that rented rooms to tourists. After a hearty meal, vodka and violins emerged, and my interest was peaked. Now, I thought, away from the rehearsed staged performances, I will experience "authentic" Górale music. I gained permission to set up my recorder and for the first time that day began to make audio documentation of events. I noted the names of two of the violinists and singers, Stanisława Szostak and Władysław Trebunia-Tutka, who exchanged *prym* responsibilities.

The first piece performed was a *wierchowa*, first sung and then played by three violins and a *basy*. Setting up my recorder while the musicians began, I was able to record only the very end of the sung portion and then the instrumental repetition of this piece (fig. 1.28, CD track 15). Szostak initiated the next piece and played *prym*, this time a *Sabałowa* (fig. 1.29, CD track 16). Almost immediately after the *Sabałowa* tune ended, Szostak started another tune, the ensemble joined her, and after the first repeat she sang "Mój Janicku, nie bij ze mnie . . ." (My Janik, don't beat me . . .) (fig. 1.30, CD track 17). The tune is one of several in Podhale with twelve-beat phrase structures (six measures in 2/4 time). Although this extended phrase length is not as typical as the ten-beat phrases of most *wierchowe*, this *kołysanka* or lullaby (cradlesong) is generally considered a tune and song from Podhale. The accompaniment with second violins and *basy* playing chords on the beat, and the vocal polyphony with the male and female voices in the same octave, are clearly in the Górale style. The melodic emphasis on the minor third contrasts with the prominent D to G# tritone in the previous *wierchowa*. I have since documented many versions of this beautiful lullaby with its disturbing hint of domestic violence.

Up to this point all the music performed at this impromptu session was muzyka Podhala, but after a short pause in the playing

Figure 1.28. *Wierchowa*, probably Władysław Trebunia-Tutka on *prym* (ac19.vii.92.1). *CD track 15*

Figure 1.29. *Sabałowa*, Stanisława Szostak, *prym;* Władysław
Trebunia-Tutka, 2nd *prym* and *sekund* (ac19.vii.92.1). *CD track 16*

Mój Janicku nie bijze mnie,
w kołysecce kołys ze mnie.
Bo mnie mama nie bijała,
W kołysecce kołysała.

My Janik don't beat me,
rock me in the cradle.
Because my mama did not beat me,
she rocked me in the cradle.

Figure 1.30. "Mój Janicku nie bij ze mnie," Stanisława Szostak, lead singer and *prym* (ac19.vii.92.1). *CD track 17*

Szostak proclaimed, "Zagromy se Słowaskom" ("Let's play something Slovak"), signaling a shift across a political—and potentially musical—border. She then began playing a tune in triple meter; Władysław Trebunia-Tutka joined her, playing accompaniment (*sekund*) on the offbeats (2 and 3) in the third bar (fig. 1.31, CD track 18), followed by the *basy* player on the downbeats. After three repetitions, Szostak changed into a new triple-meter Slovak tune without pausing (not on the CD). To my ear, the *sekundy* and *basy* did not play with the same confidence on this Slovak medley as they did when playing muzyka Podhala, and Szostak played the simple tune without variation.

The next music performed was an a cappella *pasterska* in a characteristic Górale style: one singer began alone (once again it was Szostak who initiated this performance), singing in full voice a slowly cascading melody with a prominent tritone above the tonic. Others joined in, harmonizing usually at intervals of thirds and fifths below the lead singer. At the end of each phrase, all voices came together in unison on the last note (fig. 1.32, CD track 19).

What followed again moved away from what is considered muzyka Podhala. First was a tango, sung by Trebunia-Tutka while Szostak played the melody. Next came a csárdás, "Hej ta helpa," considered to be from Slovakia (fig. 1.33, CD track 20). A few of the women who were helping to clear the dinner table joined in the singing. If one listens carefully to the audio example, one can hear that men and women sing parts separated by an octave, not in the same octave range as when singing muzyka Podhala. On many occasions I have noticed Górale musicians making this striking stylistic change to accompany repertoire shifts into music from elsewhere. Also audible is a double pulse with each bow stroke by the *sekundy* and *basy* (bowings are marked in fig. 1.33). This type of csárdás is a Slovak-style version of Hungarian csárdáses that are very popular in Podhale. The style is characterized by the double-pulse *düvö* bowing during the first half, and then, for the second half, the piece speeds up and is accompanied like a polka (1:45 track 20): the *basy* is on the beat while the *sekundy* play off the beat. After a few repeats Szostak shifted into the fast polka-like section of another csárdás associated with Slovakia called "Aniczka" (not on the CD).

After a few moments Stanisława Szostak launched into another *pasterska* (fig. 1.3, above). On the CD track 21, one can hear a few

Figure 1.31. "Slovak tune" (waltz), Stanisława Szostak, *prym* (ac19.vii.92.1). *CD track 18*

Figure 1.31. *Continued.*

women some distance from the microphone joining her, and then Władysław joins and harmonizes below. All singers end in unison, with men and women in the same octave. As is common in most Górale music forms, the first line of poetry is answered by a second repeated line, resulting in a poetic ABB form. But unlike many *pasterska* tunes, the melodic structure of this example is the same with each line (AAA). As the singing faded Władysław Trebunia-Tutka played the same melody using double stops on his violin (not on the CD). The other instrumentalists accompanied Władysław, who, after one repeat of the *pasterska*, launched into a metered *wierchowa* that seemed to lift those gathered out of the contemplative mood produced by the *pasterska*. When finished, the musicians agreed that they should get back to the festival, and they began to pack their instruments. Szostak thanked our hosts for

Figure 1.32. *Pasterska*, Stanisława Szostak, lead singer (ac19.vii.92.1). *CD track 19*

Figure 1.33. "Hej ta helpa" (csárdás), probably Stanisława Szostak on *prym* (ac19.vii.92.1). *CD track 20*

Figure 1.33. *Continued.*

dinner as I stopped my recorder and packed it back into my shoulder bag.

First experiences often have profound impact on one's understanding, and my first day in Podhale was no exception. Not only did I meet some of the individuals I have continued to visit and communicate with for more than a decade, but I was also faced with some of the cultural contradictions that would motivate and shape my subsequent research. For example, on the festival stage, troupes from Podhale performed only muzyka Podhala with the exception of a closing polka. However, the offstage music event described above contained a much lower percentage of muzyka Podhala: six pieces were clearly within the canon, while four were from outside Podhale in origin or style. Yet at the time I misprized the festival stage performances in favor of the spontaneous offstage performances around the dinner table that I interpreted as more "traditional" or "authentic." Which performance context better represented the music of Podhale?

Since that Sunday in 1992 I have revisited my conceptions and misconceptions of muzyka Podhala, as well as my notions about what it means to be Górale from Podhale and to be a musician. I have also come to recognize the important place of festivals, tourist shows, and the impact of scholars such as Szurmiak-Bogucka, Mierczyński—and potentially myself—on this music-culture. In the pages that follow I show how this thing called muzyka Podhala is invented and how tourist festivals play an important role in this ongoing invention, as do the offstage instances where musicians consciously play outside the canon, as witnessed that Sunday afternoon around a dinner table in a Podhalan village.

2

Making History

Ja myślę, że dla nas generalnie, muzycznie bliżsi są Słowacy. Słowacy są bardziej bliżsi niż polskie regiony leżące na północ od Podhala. No na przykład z Liptowem, zaraz po drugiej stronie Tatr mamy przynajmniej piętnaście wspólnych melodii. Ja jestem, moje serce jest . . . , generalnie mnie zawsze ciągnęło na południe, na tamtą stronę, zawsze to robiło na mnie wrażenie, czy jak słuchałem rumuńskiej muzyki, czy mołdawskiej, czy ukraińskiej czy huculskiej, czy Słowaków słuchałem czy Węgrów—to zawsze mnie ciągnęło w tamtą stronę. Nie wiem dlaczego.

I think that for us generally the Slovaks are musically the closest. Slovaks are much closer than are the Polish regions lying on the northern side of Podhale. Well, for example, with Liptów, immediately on the other side of the Tatras we have at least fifteen common melodies. I am, my heart is . . . , generally always pulled to the south. On that side, it always impressed me, or when I heard Romanian music, or Moldavian, or Ukrainian or Hucuł,[1] or listened to Slovaks or Hungarians— that always pulled me to that side. I don't know why.

[. . .] Somewhere in the sub-

[. . .] Gdzieś w podświadomości tkwi w góralach to, ze
jednak nie jesteśmy już wszyscy
czysto polskiego pochodzenia.
Zresztą cala Polska nie jest czysto
polska, bo Polska jest dla Europy
jak "hall" gdzie się wszyscy prze-
chodzą, a Podhale szczególnie,
przecież tutaj przyszli Rumuni—
pasterze wołoscy, tu byli Niemcy
blisko, różne narodowości się
przewijały, i Słowaków jest dużo i
węgierskie są ślady. Tak więc w
podświadomości górali było prze-
konanie, że oni 100 procentów
Polakami nie byli, chociaż byli pa-
triotami polskimi zawsze . . .
—Jan Karpiel-Bułecka

consciousness of Górale resides
the idea that we are not of entirely pure Polish origins. After
all, all of Poland is not pure Polish, because Poland is for Europe
like a "hall" where everyone
passes through, and especially
Podhale. After all, here came Ro-
manians—Wallachian[2] shepherds,
close to here were Germans, different nationalities came and
went, and Slovaks are many and
there are Hungarian traces. Yes,
therefore in the subconsciousness
of Górale was the conviction that
they were not 100 percent Polish,
although they were always Polish
patriots . . .
—Jan Karpiel-Bułecka[3]

One way or another people create the social realities and fic-
tions that they inhabit. The popular notion that Poland is a relatively homogeneous nation-state results, at least in part, from
ethnic genocides and expulsions during World War II, followed by
a government policy and ideology of social integration after the
war. The wartime genocide was real; the policy of social integration
was legislated fiction that, over the years, did create a conceptual
reality (Kenney 1997, 144).[4] Yet, as Jan Karpiel-Bułecka suggests,
in Podhale the myth of homogeneity meets challenges.

The history and geography of Podhale make it a special case,
however. In general, the borders of Poland have been indefensible
and highly malleable ("Poland is like a 'hall' or corridor through
which Europe passes," to paraphrase Karpiel-Bułecka), but the alpine ridges of the Tatras form one of Poland's few natural borders.
Did this unique characteristic result in the inhospitable Tatras becoming a harbor for something essentially (genetically) Polish? Polish nationalism was in full flower during the late nineteenth and
early twentieth centuries when Poland was still partitioned, an era
when nationalisms throughout Europe tended to imagine that the
essence of a nation resided in the folkways of presumably isolated
peasants. The rugged mountaineers of Podhale have filled this role
on occasion, bolstered by the most persistent ethnographic trope

that Górale life-ways are the results of centuries of mountain isolation (for versions of the isolation trope, see Gutt-Mostowy 1998,
16; Ćwiżewicz and Ćwiżewicz 1995; Czekanowska 1990, 84; and
Benet 1979 [1951], 130). Yet almost from the beginning of the
ethnographic study of Podhale a more complex theory emerged
that challenges the notion of isolation.

My interpretation of Podhalan history begins with the premise
that mountains are mysterious places. On the one hand, they form
borders that divide; on the other, they can become magnets that
ultimately bring together disparate peoples. This is illustrated by
the social and political history of the Carpathian Mountain chain,
which became a conduit of people and cultural practices between
the Balkans and the High Tatras. The harsh climate of the Tatras
may have been a deterrent to most, but it was a refuge of last resort
for others who traveled there to avoid various forms of oppression.
For example, legend has it that some came to the Tatras to avoid
serfdom, and Górale of Podhale did avoid being fully incorporated
into a feudal system (Gromada 1982, 107; Benet 1979 [1951], 130).
In this way the Tatras can be seen as a sort of magnet that pulls
people in—a metaphor used by Górale Tadeusz Styrczula-Maśniak
when he explained to me how the tall mountains attracted people
from as far away as Romania and Yugoslavia in the sixteenth and
seventeenth centuries (personal conversation, 15 January 1995,
Kościelisko). The more common ethnographic trope of mountain
isolation is, I believe, an invented tradition or historical narrative
made by the most recent wave of migrant travelers who were drawn
to the Tatras in increasing numbers beginning in the late nineteenth century. This new class of migrants falls within the broad
and ever-changing category of "tourists," and if the Tatras ever
were isolated, tourists have transformed Podhale into one of the
most international and diverse regions of Poland today.

Whether formed in an environment defined by diversity or
isolation, eventually the concept of an ethnic category "Górale"
emerged. In this chapter I interpret what I believe was the creation
of this ethnic category together with the cultural practices, especially as expressed in music-culture, that define this ethnicity. Recognizing that social, political, and cultural histories are made by
people, I call this chapter "Making History." These histories are
made in a series of overlapping narratives not only by historians,
ethnographers, folklorists, and other scholars but also (and more
importantly) by the individuals and groups who migrate, fight bat-

tles, write songs, marry, raise children, and so forth. My emphasis is deliberately on the "making" rather than the "discovery" of histories, ethnicities, and music-cultures. Much about human society is invented and imagined (Hobsbawm and Ranger 1983; Anderson 1991 [1983]). Included among the makers and inventors are ethnographers, who, as Fabian (1983) has suggested, are capable of creating the very thing they present as discovery. That histories, and ethnicities, are imagined, invented, and made by people does not render them any less real or meaningful. Instead, the effect is to place the responsibility of human society back into the hands of people, rather than to surrender it to depersonalized ideas about "nature" or "accidents of history."

This chapter considers historical narratives about migration to the Tatras that resulted in the region being unusually diverse in this ostensibly homogeneous nation. Following this I explain what I am calling the "new migration" of leisure travelers and urban dwellers to Podhale in the nineteenth and twentieth centuries. This new migration set up what John Comaroff calls "relations of inequality" (1996, 166) that initiated the making of a modern ethnicity—Górale. Key to my understanding of Górale is a *situational* rather than an *ascriptive* approach to ethnicity (Vermeulen 1984, 7). In the third chapter I extend the concept of "making" to music-culture and show that the making of mountain music—muzyka Podhala—paralleled and facilitated this making of Górale ethnicity.

Interpreting Locality: Historical Narratives and Discourses on Ethnicity

Byliśmy pod zaborem austro-węgierskim i monarchy. . . . Pod cesarzem Franciszkiem Józefem. . . . I granic tu na Węgry nie było. Więc tu była bieda bo tu po północny strony Tatr, ziemia kamienista; rodził się tylko owies i ziemniaki, jak był dobry rok. Bo jak był mokry rok, to ziemniaki się nie urodziły. Jak był suchy rok, to znowu ziemniaki były, a nie było owsa. A po słowackiej stronie, było bogactwo, bo tu

We were under the Austro-Hungarian partition and monarchy . . . Under the emperor Franz-Joseph. . . . And there was no border here with Hungary. Therefore, it was poor here because here on the north side of the Tatras, the soil is rocky; only oats and potatoes grew, if it was a good year. But if it was a rainy year, potatoes did not yield. If it was a dry year, again there were potatoes, but no oats. Now on the

południowa strona Tatr, i tam rosły nawet winogrona, prawda, i dwory bogate były. No to na wsi górale zbójowali. —Tadeusz Gąsienica-Giewont	Slovak side, it was rich, because that is the southern side of the Tatras, and there even grapes grew, it is true, and the manors were wealthy. Well here in the villages, Górale became brigands [*zbojniki*]. —Tadeusz Gąsienica-Giewont[5]

When seeking to understand how an ethnic group is made, one looks to location, settlement records, migration patterns, and language groups. One also considers how people, who are grouped as an ethnicity, think about, talk about, and interpret their own history, their relationship to locality, and their relationships with other people. In other words, one engages historical narratives and their related discourses. The distinction between narrative and discourse is subtle but significant. Narratives are the stories people tell about themselves and about others: the W people migrated to X at Y time for Z reasons. Discourses draw from these narratives to make claims about the character, proclivities, nature—the ethnicity—of W people: the ethnicity of W can be understood considering X, Y, and Z. Narratives are histories, the presentation of selected facts and myths to support one's ideas about oneself or another. Discourses are the interpretations of that historical narrative, the efforts to give meaning to the narrative.

Geography emerges as a central component of narratives and discourses about Podhale and Górale, as is seen in Gąsienica-Giewont's words above. The very qualities that make the Tatras a tourist destination today were the qualities that made the region the last place in the area to be settled. The steep northern side of the alpine Tatras were good for nothing but growing potatoes and oats, and for hiding brigands. Tadeusz Gąsienica-Giewont's explanation of the context for Podhale's legendary brigands illustrates the sense of history and geographic place important to many Górale musicians today. That brigands, or *zbójniki*, were less active, if active at all, on the Polish side of the Tatras, and that technically there was a border through the Tatras between Hungary and Austrian Galicia, does not diminish the mythic veracity of Gąsienica-Giewont's narrative. The verifiable rugged topography of the Polish Tatras and the sense of frontier living are essential myths transmitted among Górale in song, dance, and oral history.

At the time of the interview excerpted above, Tadeusz

Figure 2.1. Tadeusz Gąsienica-Giewont in 1995.

Gąsienica-Giewont (1915–1999) was regarded as the oldest Górale musician alive and was respected for his knowledge of music and Górale traditions in general (fig. 2.1). Younger, more nimble musicians readily deferred to Gąsienica-Giewont's authority at music sessions. While he wielded his bow and navigated the strings of his violin with arthritic fingers, and tuned with failing hearing, the most technically proficient musicians in the community would listen intently to his playing as if for truth that they vitally needed to hear. I spent many hours with Gąsienica-Giewont as we endeavored to record as many tunes as he could remember. His playing was invariably interspersed with explanations of history and context for muzyka Podhala, explanations that contained truth that I vitally needed to hear. One truth Gąsienica-Giewont taught me is that the essence of what it meant to be Górale and to play muzyka Podhala is not found in undisputed verifiable origin histories, genetic traits, or migration and settlement patterns. The truth, at least in the way that it impacts the individuals who call themselves Górale (or are labeled Górale by others, in some cases) and who make the sounds recognized as muzyka Podhala, may lie in conflicted interpretations of the past and present, in conflicting narratives and discourses. Górale ethnicity is situational, not ascribed by genetic heritage. In this way Górale and muzyka Podhala are continually made (and remade), not discovered. Being situational they are ever changing to accommodate present need. Following Gąsienica-Giewont and other Górale, my narratives and discourses about Górale and their music-cultural practices will often wander across the border that separated Galicia from Hungary, and now Poland from the Slovak Republic.[6]

Making History: Narratives about Settling the Tatras

History is made by repeating historical narratives. The narratives I repeat here, like the narratives and discourses on Górale cultural practices and ethnicity, all include the Tatra Mountains as a defining factor. The poor climate and soil conditions of Podhale caused it to be settled late in Central European history, whereas the surrounding regions received permanent settlements relatively early. The northern edge of Podhale was settled as early as the thirteenth century, but most of Podhale was settled from the fifteenth to eighteenth centuries. In my interpretation of history in Podhale, I add yet another migration trend that is not generally included in histories of the settlement of Podhale but which is central to my understanding of Górale musical practices. This trend is the seasonal migration of people to the Tatra regions as tourists from as early as the sixteenth century, and specifically to Podhale from the nineteenth century to the present. The later phases of this trend were accompanied by the permanent migration of lowlander Poles to Podhale to work in the growing tourist industry.

The Tatras lie in the upper arch of the Carpathian Mountain range that forms a crescent extending from what is today Romania reaching toward the Balkans, through the southwestern edge of Ukraine, across southern Poland and the northern Slovak Republic before descending to Vienna and Bratislava (see fig. 1.1). During its early settlement history, the Tatra region was an uncertain borderland between Hungary and Poland, although Podhale was considered part of the kingdom of Poland. When Poland was partitioned in 1772 between Prussia, Russia, and the Austro-Hungarian Empire, the entire Tatra region became a part of the Austro-Hungarian section, with Podhale as part of the Austrian crown land

Figure 2.2. Map of migrations to the Tatra regions.

of Galicia, and the Slovak Tatras were administered by Hungary. The partition of Poland lasted until 1918 and would be familiar to older Górale such as Gąsienica-Giewont from the oral histories of their elders if not from their own experiences.

Today driving along the E50 highway in the Slovak Republic from Orawa, through Liptów and into Spisz, one is graced with dramatic views of the high Tatras that rise abruptly out of a broad expanse of gentle hills and valleys. By contrast, views of the Tatras from the northern Polish side are fleeting, as roads wind in and out of small valleys and over mountain passes. The more gentle terrain of the southern exposure attracted the earliest intensive settlement (fig. 2.2). As Gąsienica-Giewont said about the Slovak side, "there even grapes grew," and they still grow. Present-day Górale regularly cross the border to the south side of the Tatras to buy the sweet red wine pressed from local grapes.

From the eleventh to the fourteenth centuries the upper Spisz area was first settled by Rusyns from the Carpathians that now lie in Ukraine, and Poles from the Sądecki region to the north. The

Slavic-speaking ethnic Rusyns are also sometimes called "Ruthenians" in English and are most commonly, if mistakenly, known as "Ukrainians" in America (Kuropas 1986, x; Magocsi 1975, 1994). The kingdom of Hungary was the dominant political force in the region at the time, and some ethnic Hungarians also settled parts of Spisz. Invasions by Tatars in the thirteenth century encouraged Hungarian kings to resettle Saxons (Germans) in Spisz in order to make the region less accessible to marauding troupes (Radwańska-Paryska and Paryski 1995, 410–411; see also Magocsi 1975, 215). On the other hand, from the thirteenth to fifteenth centuries, the persistent attacks farther south and east by Tatars and later by Ottoman armies were also a strong motivation for migration from the Balkans up along the Carpathian chain into Spisz, and perhaps Podhale.

From the twelfth century on, Slovaks, and possibly Rusyns and Wallachians, settled the Liptów region that lies to the west of Spisz and directly south of the Tatras. Already by the fourteenth century many of this area's villages and towns existed. Orawa, wrapping around the western side of the Tatras and extending into Poland, was settled at the same time primarily by Slovaks and Wallachians. Orawa Castle existed by the end of the thirteenth century, and close to forty settlements were established in the area by the fifteenth century (Radwańska-Paryska and Paryski 1995, 411). The upper part of Orawa was settled much later, in the sixteenth century, primarily by Poles.

The area between Kraków and Podhale was inhabited by Poles from early on, but settlements did not extend southward into Podhale until the thirteenth, or possibly the twelfth, century. Podhale was first settled in its northern edge—in the relatively flat and fertile land of the Nowy Targ valley—beginning with the founding of the villages of Ludźmierz, Rogoźnik, and Szaflary, all dating from the thirteenth century. It was several centuries before intensive settlement of the southern portions of Podhale close to the Tatras began (fig. 2.3) (Radwańska-Paryska and Paryski 1995, 411; see also Kotoński 1956, 13; and Wrazen 1988, 46). The villages of Czarny Dunajec, Ciche, and Chochołów, all along the western edge of Podhale, were settled in the fifteenth and sixteenth centuries. Biały Dunajec, in the geographic center of *Skalne* Podhale, was also settled at this time (1579). Several of the villages that are of special significance to the subject of this book were not settled until the seventeenth and eighteenth centuries: Witów, Poronin, and Bu-

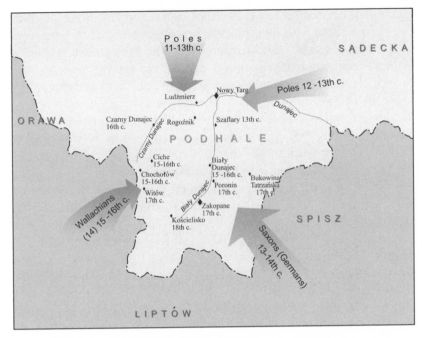

Figure 2.3. Map of the settlement of Podhale, showing three primary waves of immigration to *Skalne* Podhale (Kotoński 1956, 14; Wrazen 1988, 46).

kowina Tatrzańska were founded in the first half of the seventeenth century; Zakopane was founded in the second half of the seventeenth century (1670);[7] and Kościelisko was established in 1790. All these most recent villages are nestled close to the Tatras in the rugged southern extremes of Podhale.

Discourses on Ethnicity

Among historians and students of the cultural practices of the Tatra regions, there is general agreement about the above historical narrative representing the settlement of this part of Europe: over centuries the Tatra regions were a magnet for diverse peoples—Poles, Hungarians, Saxons, Slovaks, Rusyans, and Wallachians. But who settled Podhale specifically? Who decided (or was forced) to eke out a living in the least hospitable northern side of the cold Tatra Mountains, the last region in the Tatras to be settled? Who became today's Górale of Podhale? These questions are the basis of disagreement between interpretive approaches and engender different discourses about Górale ethnicity. Some believe that the different peoples who settled the broader Tatra regions came together in Podhale and eventually formed a new ethnic group. A second approach claims that Podhale was settled almost exclusively from the north by Slavic Poles, although the surrounding regions were ethnically heterogeneous. The first group interprets Podhale as a multiethnic melting pot, the second as an enclave of relatively pure Polishness in an otherwise diverse borderland. Both interpretive discourses have internal conflicts. If Podhale were an ethnic melting pot, why is the new Górale ethnicity so resistant to accepting new immigrants into their number? On the other hand, are not claims of ethnic purity really discourses about racial purity? Yes, "ethnicity" and "race" are themselves closely related discourses that cannot be completely separated (see Sollers 1996, xxix–xxxv), but I consider race to be overwhelmingly genetic, and ethnicity to be overwhelmingly cultural. This cultural definition of ethnicity constitutes the third interpretive approach that concentrates on cultural practices (which demonstrate diversity in Podhale rather than anything specifically "Polish") and de-emphasizes the actual genetic heritage of Górale. All three views ultimately bring to the fore the nature of ethnicity itself.

Before considering these three interpretive approaches to the settlement of Podhale and hence Górale ethnicity, I will muddy the waters with observations on the current makeup of Podhalan society. Conspicuously absent from most historical narratives of the settlement of the Tatras are Jews and Roma. Jews figure prominently in Górale folklore, and senior Górale tell me about Jewish musicians and weddings, but the genocides and dislocations of the Second World War severely reduced the size of the Jewish community in Podhale as in the rest of Poland and Central Europe. The impact of any surviving or reviving Jewish community on current muzyka Podhala is not at all evident to me. Roma, on the other hand, remain an important group in the region and several Roma bands perform in Zakopane restaurants today. While many Górale musicians play music associated with Roma music-culture, few actually play with Roma musicians. As elsewhere in Central Europe, in Podhale Roma live in a largely separate parallel society. Failure to account for these significant groups of people in Podhale and surrounding regions points to the fact that the question of Górale ethnicity is politicized. Certainly this is the case in Podhale today, where who is and who is not Górale is a social, cultural, and political point of everyday conversations and effects how business is done, how elections are won, and how music is made. The exclusion of Jews and Roma from the consideration of Górale ethnicity and the settlement history of Podhale reminds us that ethnicity itself is a boundary-making enterprise which creates sociopolitical groups that are only as inclusive as they are exclusive—one is either in the group "Górale" or not. I am more interested in how these boundaries are made and maintained than in any genetic makeup of Górale bloodlines (Barth 1996 [1969]). Yet discourses on Górale identity revolve around the three interpretive approaches outlined above, so I return to them here.

The first and most common discourse encompasses a "melting-pot" theory. This discourse accounts for the clear cultural links with Carpathian regions, extending down into the Balkans, by concluding that Poles, Rusyns, Wallachians, Hungarians, Germans, and Slovaks moved into Podhale itself, where they eventually intermingled and thus created a separate ethnic group. This interpretive approach is upheld by many scholars of cultural practices, including ethnomusicologists (see Kotoński 1956, 14; Dahlig 1991, 83–84; Wrazen 1988, 46–47; Ćwiżewicz 2001, 29–30), as well as by some historians and ethnographers (e.g., Gromada 1982, 107; Lehr and Tylkowa 2000, 23–26, 79). The most nuanced version of this interpretation was provided by ethnographer Kazimierz Dobrowolski (1938; see also Antoniewicz, Dobrowolski, and Paryski 1970) who downplayed the influence of Germanic peoples in Podhale while emphasizing the impact of Wallachians. Politically and ideologically I find the melting-pot discourse to be the most attractive because of the suggestion that diverse peoples can create a society together. This fits nicely with my liberal, and perhaps American, sensibilities which would like to believe that all people can live together despite their varied backgrounds. My own utopian tendencies are challenged, however, by the exclusionary quality of Górale ethnicity today. We are left to ask, as Fredrik Barth did in 1969 (1996 [1969], 294–295), why ethnic boundaries persist even as interethnic contact increases.

The second interpretive discourse of Podhale as an ethnically pure enclave does not deny the cultural influences of heterogeneous people on the folklore of Górale. Nor do the scholars who support this view dispute the presence of diverse groups in the broader Tatra regions. At issue is the genetic heritage of those who

settled Podhale itself and who now call themselves Górale of Podhale (*górale podhalańscy*, see Kotoński 1956, 14). This discourse was
upheld by the dedicated historians of the Tatras Witold H. Paryski
and Zofia Radwańska-Paryska, and by native Górale historian Jan
Gutt-Mostowy. These historians claimed that Podhale was settled
almost exclusively by Slavic Poles from the north (Radwańska-
Paryska and Paryski 1995, 410–411, 679; Gutt-Mostowy 1998, 16,
23–27). I have the utmost respect for these individuals and for their
scholarship,[8] although I find the claim of ethnic (read "racial") purity in Podhale to be problematic. First, ethnic purity is always a
problematic proposition especially in a region of Central Europe
that has experienced and continues to experience such widespread
migration and nomadic to seminomadic lifestyles. Second, such an
approach to ethnicity is too rigidly ascriptive and linked to equally
problematic concepts of race.

The third interpretive discourse I have identified in the literature charts cultural connections between Górale of Podhale and
the different societies and people along the Carpathian Mountains,
and downplays the role of race or genetic heritage (e.g., Kolberg
1968b, 449, 451, 455; Zejszner 1845, 34; Czekanowska 1990, 39).
These cultural connections are clearly demonstrated by Adolf Chybiński in his article originally published in 1933, "O źródłach i
rozpowszechnieniu dwudziestu melodii ludowych na Skalnym Podhalu" (On the sources and diffusion of twenty folk melodies from
Skalne Podhale) (1961 [1933], 113–143). In this article he docu-
ments clear similarities between twenty melodies common in Podhale and melodies from Romania (Wallachia), Slovakia, Hungary,
and Moravia, usually locating the similar melody in a specific village or region. He calls Podhale a borderland and considers the issues addressed in his article to be borderland issues (1961 [1933],
113). Music in Podhale is Polish, he writes, but is balanced by influences from beyond Poland. These cultural influences arrive in
the borderlands of Podhale in two ways: people from elsewhere
"wandering" to Podhale, and Górale from Podhale wandering south
into Slovakia (113–114). Chybiński's "Twenty Folk Melodies" article
is especially useful for making sense of a Polish folk region that otherwise seems ill fitted with the rest of Poland. His detailed tracing of
twenty melodies also situates Podhale culturally within the Carpathian crescent, a theme confirmed and expanded on by the International Commission for Studies of the Carpathian Folk Culture,
founded in 1959 under the leadership of Oskár Elschek and Alica Elscheková (see Elscheková 1981; and Wrazen 1988, 33–34).

This third discourse—the cultural approach to ethnicity—is attractive for the scientific rigor employed to detail the cultural connections along the Carpathian chain. The primary distinction from the first two discourses is that the third privileges cultural practices over race and allows one to focus on ethnicity as an invented classification system that is socially constructed and maintained, and that is culturally articulated. The recognition that cultural practices flow freely across political and ethnic borders, and that we therefore cannot assume a one-to-one relationship between ethnicity and cultural practices (Barth 1996 [1969], 299) does not eliminate the value of this approach. Instead, the challenge is to interpret this flow of cultural practices as part of the defining nature of ethnicity. Ethnicity is necessitated by, and constructed within, the context of social interaction (Cole 1984, 97). Ethnicity is a means for imagining social groups and boundaries that are contextually dynamic (Pieterse 1996, 33). The first and second discourses on Górale ethnicity are *ascriptive* (Chapman 1993, 19–20; Vermeulen 1984, 7); that is, they define ethnicity as a fixed attribute associated with heritage, race, and place. Ethnicity in these ascriptive approaches is the sum total of the ethnicities of a given people's ancestors. Although I agree that ethnicity is in part ascribed, or what Steve Fenton (1999, x) might call "material" or "grounded," the meaning and significance of such ascribed circumstances of heritage for any one individual or group are highly malleable and negotiable within society.

A more useful approach is to consider ethnicity as a *situational* construction dependent on social, economic, and political circumstances. Fenton's (1999) similar model calls this a "symbolic" or "constructed" approach to ethnicity. A situational approach interprets ethnicity as a conscious thought process, even a strategy or tool, with which people construct ethnic boundaries for themselves and for others. Moreover, ethnicity is social and relational—a way for individuals to group themselves and to be grouped by others into a collection of people believed to be fundamentally similar. As social situations change, ethnicities are re-created (Eriksen 1993, 1). Even ancestry is socially negotiated, leaving some ancestors to be forgotten while raising up others to be revered as somehow essential for a group's identity (Fenton 1999, 6–7). Situational and malleable, yes, but this does not mean that ethnicity is easily changed like a set of clothes—although individuals do put on and shed certain markers of ethnicity (such as dialect, eating habits, music, and even costumes) to accommodate particular situations.

Like other cultural institutions, ethnicity takes on a life of its own and can be slow to change, often requiring generations to do so. With this approach to ethnicity, the debates about who settled Podhale are more important as discourses—as socially negotiated constructions of ideas about what it means to be Górale—than they are informative about genetics. The cultural focus of the third discourse is preferable, because it is through cultural practices that social ideas are expressed.

Why and how was the modern ethnicity "Górale" constructed? What were the social and economic conditions that encouraged the creation of this ethnicity? My argument has been that cultural diversity has long been a defining characteristic of the Tatra regions, including Podhale. What is needed, however, to forge diversity into a distinct, recognizable, and definable ethnicity, is a "politics of difference," a potentially threatening economic or social force that persuades individuals of "a need to confirm a collective sense of identity" (Wilmsen 1996, 4–5). This social force usually emerges in the form of a dominant group that is both politically and economically more powerful than other groups. In the nineteenth century a new and very different wave of migration to Podhale introduced such a group, and redefined the discourse on Górale ethnicity.

The Missing Narrative: The "New Migration"

Już od pewnego czasu corocznie znaczniejsza liczba podróżnych odwiedza Tatry. Podhalanie za chlubę sobie poczytują rozmawiać z panami, i uprzejmą uniżnością i chętliwością jednają ich serca. Powszechnie wychwalając swoje wirchy, zalecają wyborne wody kryniczne, pod niebiosy wynoszą żentycę wszystkie choroby uzdrawiającą, opisują swój kraj ubogi; daléj dziwią się nad budową pojazdu i zaprzęgiem podróżnego. (Zejszner 1845, 36)

For quite some time now, there have been more people visiting the Tatras. The number of people is growing on a yearly basis. Górale proudly speak with the distinguished visitors, winning their hearts with their polite deference. Persistently praising their mountains, they recommend their exquisite spring water, they extol their sheep's buttermilk that will cure any sickness. Górale describe their poor country and question the tourists about the construction of their carriages and horses' tack. (Zejszner 1845, 36)

Missing in most historical narratives about the settlement of Podhale and in other discourses on what this means for Górale ethnicity are narratives about modern history and what I call the "new migration." I claim that this ongoing new migration, most often treated as irrelevant to discourses on ethnicity, is indeed redefining the ethnicity debate in Podhale and is therefore a primary focus of my thesis. The new migration shares much with the earlier phases of historic migration to, and settlement of, Podhale: the new migration is predominantly Polish although increasingly international; it is seasonal but related to work in ways that are distinct from earlier seasonal migrations for work; and it is resulting in permanent settlement in Podhale by some.

The new migration of which I write is the migration of tourists to Podhale together with a new wave of settlement primarily in Zakopane to staff the growing tourist service industry. Embracing relatively recent scholarship that recognizes the sometimes uneasy, sometimes blissful marriage between tourism and ethnographers (Bendix 1989, 1997; Kaeppler and Lewin 1988; Suppan 1991; DeWitt 1999), I include early scientific travelers and ethnographers in this new migration category. Beginning in the early nineteenth century, gaining speed in the last quarter of that century, and continuing through the twentieth century with the major interruptions of two world wars, the migration of tourists to and from Podhale is changing the cultural landscape. As suggested above, the new migration shares many characteristics with previous migration and settlement patterns, and I believe it is informative to interpret it in the context of the historical settlement of Podhale. I consider together temporary tourists and new permanent settlers in Podhale because they are symbiotic—one requiring the other. And in the context of centuries of migration to Podhale, the two related groups are not so different from fourteenth- to sixteenth-century Wallachians who migrated to Podhale seasonally. We do not know how many Wallachians settled permanently in Podhale, but their cultural influence was dramatic. The same can be said about the new migration, which offers new challenges to Górale ethnicity and to Górale music-culture.

The new migration is not monolithic, although, at least initially, it exhibited some general characteristics that distinguished it from all earlier migrations to Podhale. Instead of coming to Podhale to try to make a living, the early tourists of the new migration came for recreation, for health reasons, and for scientific research. Contrasting with earlier migrants and settlers in Podhale who were generally poor, these new migrants were often of an elite class and possessed disposable income. Perhaps because of these fundamental distinctions, one effect of the new migration of tourists is a raised self-consciousness among Górale—a new sense of group or ethnic identity in the face of difference amplified by inequality. I argue that these new migrants, their historical narratives and discourses on ethnicity, created the Górale ethnic group as it is understood today, and that in the process they closed off the possibility of new migrants to Podhale becoming Górale themselves.

Like the settlement of the Tatras, tourism to the area was first from the more gentle southern approaches of what is now the Slovak Republic. The earliest documented excursion into the Tatras was by princess Beata Łaska and her new and younger husband Olbracht Łaski in 1565. They approached the Tatras from the Slovak Spisz town of Kezmarok and traveled up the Kezmarok valley in the southeastern edge of the Tatras. Earlier recreational tours were probably made to the Tatras, but none are documented. Toward the end of the sixteenth century additional excursions from Spisz into the Tatras are documented, but they probably only went as far as the mountain valleys. Documented excursions to the Tatra peaks began in the seventeenth century (Paryski 1991, 7).

Student and scientific research trips into the Tatras from the northern Polish side began toward the end of the eighteenth century and continued into the nineteenth century at a time when mountain tourism was a new phenomenon in the Western world. Before this time in Europe, mountains were viewed as places to be feared and avoided (Hall 1991, 41). By the early nineteenth century the largest and very beautiful mountain lake, Morskie Oko ("eye of the sea"), had become a popular tourist attraction. One of the first mountain shelters for tourists (rather than for shepherds) in the Tatras was built at this lake in about 1827 (Radwańska-Paryska and Paryski 1995, 767–768). Other mountain shelters for tourists were built in the last half of the nineteenth century. Today a system of hostel-type shelters run by the Tatra National Park is so popular that rooms during peak seasons must be reserved several months in advance.

The publication of tourist travelogues and travelers' recollections in the early nineteenth century contributed to the popularization of the Tatras among Polish society (for commentary and analysis of early tourists publications, see Kolbuszewski 1982; and Paryski 1991, 10). Within the writings of these early tourists are descriptions of Górale cultural practices, including music-culture as seen in Goszczyński's writings (1853), suggesting that the attraction to the Tatras and Podhale was not limited to the spectacular mountain scenery and the presumed health benefits of mountain air. I interpret this era as the beginning of ethnographic interest in Podhale.

A watershed moment for tourism in Podhale came in 1873 with the founding of the Towarzystwo Tatrzańskie[9] (Tatra Society) by a group of distinguished guests in Zakopane including Ludwik Eichborn, a banker from Berlin; Feliks Pławicki, a retired captain of the Austrian army and member of the regional *sejm* (congress) in Lwów; Dr. Tytus Chałubiński from Warsaw; and the parish-priest of Zakopane, Józef Stolarczyk. The Towarzystwo Tatrzańskie was the first tourist organization in Poland and the first among Slavic peoples. The goals of the Towarzystwo Tatrzańskie were (1) to popularize the mountains by building trails and lodges, organizing guided tours, and publishing information; (2) to advance scientific research in the mountains and to disseminate information from this research; (3) to protect the mountain ecology; and (4) to provide economic assistance to people of the mountain areas (Anonymous 1963, 5; Kulczycki 1970, 77–89; Paryski 1991, 15–18). The makeup of the early membership of the Towarzystwo Tatrzańskie and the members' goals for the society are informative. The founding members were not Górale but were guests in Zakopane, a formerly insignificant village between Kuźnice and Witów but now increasingly the focus of visitors' attention. These guests were also Polish inteligencja, not just from Galicia but from the other partitioned regions of Poland and from abroad as well. The development of tourism up to the Second World War was predominantly done for and by inteligencja including university students and some of Poland's leading artists, a trend that dramatically influenced Podhalan society (fig. 2.4).

During the last quarter of the nineteenth century, after the founding of the Towarzystwo Tatrzańskie, Podhale experienced a rapid increase in the numbers of tourists. Accurate records of the numbers of people traveling to the region of Podhale at this time are not available, but we do have good records from Zakopane, which was already the center of tourist activity. In 1873 about 400 guests came to Zakopane; by 1880, 638 guests were recorded; in 1886 the number jumped to 3,123; and in 1900, 8,011 tourists traveled to Zakopane. The arduous journey to Zakopane was greatly eased with the completion of the railroad line to the village in 1899, after which time the number of tourists increased steadily to about 13,000 guests in 1913.

The outbreak of the First World War in 1914 brought tourism

Figure 2.4. Bartuś Obrochta (*front*) and his ensemble, at the twentieth anniversary of the Towarzystwo Tatrzańskie, at Morskie Oko, 1893. Courtesy of the Muzeum Tatrzańskie, Zakopane.

to a halt, but the development of tourism between the wars out-paced previous growth. In 1918 there were 9,373 guests, and the number increased to 60,590 in 1938 (Paryski 1991, 21; Jackowski 1991, 23). Records concerning how many tourists came to Zako-pane from outside Poland are also available beginning in 1918 (Jac-kowski 1991, 23). In that year there were 22 guests from across the border. This number increased to 2,633 in 1938. Obviously the tourists migrating to Podhale were overwhelmingly Polish, and even many of the tourists from abroad may have been Polish. During the interwar period the Polskie Towarzystwo Tatrzańskie (Polish Tatra Society, formerly the Towarzystwo Tatrzańskie) and the Związek Podhalan (Podhalan Alliance, discussed below) were actively encouraging Polish emigrants to return to Podhale for vacations, essentially to become tourists in their homeland. For example, from 1927 to 1938 Stefan Jarosz was engaged by the Polskie Towarzystwo Tatrzańskie and the Związek Podhalan to establish sister organizations in America and to promote tourism to Podhale. His success is evidenced by the continuing activities of the Związek Podhalan w Północnej Ameryce (Podhalan Alliance in North America), an organization he was instrumental in starting in America (Gromada 1982, 112–113; Wnuk 1985, 35–41).

The development of tourism in the region was again interrupted by war in 1939, and the eventual adoption of Marxist-Leninist communism as the official state ideology in 1948 altered the nature of tourism for the next four decades. To a great extent tourism was socialized, with the government determining when and where most individuals would vacation. As longtime resident of Zakopane Marek Jenner told me with a dry sense of humor forged in the communist era, the government told each worker when he would vacation, to what vacation house he would visit, in what room he would stay, and in which bed he would sleep (interview, 11 April 1995, Zakopane, ac11.iv.95). Often the vacationing "worker" stayed in one of the many vacation houses that today line the streets of Zakopane, built by the Fundusz Wczasów Pracowniczych (Fund for workers' vacations) that was established in 1949 by the Sejm. The state also ran the travel agency "Orbis," which already existed before the Second World War but now enjoyed a complete monopoly (Dawson 1991, 192; Kulczycki 1970, 166–177). Thus Podhale was consciously developed by the communist government as a resort area and tourist destination. Although still a popular place for artists and "working intellectuals," the face of tourism in Zakopane began to change as laborers and others flocked to the Tatras in increasing numbers. Already in 1948, 150,000 people visited Zakopane; 922,000 in 1960; and over 3 million annually by the mid-seventies (Warszyńska 1991, 38).

Summarizing this survey of the "new migration" thus far, one can divide tourism to Podhale into three waves. The first wave began in the late nineteenth century and lasted until the First

World War. This wave established Podhale as a tourist destination primarily for Polish inteligencja, and corresponds with the "Young Poland" movement of intensifying Polish nationalism. The second wave occurred between the two world wars, an important period for reestablishing Polish national identity. The third wave rose after the chilling effects of the Second World War and a period of Stalinism in Poland (roughly 1948 to 1956; see Kenney 1997, 140). The foundation for this third wave was set during the Stalinist period with the establishment of the Fund for Workers' Vacations. During communism, Podhale was transformed into a tourist destination for all Poles, not just the elite, and hence the mass tourism of the 1970s. This wave subsided with the imposition of martial law in 1981 in an effort to silence Poland's anticommunist SOLI-DARITY movement.

A fourth wave may be rising now since the end of communist control in 1989 as Zakopane and all of Poland experience rapid privatization. The tourist infrastructure established during the communist era remains. The state-owned vacation houses of Zakopane still operate, but they compete with private hotels. Orbis still has its office in the center of town, but small private travel agents also line the streets. While I was living in Poland from 1994 to 1995, an icon of American capitalism, a McDonald's restaurant, was constructed on Krupówki, Zakopane's main business street. The advertisements for the opening of the fast-food restaurant suggested an affinity between Górale and Native Americans (fig. 2.5). This American franchise was preceded by a Levi's clothing store, an Italian shoe store, and a French pastry chain, all on Krupówki Street. The globalization of Zakopane also extends to the people who visit there. Krupówki is closed to all but pedestrian traffic, and during peak tourist seasons it is crowded with people. Strolling along this street one can eavesdrop on conversations in German, French, Italian, English, and Japanese, as well as in Polish. Despite the increase in international tourism to Zakopane in post-communist times, informal estimates are that the sheer numbers of tourists in Podhale have actually decreased since the mid-1970s. In a sense, this newest wave of tourist migration to Podhale is returning to models from centuries ago: the majority of migrants are Polish, but the international component may leave the most distinctive traces.

The dramatic numbers of tourists visiting Zakopane is, of course, only part of the story. This book is not about tourists per se

Figure 2.5. Advertisement for the opening of the McDonald's in Zakopane, 1995. The banner at top reads: "If Janosik lived, he would eat and drink here." Used with permission from McDonald's Corporation.

but about Górale of Podhale. Just as in centuries past when some of the migratory shepherds who passed through Podhale ultimately settled there, some of the "tourists" who have been visiting Podhale in earnest since the mid-nineteenth century eventually put down roots. The first notable tourist to build a home in Zakopane (from 1877 to 1878) was Walery Eljasz-Radzikowski, an artist and one of the founders of the Towarzystwo Tatrzańskie (see fig. 0.2 for an example of Eljasz-Radzikowski's art). Others followed suit, including Dr. Tytus Chałubiński in 1879. The trend of important artists establishing residences in Podhale continued throughout the twentieth century up to the present time, including composer Karol Szymanowski who first came to Zakopane around 1894 as a boy and resided there from 1930 to 1935, and composer Henryk M. Górecki who built a home near Zakopane in the 1990s.

Poland's inteligencja were not the only strata to move permanently or semipermanently to Podhale. Especially in the twentieth century after the railroad was built and as hotels and health resorts began to proliferate, workers from outside Podhale began to settle in the region in increasing numbers. They came to work in the hotels, restaurants, and shops that sprang up to serve the swelling tide of tourists. This explains the expeditious rise in the number of people living in Zakopane beginning in the late nineteenth century, but growing most rapidly between the two world wars. Just over 2,000 people lived in the village in the 1870s. This number rose to more than 5,000 by 1900 and almost 8,000 in 1914 when the First World War began. The era between the two wars, as more and more service workers were moving to Zakopane, was by far the greatest period of growth as the population swelled to around 23,000 people. During the Second World War the population was reduced to only 13,752 by 1946, but the number rapidly increased after the war as workers came to staff the new state-run hotels and vacation homes, and to provide other services. The population was again over 20,000 by 1950 and then rose at a moderate pace to around 30,000 in the 1990s, although at any moment the number of people actually in Zakopane might be doubled or tripled by tourists.[10] I have located no reliable statistical data on the subject, but anecdotal evidence suggests that Zakopane now has more residents from outside Podhale than old family Górale (Marek Jenner, interview, 11 April 1995, Zakopane, ac11.iv.95, and confirmed in informal conversations with other Zakopane residents). At least in some parts of Podhale, Górale have become a minority in their own home region.

The New Migration and Modern Górale Ethnicity

The new migration to Podhale is key to understanding modern Górale ethnicity in two ways. First, the new migration was of a fundamentally different sort than earlier migrations, and it created in Podhale new social interactions that resulted in new negotiations of ethnicity. The early settlers in Podhale were presumably poor and dispossessed, more or less forced to the shadowy north side of the Tatras where living was certain to be difficult. Others sought autonomy and to escape serfdom. The new migration, on the other hand, was led by Polish inteligencja traveling to the Tatras in increasing numbers by the end of the nineteenth century for leisure and for the healing powers of sulfur springs and fresh air. Second, these new migrants took an active interest—even ethnographic interest—in Górale cultural practices resulting in cultural codification and a new discourse on ethnicity.

To illustrate these points, I return to the Chałubiński monument that I introduced at the beginning of this book (see fig. 0.1). Chałubiński represents the first wave of new migrants and the beginning of the intensive development of Zakopane as a tourist destination. As I interpreted the monument in the introduction, Chałubiński's identity is "unmarked" (read "normal" or not "ethnic"), while at the base of the monument sits Sabała, a prototypical Górale so marked with costume and musical instrument, both defining symbols of his ethnicity. Although there is little indication of sartorial style for Polish elite on this monument, we know that such cosmopolitan style has changed substantially since the late nineteenth century. Yet a full century after the monument was erected (1903) Górale men dress exactly as Sabała is depicted in bronze, at least when they self-consciously dress *as* Górale. At such moments a Górale musician may even pull out a folk violin (*złóbcoki*) like the one held by Sabała (fig. 2.6). How did such dress become a symbol of Góraleness? How can it be that such a symbol has changed so little in the course of one hundred years?[11]

The politics of difference introduced by the new migration helped to codify symbols of difference, especially among the less mobile, less privileged indigenous inhabitants of the Tatras. The relationship between Sabała and Chałubiński is indicative of the relationship between Górale and tourists. Although Chałubiński's writings suggest that he admired the skill and knowledge of Sabała, the Górale was the physician's guide, helper, and local facilitator;

Figure 2.6. Władysław Trebunia-Tutka playing a złóbcoki. Józef
Staszel (*seated*) plays a standard violin (Poronin 1992).

Sabała was an early employee in the tourist services industry.
Chałubiński came to Zakopane to enjoy the fresh air and mountain
scenery, and then he returned to his work in Warsaw. He was mobile and in a different social class than the Górale he visited. This
social distance allowed Chałubiński and others to consider the differences between themselves and Górale, to begin the ethnographic process of recording cultural practices of Górale, and sub-
sequently to define the symbolic capital of Górale ethnicity. In this
way tourism and ethnography participate in the making of a modern ethnicity—Górale. Part and parcel with the making of an ethnicity is the making of the cultural practices by which that ethnicity
is maintained. This includes muzyka Podhala in the case of the
ethnicity Górale.

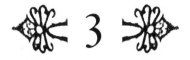

Making Mountain Music:
A History of Ethnography
in Podhale

GIEWONT: I góralskiej muzyki żaden z kompozytorów nie mógł napisać. Bo to był ksiądz Chybiński w XIX wieku, który napisał góralską muzykę, ale w tempie mazurka, oberka, w takim tempie. Pierwszy dopiero kompozytor, który 130 zapisał melodii góralskich. [...] To chodził z Bartusiem Obrochtą. Kompozytor dwa lata grał po weselach; Mierczyński, Stasiu Mierczyński [...]

COOLEY: Pan zna go, nie?

GIEWONT: Znałem go, bo on już nie żyje dawno. Bo to, on chodził z Bartusiem Obrochtą po weselach dwa lata, jako sekundzista bo był skrzypek super i kompozytor. I dopiero on napisał w tempie takim jak powinna być góralska muzyka.

GIEWONT: And no composer knew how to write Górale music. Well, there was this priest Chybiński in the nineteenth century who wrote Górale music, but in mazurka and oberek time [in triple meter]. The first composer who wrote 130 Górale melodies [...] traveled with Bartuś Obrochta. The composer played at weddings for two years; Mierczyński, Stasiu [Stanisław] Mierczyński [...]

COOLEY: You know him, no?

GIEWONT: I knew him, because he has not been alive for a long time. He went with Bartuś Obrochta to weddings for two years and played accompaniment, because he was a super violinist and a composer. He was the first one to write the meter

COOLEY: To dobre, co on pisał? GIEWONT: On dobrze napisał muzykę góralską. Tak samo, jeszcze pamiętam Szymanowskiego. Bo Szymanowski jak przyjeżdżał to wieczór [. . .] był Obrochta zawsze. Pamiętam Szymanowskiego. Pamiętam dobrze Witkiewicza, bo przecież . . . im graliśmy.
—Tadeusz Gąsienica-Giewont and Timothy J. Cooley

as it should be for Górale music. COOLEY: It is good, what he wrote? GIEWONT: He wrote Górale music well. In the same way I still remember Szymanowski. Because Szymanowski arrived in the evening [. . .] and Obrochta was always there. I remember Szymanowski. I remember well Witkiewicz because . . . we played for them.
—Tadeusz Gąsienica-Giewont and Timothy J. Cooley[1]

Past musical folklorists, ethnographers, composers, and others who took an active interest in Górale music-culture are alive today in the memories of Górale musicians. Tadeusz Gąsienica-Giewont was a maturing boy when many influential Polish artists, classical musicians, and ethnographers were active in Podhale, including painter and writer Stanisław Witkiewicz (1851–1915), composer Karol Szymanowski (1882–1937), and musical folklorist Stanisław Mierczyński (1894–1952). These individuals have entered the historical narratives Górale tell about themselves. But Gąsienica-Giewont did not, and other Górale do not, accept uncritically what visitors have written about their music-culture. For example, he was critical of a nineteenth-century priest he called Chybiński (probably meaning a priest named Janota)[2] for transcribing Górale music in mazurka and oberek time—in 3/4. With extremely rare exceptions Górale music is represented today in duple time. Another senior Górale musician, Józef Styrczula-Maśniak, preferred the transcriptions made by a later musical folklorist, Włodzimierz Kotoński (fieldnotes 1992, IV:22). These comments were not isolated. Time and again Górale musicians would mention past and living musical ethnographers when we talked about muzyka Podhala. This is just one indication of how musical ethnographers— usually part of the new migration to Podhale considered in the previous chapter—are implicated in the making of the modern mountain music called muzyka Podhala.

Like Górale ethnicity, Górale music-culture responded to the changes in society brought on by the new migration of tourists to Podhale and the musical ethnographies that were a by-product of this trend. Gąsienica-Giewont's criticism of a nineteenth-century

writer who represented Górale music in triple meter raises an interesting question. Oskar Kolberg and others, as I will show, also
documented many triple-meter tunes in Podhale. Has the repertoire of musicians in Podhale changed from mazurkas and obereks—styles common in much of Poland—to the more distinct
genres of muzyka Podhala, or have representations of Górale repertoire changed over time? Of course, any living music-culture is
in a constant state of change, but what motivates musicians to move
from general and widely popular styles to a rarefied style recognized as regional? This appears to be exactly what happened in
Podhale in a process familiar in many traditions by the name of
"revival" or the related phenomenon Slobin (1992, 11) calls "vali-
dation through visibility," which occurs "when a higher profile
causes a local or regional population to reconsider its own
traditions, and the occasion for this moment is usually outside promoting." A comparable example is the revival of "old-time" music
in America brought about by increased visibility owing to commercial "hillbilly" recordings and bluegrass music (Cantwell 1984,
190–191). I argue here that similar social and cultural forces resulted in the rising visibility of certain styles and repertoires in
Podhale. These styles and repertoires were codified, canonized, and
promoted by outsider interests with the cooperation of key Górale
musicians to create muzyka Podhala.

From the perspective of its impact on Górale music-culture,
ethnography of Podhale can be divided into four main historical
periods (which overlap imperfectly with the phases of tourist migration to Podhale described in chapter 2): (1) writings from the
early nineteenth century to Chałubiński's "discovery" of Zakopane
and the founding of the Towarzystwo Tatrzańskie (Tatra Society)
in 1873; (2) from 1873 to World War II in 1939; (3) after the war,
during the communist era in Poland (Szurmiak-Bogucka and Bogucki 1961; see also Chybiński 1961, 166–185; Lewandowska 1982;
Styrczula-Maśniak 1991, 7–128; Wrazen 1988, 19–36); and (4) current and recent research, primarily since 1980.

First Period: To the Late Nineteenth Century

A few ethnographic references to Podhale were written before the
nineteenth century, but the first substantial information about music in the region is from the first half of the nineteenth century
when the Tatras were first becoming a tourist destination. The

Figure 3.1. *Nuta* (from Gorączkiewicz 1829, as reproduced in Chybiński 1961, 168).

Figure 3.2. *Nuta* (from Gorączkiewicz 1829, as reproduced in Chybiński 1961, 168–169).

earliest published music from Podhale appears in a collection of thirty-four krakowiak dance tunes arranged for piano by Wincenty Gorączkiewicz (birth and death dates unknown) and published in Vienna in 1829.[3] The final four dances in this collection are based on Górale tunes from Podhale, and although they were most certainly altered with added cadences and "corrected" tonality (Chybiński 1961, 167–169), they bear some resemblance to muzyka Podhala today (figs. 3.1–3.4). For example, augmented fourths above the tonic, a common sound today in Górale music, are conspicuously present in figures 3.2 and 3.3. The phrasing structures of two of Gorączkiewicz's dances are also similar to common structures in Górale music as represented in the early twentieth century and as I have heard it in the late twentieth century. The four-bar phrases in 2/4 meter of figure 3.1 are similar to a *krzesana*, and the

Figure 3.3. *Nuta* (from Gorączkiewicz 1829, as reproduced in Chybiński 1961, 169).

Figure 3.4. *Nuta* (from Gorączkiewicz 1829, as reproduced in Chybiński 1961, 169).

five-bar phrases in figure 3.4 suggest a *wierchowa*. However the melody in figure 3.4 is tonally centered around an A, with a B♭ and C♯ above, a mode I have not encountered in muzyka Podhala. The remaining two tunes have phrase structures that are unusual in muzyka Podhala, and I recognize none of the tunes as currently played by Górale. Finally, with no information about how these particular tunes were collected, in what villages, from whom and by whom, they remain historically interesting but problematic early representations of Górale music. At best they suggest that *krzesana*-like and *wierchowa*-like structures, and a propensity for augmented fourths, were musical characteristics found somewhere in Podhale, sometime in the first few decades of the nineteenth century.

A complementary early example of ethnographic information about Górale music-culture is a travelogue written during a journey to Podhale in 1832 by the romantic Polish poet Seweryn Goszczyński (1801–1876). In his diary, published twenty-one years after his trip in 1853 as *Dziennik podróży do Tatrów* (Diary of a journey to the Tatras), he chronicled his experiences and impressions of the Tatras, and of Górale and their ways, including two entries that deal specifically with music and dance. He makes no pretense at being a "scientist," but he goes as one "begging with or for songs, poems of the spirit" (Goszczyński 1853, ii). Nevertheless, he gained the nickname "father of Podhalan ethnography" (Radwańska-Paryska and Paryski 1995, 354), and, although romantic, his descriptions are informative, providing the earliest account of contexts for Górale music and even early musings on Górale ethnicity.

In a section dated 22 June 1832 and entitled "Pasterstwo w Tatrach—Pieśni pasterskie" (Shepherding in the Tatras—shepherds' songs), Goszczyński struggles with Górale's heritage based on their lifestyle (1853, 138–139). He notes that they are farmers and shepherds, and probably more shepherds than farmers. Farming he considers to be a Slavic trait that associates Górale with the predominantly Slavic Poles. Shepherding, on the other hand, Goszczyński associates with peoples from "the east," and he extends his comparison to the "Arabs." He goes on to describe Górale shepherding techniques involving one or two head shepherds and their apprentices, who take the village's sheep into high mountain pastures when the pastures are free of snow—usually from May to September (139–141). While in the mountains the shepherds (all male) live in small huts where sheep's milk is made into cheese and smoked. They work all day and party at night, including playing music and dancing. On a few occasions during the season, such as the last day of May, the village women and girls dress in their finest clothing and walk up from the villages to join the shepherd men and boys for a holiday of food, drink, music, and dance (142–143). Incidentally such gatherings are memorialized today by Górale in staged performances.

Goszczyński goes on to transcribe the texts of seven Górale songs, plus fractions of a few additional songs he describes as being "in the spirit of krakowiaks" (1853, 145). The seven texts represented as Górale have, without exception, twelve syllables per line, each divisible into two six-syllable halves. The following poem from Goszczyński (147) illustrates this poetic structure:

Héj! ładnaś dziewcyno,	Hey! girl you're lovely,
ładnaś i do smaku,	lovely and pleasing,
Nie zal mi puść z tobą	I don't regret leaving the mountains
z hory taj do światu	with you for the world.
Ja pudę po wirsku,	I'll go over the peaks,
ty pudzies doliną,	you'll go in the valley,
Jak się nie zendziemy,	If we don't meet,
to se wezme inną.	I'll fetch myself another.

Six-plus-six syllable lines are by far the most common poetic meter of Górale songs documented throughout the twentieth century (see Chybiński 1961, 427–507; Sadownik 1971 [1957]; Cooley and Spottswood 1997a, 1997b). The topics of the poems in Goszczyński's diary are also familiar in Górale poetry from the twentieth century; they speak of shepherding, they combine pastoral scenes with expressions of longing for a loved one, and one song is about conscription into the army. What follows on pages 148 to 150 of Goszczyński's diary are "fragments" of sixteen krakowiak-like songs. Eight of the songs have four lines, and eight have only two. Ten of the sixteen contain lines of twelve syllables each divisible into two six-syllable halves (6 + 6, 6 + 6). Three of the remaining six texts contain four lines of six syllables each, and could also be represented as two lines of twelve syllables each. Two have four eight-syllable lines, and one has four seven-syllable lines. Thus, with only three exceptions, all the poetic structures are identical to the songs Goszczyński represents as distinctly Górale. Nor does the poetic content distinguish the sixteen krakowiak-like songs from the Górale-style songs; they, too, contain pastoral scenes, and are about love and courtship, certainly common song themes around the world. Perhaps the most significant information contained in this section of his diary is that, to his ear, some songs were distinctly Górale, and therefore Górale music was somehow distinguishable from other kinds of music. And if we trust Goszczyński's ear, we also know that so-called Górale music was not all the music that Górale sang: they sang "something like krakowiaks" and other songs that were, in his opinion, "passages from Hungarian songs" (Goszczyński 1853, 150).

In a separate entry dated 25 June 1832 and entitled "Muzyka i taniec góralów" (Music and dance of Górale), Goszczyński not

only describes music and dance, but he also addresses its importance in the lives of Górale (1853, 151–155). He lists the instruments used: violin, fiddle, double-bass, bagpipes, flutes, and whistles, noting that the violin, double-bass, and fiddles (*gęśle*) were
most common for music in homes, and were also necessary for
dances. Shepherds preferred flutes, and they also used long wooden
horns (alpine trumpets) (152). He admits that he is not qualified
to transcribe the melodies, and his discussion of music sound is
vague—more poetic than descriptive—referring to the music as
having a narrow scale and being monotone (*jednotonność*), and the
songs as being gloomy and strained (152).

Goszczyński's diary does allow for a comparison of the materials of Górale music-culture in the 1830s with those in the twentieth century. All the instruments described by Goszczyński are still
in use in Podhale, although the *basy* is much more common than
the double-bass. Violin ensembles are still the primary instruments
for dancing, and occasionally individuals play on "fiddles," which
Górale call *złóbcoki* instead of the generic Polish term *gęśle* (fig. 3.5).
I take his consistent listing of both violins and *gęśle* to indicate that
standard violins and locally made *złóbcoki* were frequently used together in string bands. Flutes that fit Goszczyński's description are
also common despite the relative paucity of shepherds. I also documented the use of alpine horns in Podhale, not in a shepherding
context but for ceremonial functions at festivals and at a funeral.

Goszczyński goes on to describe his impressions of a dance
"suitable for men only, when male Górale lock in a circle of dancers, making in the center various jumps, and together flinging axes
up high again and again, and catching them in the air with amazing
adroitness. This is a fitting male character dance, recalling ancient
war dances."[4] The dance Goszczyński described is clearly the *zbójnicki* that is still danced today. I find his description significant
because it suggests a dance that is choreographed, at least to some
extent: "*together* flinging axes up high again and again . . ." In the
early twentieth century the director of the Tatra Museum in Zakopane, Juliusz Zborowski, believed that this dance in particular had
lost its spontaneity and become more stylized for staged tourist
performances (Zborowski 1972 [1930], 331). Goszczyński describes
a *zbójnicki* dance observed in 1832, almost a century earlier, that is
already uniform, although this does not necessarily rule out spontaneity.

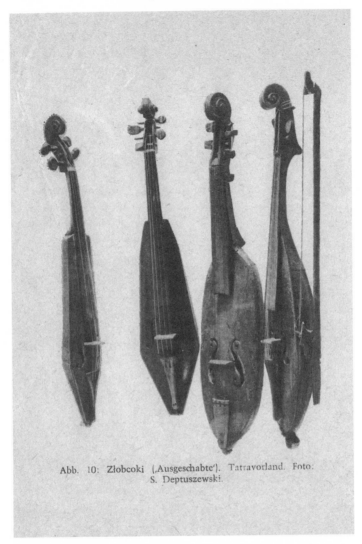

Abb. 10: Złobcoki („Ausgeschabte'). Tatravorland. Foto: S. Deptuszewski.

Figure 3.5. *Złóbcoki*. Photograph by S. Deptuszewski, courtesy of A. Szurmiak-Bogucka.

The next contribution to ethnographic literature on Górale music is Ludwik Zejszner's *Pieśni ludu Podhalan, czyli górali tatrowych polskich* (Songs of the folk of Podhale, or the Tatra Górale of Poland). Zejszner (1805–1871) was not an ethnographer by profession but a geologist and paleontologist. Zejszner did his collecting in Podhale in 1838, just a few years after Goszczyński visited Podhale, but Zejszner's book was published in 1845, before Goszczyński's diary. Containing 737 song texts, Zejszner substantially increases our knowledge of early-nineteenth-century Górale poetry, although he provides no musical transcriptions. Similar to Goszczyński, he describes the music as being monotone, melancholy, and not particularly pleasant. I am not sure how to account for Goszczyński's and Zejszner's similar derogatory opinions about Górale music other than to wonder if the music was so exotic to these early visitors that it all sounded the same, and thus they were unable to comprehend its subtleties and beauty. In the early twentieth century, although the music played by Górale had come to be celebrated by many visitors, exoticizing commentaries even more derogatory than Goszczyński's and Zejszner's were still found. For example, painter Wojciech Kossak in 1913 described the playing of Bartuś Obrochta's band as "naïve jangling music" that induced shepherds to "break out into mad trance-like dervishes" (quoted and translated in Jabłońska, Liscar, and Okołowicz 2002, 99).

Zejszner's description of Górale dancing suggests that, at least in the early nineteenth century, its general structure and format were very similar to Górale dance today. He also observed that Górale dance resembled Slovak dance:

Taniec zupełnie właściwy Podhalan, różni się od tańców właściwych mieszkańcom równin: zbliża się do Słowackiego. Piękny, rosły chłopak, w opiętych białych spodniach, zrzuciwszy gunię, występuje na środek izby, i zaczyna taniec przebiérając nogami w najrozmaitszy sposób: skacze i tupie, czasem poświstuje lub wykrzykuje.[5] Jedna albo dwoje dziéwcząt, krokami drobnemi, tańczą wokoło

Dance styles characteristic of Górale differ from the dances of the flatlands: it is similar to Slovak forms. A handsome, tall lad, fitted with white pants, having tossed off his overcoat, comes into the center of the room, and begins dancing intricate and skillful footwork: he jumps, stamps, sometimes whistling or yelling commands. One or two girls, with delicate small steps, dance around the

mężczyzny popisującego się na środku izby: to zbliżają się do niego, to znów oddalają. Muzyka towarzysząca na skrzypcach, nie należy do zbyt przyjemnych. Monotonna jest i melancholiczna; a gdy nadejdą szybsze akordy, wtedy chłopak porywa zwinną tancerkę, i wykręca ją z niewymowną prędkością. Zebrani w karczmie przypatrują się: chwalą zwinność, weselą się, piją lub namawiają dziewczęta do przyszłego tańca. Jestto raczéj popisywanie się nie taniec ogólny. Taniec zbójecki różni się tańca zwyczajnego, skokami śmielszemi, a muzyką bardziéj poważną, zapowiadającą.

Tancerz między odstępami zwykł śpiewać dwa wiérsze, wyjątkowo cztéry, a widzowie i słuchacze cieszą się dowcipem tych śpiewek, a cóż dopiéro ich przystósowaniem. (Zejszner 1845, 34)

young man as he shows off in the middle of the room: now they get close to him, and then again dance away from him. The violin music accompanying this does not belong to the most pleasant of music. It is monotone and melancholy; and once they pick up the tempo with quick chords, then the boy takes the agile girl he is dancing with and spins her with unspeakable speed. Those gathered in the inn look on, commenting and praising their agility. They are joyful and merry as they drink and convince the girls to dance the next dance with them. This is a form of showing off, and not social dance for couples. The brigands dance differs from their normal dancing with daring jumps, and the music is very serious, menacing.

During breaks the dancer sings two verse couplets and sometimes four verse couplets, and the onlookers and the listeners laugh at the humorous meaning of the songs, and even more at their pertinence. (Zejszner 1845, 34)

Zejszner's most significant contribution concerning Górale music-culture is to our knowledge of poetic forms of Górale songs from the first half of the nineteenth century. Zejszner divided his collection into four sections: songs about love (478 examples), wedding songs (22 examples), shepherding songs (103 examples), and songs about *zbójniki* (137 examples). From this alone one can see that the poetic content of the songs is quite similar to those collected by Goszczyński. Concerning the structure of these song texts, the most striking feature is the preponderance of twelve-syllable lines, divisible into two six-syllable halves. For example, reproduced and translated below is song no. 110 from Zejszner's section 1, songs about love:

| Zapłać mi karczmarko co ci karczmę zdobię, | Innkeeper lady, pay me for adorning your inn, |
| Całem gardłem śpiewam a nóżkami drobię. | With my entire throat I sing and with my legs I dance. |

Of the 150 songs sampled, 80 had this structure. The next most common poetic structure was two pairs of six-syllable lines. Twenty-four poems out of those sampled had this structure. Song no. 57 from section 3, shepherding songs, exemplifies this:

Idą cie owieczki	The sheep walk
Z wierzka do uboczki,	From peak to mountain side,
Jak się pięknie roją,	How nicely they cling together,
Bo się nocki boją.	Because they fear the night.

These six-syllable poetic lines conceivably serve the same musical function as twelve-syllable lines divided into two six-syllable halves. The only reason some songs are represented as having twelve-syllable lines, and others pairs of six-syllable lines, seems to be rhyme scheme. Of the 150 songs I analyzed, a total of 104 used some form of six-syllable units. The collections of Zejszner and Goszczyński firmly establish six-syllable units as the most common form of Górale poetry in the first half of the nineteenth century. This characteristic, however, does not distinguish Górale poetry from other Polish forms, nor from poetry throughout Central Europe (see Slobin 1996a, 249). For example, the krakowiak genre from north of Podhale around Kraków also uses six-plus-six syllable lines, as do many songs in Transylvania.

The next source of information about Górale music and dance was a manuscript dated 1851 by Gołaszcziński, an individual about whom nothing is known except what was gleaned from this manuscript. The manuscript was lost during the Second World War and is known to me only in a description by Karol Hławiczka published in 1936 in the journal *Muzyka Polska*.[6] According to Hławiczka, Gołaszcziński's manuscript contained two main parts: first, a description of dance and, second, a description of thirty-one dance songs and tunes, complete with transcriptions of the tunes arranged for violin and piano, performance notes, and information about the origin of the songs. Unfortunately Hławiczka's review of the manuscript includes reproductions of only four of the tunes and twenty-two fragments of song texts. Hławiczka also directs readers to other sources for additional items from

Gołaszcziński's manuscripts, and in these sources I have located a variation of one additional tune said to be from Gołaszcziński's manuscript. This leaves me with a total of five tunes that I can say with some certainty were noted by Gołaszcziński in the mid-nineteenth century (figs. 3.6–3.10).

Much in Gołaszcziński's description of music and dance is consistent with the core music and dance repertoire of the muzyka Podhala complex. He also describes significant variations, especially in villages lying on the edges of Podhale. His description of dance focuses on the *drobny*, a particular dance step and tune type that is part of the *góralski* genre dance cycle, and the *kozak*, probably referring to the *zbójnicki* (brigands') dance. My interpretation, however, of Gołaszcziński's observations of dance is severely limited because my knowledge of his work is filtered through Hławiczka's review. I cannot know if in Podhale Gołaszcziński only saw the *drobny* danced and not other components of the *góralski* cycle such as the *ozwodny* and *krzesany*. The term *drobny* today is often used interchangeably by Górale with *krzesany*, and maybe in Gołaszcziński's time *drobny* encompassed those dances called *krzesane* today. Three of the four music transcriptions we have from Gołaszcziński's manuscript are structured more like an *ozwodny* than a *drobny* or *krzesany*. Perhaps he is using *drobny* to refer generally to what Górale today call *góralski* or *po góralsku*. His descriptions of dance suggest that this is the case. Nor can I know if the *kozak* he witnessed differs significantly from the way the *zbójnicki* is danced today.

Particularly interesting is Gołaszcziński's topography of dance in which he attributes the *drobny* and *kozak* to specific villages: Bukowina, Poronin, Zakopane, Kościelisko, Bystre—all villages in Podhale close to the Tatras. He goes on to describe Górale in the northwestern edge of Podhale around Czarny Dunajec (bordering Orawa) as dancing these Górale dances, but also as dancing krakowiaks, *stajeras* (a fast triple-meter dance), waltzes, and polkas. Thus we are provided with an image of dances that are still considered specific to Górale (*góralski* and *zbójnicki*) as being common in the Podhalan villages closest to the Tatras in 1850. We also learn from Gołaszcziński that other dances (including the Bohemian polka that became popular internationally only in the 1840s) were danced on the periphery of Podhale, especially the northwestern edge that happens to be geographically the least rugged approach to Podhale.

Figure 3.6. *Nuta* from the border of Orawa in the area of Czarny
Dunajec (Gołaszcziński in Hławiczka 1936).

O Jasiu, moj Jasiu,
wywiadż że mię z lasu
z lasu dębowego,
bo nie wyjdę z niego.[7]

O Johnny, my Johnny,
lead me out of this forest
out of the oak forest,
for I will not find my way out.

Figure 3.7. *Podhalańska* or *drobna* from around Nowy Targ
(Gołaszcziński in Hławiczka 1936).

Hej, nie chciała Marysia,
hej, we wianecku chodzić.
Hej, wolała Jasiunia,
hej, za rącycke nosić.

Hey, Mary did not want,
hey, to wear her wreath.
Hey, so she preferred,
hey, to hold Johnny's hands.

Figure 3.8. Wedding song, *cepowiny* (capping ceremony)
(Gołaszcziński in Hławiczka 1936).

Czemuś ty, Janicku
owiesku nie siejes;
czyci się nie rodzi,
czy go nie rod widzis?

Why, Johnny, aren't you
sowing your oats;
don't they germinate for you,
or don't you like them?

Figure 3.9. Carpathian *nuta* (no specific village given)
(Gołaszcziński in Hławiczka 1936).

Figure 3.10. *Nuta* from Ostrowska as found in Mierczyński 1930,
no. 13.

The song texts also reveal a similarity to the core repertoire still prevalent today in Podhale. Eight of the twenty-two song texts and fragments provided in Gołaszcziński's manuscript as represented by Hławiczka conform to the six- and twelve-syllable line standard established above as the most common. Of course, the remaining fourteen songs that do not conform to this standard show that other poetic forms were present, as is still the case today.

The five tunes from Gołaszcziński available to us present a similarly mixed picture. I have reproduced the five tunes in figures 3.6 to 3.9, which are from Gołaszcziński as represented by Hławiczka,[7] and figure 3.10, which is a variation found in Mierczyński, cited by Hławiczka, of a tune reported to have been in Gołaszcziński's manuscript.

Figures 3.7, 3.9, and 3.10 are typical Górale tunes of the *oz-wodna* type, exhibiting five-bar (ten-beat) phrases, descending melodic shapes with raised fourth-scale degrees. Although I do not recognize the tunes specifically, they are in the *ozwodna* tune family still prominent in muzyka Podhala and therefore demonstrate continuity since the mid-nineteenth century to the present.

Figures 3.6 and 3.8, on the other hand, are not tune types performed in the core repertoire of Górale music today. The eight-beat phrase structure of figure 3.6 suggests a *krzesana*-like tune, although the rising melodic shape is not typical for Górale tunes, and the rhythmic motif | ♪ ♪ ♩ | ♪ ♩ ♪ | in the second line strongly suggests a krakowiak. The tune is also not unlike tunes from Orawa, which is not surprising since Gołaszcziński does indicate that this tune is from the Czarny Dunajec area bordering Orawa. The wedding song of figure 3.8 is not a tune used by Górale for weddings today, nor was it used in the early or mid-twentieth century as documented by Mierczyński (1930) and Szurmiak-Bogucka (1974). Thus figure 3.6 represents the periphery both geographically and musically to core Górale music-culture, and figure 3.8 presents a discontinuity with twentieth-century Górale music-culture.

To summarize, Gołaszcziński's manuscript offers a complex image of music-culture in mid-nineteenth-century Podhale with tunes, poems, and dances very similar to core muzyka Podhala as defined in later generations, and with other popular dances also present at least in the outer limits of Podhale.

The next source of information about music in Podhale is a nineteenth-century manuscript housed in the Ethnographic Museum in Kraków believed to be in the hand of Eugeniusz Janota, a priest, naturalist, and geographer who spent a great deal of time in the Tatras from 1852 until his death in 1878. The small portfolio is not dated, but a museum catalogue card puts the date at "around 1880" suggesting that it was created toward the end of Janota's life, although it may have been created earlier. Containing seven transcriptions (two instrumental and five songs) the manuscript is notable for the ambiguous image it provides of music in Podhale during the second half of the nineteenth century, and for the critique it has received from subsequent commentators, especially Chybiński (1922; 1961, 174–178).

Janota's manuscript is problematic for several reasons. First, the music was collected in the small village of Rogoźnik. Most ethnographies since the 1950s include this area in the ethnographic region of Podhale (e.g., Kotoński 1956), although it is technically

Ju - ha - si,   ju - ha - si   sko - da wa - syj___ kra - sy

kiej wás po - wią - zu - li   u buc - kó   za   wla - sy.

| Juhasi, juhasi skoda wasyj krasy kiej wás powiązuli u buckó za wlasy. | Shepherd boy, too bad for your good looks since they tied you to the oak by your hair. |

Figure 3.11. *Nuta* from E. Janota with suggested corrections by A. Chybiński (1961, 177).

not in *Skalne* Podhale (Chybiński 1961, 173) but in the relatively flat terrain that opens up toward Orawa, placing us once again in a cultural border region. Second, Janota's transcriptions have been deemed "unreliable" because of the relative paucity of augmented fourths above the tonic. Chybiński speculates that Janota was not familiar with "tonality" from Podhale, and reproduced the tunes Janota transcribed with proposed corrections, effectively creating what he calls "Lydian" tonality (Chybiński 1961, 175–178).[8] Figure 3.11 is a prominent example of this. The tonic is D, and the sharps above the Gs are Chybiński's suggested corrections.

Chybiński's critique of Janota's transcriptions, especially the issue of the augmented-fourth scale degree, raises interesting issues. A *raised* fourth is indeed common in muzyka Podhala, but discussions of the phenomenon in musicological studies of Górale music typically conclude that the Lydian mode is favored by Górale. However, to my ear and confirmed by a computer-aided analysis of tuning (Spafford 2002), muzyka Podhala in the twentieth century often employs an *ambiguous* fourth scale degree, somewhere between a "perfect fourth" and an augmented fourth also called a "tritone." In theoretical interpretations of intervals developed in European classical music practices, the intervals of a perfect fourth (considered very consonant) and a tritone (considered exceedingly dissonant) are imbued with great and almost polar symbolic value. Given that Górale musicians tend to play between a perfect and augmented fourth, I am compelled to speculate that scholars trained in Western classical traditions may bring a concept of tuning to music in Podhale that might not be appropriate. Short of more detailed analyses of tuning, I believe it is best to say that a tendency for a raised fourth scale degree is a feature of muzyka Podhala, although exactly how much the fourth is raised varies considerably, and what this might mean to Górale musicians remains an open question.

Leaving the important questions of location and scale aside, the transcriptions left by Janota suggest other connects and disconnects with muzyka Podhala. With the exception of the transcription reproduced as figure 3.11, the songs are not generally in the six-plus-six poetic meter style. For the most part, however, the musical meters are within the characteristic *wierchowa* or *ozwodna* genre: ten beats or five bars of 2/4 time. Melodically the overall descending shapes suggest Górale tunes as documented by many in the twentieth century. I recognize none of the tunes as current in Górale repertoire.

The final source in what I am calling the first period of musical ethnography is from the lifetime of music collecting by Oskar Kolberg (1814–1890). Kolberg was the most prolific collector of folk music and information about folk music in the nineteenth century in and around what is now Poland, and he was one of the most prolific collectors of all time anywhere. In all, he collected about twenty-five thousand songs, more than half with melodies. Within this massive body is the largest collection of songs and tunes from Podhale in the nineteenth century, but it presents a complicated image of Górale music-culture.

Kolberg's complete works are being published by the Polish Ethnographic Society (Polskie Towarzystwo Ludoznawcze), a project that began in 1961 and will include eighty volumes when complete. Volumes 44 and 45 are devoted to the mountain regions of Poland, including the Tatra regions (Kolberg 1968a, 1968b). Together they contain 2,316 songs (with and without melodies) and dance tunes. The ethnographic information, songs, and tunes gathered in these volumes is derived from Kolberg's own fieldwork in the Tatras, conducted primarily in 1857 and 1863, and is supplemented with material that Kolberg copied into his notebooks from the published and unpublished work of other collectors. For example, the section of Volume 45 entitled "Melodie zakopiańskie i podhalskie" (Melodies from Zakopane and Podhale) is actually an article published by Jan Kleczyński in 1888 and copied by Kolberg into his notebooks with annotations (see Miller, Skrukwa, and

Tarko 1973, 99–101). The two musical folklorists were corresponding when Kleczyński's work was published, but I place him in the second period of ethnographic research for reasons that I clarify below.

Analyzing Kolberg's two volumes on the mountain regions of Poland for information about Podhale is a challenge, because much of the data they contain are from several different mountain regions nor do they provide the origins of many songs. More than 300 songs and tunes are clearly identified with Podhale broadly defined. Of these, only 161 are linked specifically with *Skalne* Podhale (excluding the tunes he copied from Kleczyński's 1888 publication which are considered in detail below). Not included in this figure are the many additional tunes that may be from *Skalne* Podhale but that are not identified by Kolberg with a specific Podhalan village or the region in general.

To analyze these 161 transcriptions from *Skalne* Podhale, I first sang or played through all the tunes or did both. Then I arranged them by form including time signature, phrase length, and, when there was text, poetic meter (see Cooley 1999b, 123–125, 148–149, for the detailed results of this analysis). So arranged, it becomes clear that only about half (85) of the tunes are compatible with muzyka Podhala genres as defined by later musical folklorists and ethnomusicologists: duple meter with an occasionally mixed-metered tune, or unmetered, and with a tendency for short phrase structures. Relatively few tunes (10) in Kolberg's collection have the most characteristic phrase structure in muzyka Podhala: ten-beat phrases (five bars in 2/4 time). About the same number of poems set to duple or mixed meter tunes have the most characteristic poetic meter of six-syllable lines. Yet of these 85 tunes, I identify only 1 as specifically recognizable in twentieth-century repertoire, no. 1079, the tune known as "Marsz Madziarski" (Hungarian march) or "Hej Madziar Pije" (Hey the Hungarian drinks).

The remaining 76 tunes in the collection that I interpret as not compatible with later constructions of muzyka Podhala are triple-meter tunes (polonaises, obereks, and mazurkas) plus a few German-language songs. Kolberg also includes a large collection of wedding songs in triple, duple, and mixed meters, but none of these tunes is associated with Górale weddings in the twentieth century (see Mierczyński 1930, nos. 65, 66, 67; Szurmiak-Bogucka 1974; and chapter 7 in this book).

Kolberg's monumental work is a fitting conclusion to the first period of ethnographic representations of music in Podhale for a number of reasons. First, as with the musical ethnographers that preceded him, while some of the music he documented fits into the style recognized today as muzyka Podhala, very few tunes in his collection are still current in the repertoire. Second, his collection recognizes in mid-nineteenth century Podhale the presence of a great variety of popular and folk genres, ranging from proto–muzyka Podhala to popular Polish and international dances to German-language songs (not surprising considering that Podhale, at the time, was a part of the Austro-Hungarian Empire). I should note here that Kolberg's work has been criticized for being inaccurate (Szurmiak-Bogucka 1991, 702; Ćwiżewicz 2001, 22). This may be true, but he remains the most prolific collector in Polish history, presenting the world with more musical transcriptions from Podhale than were produced by all preceding collectors combined. Surely his collection contains something from which we can learn. I am obliged to wonder if he is dismissed by some because the Podhalan soundscape he presents is at odds with the canonized image developed in the decades after his career.

In subsequent years, as Podhale was transformed into a tourist destination, ethnographic representations began to present a much narrower image of Górale music. I argue that, during this second period of ethnographic research in Podhale, the concept of muzyka Podhala emerges as certain styles and genres were identified as being specific to Górale of Podhale. I begin my review of literature from the second period with the transitional figure Jan Kleczyński, who was closely associated with Kolberg but whose representation of Górale music differs significantly.

Second Period: Late Nineteenth Century to World War II

Ktokolwiek raz w życiu znajdował się na jednej z tych uroczych wycieczek w góry, urządzanych przez profesora Chałubińskiego, tego musiał uderzyć marszowy temat, grywany zawsze przez mejscową "orkiestrę", a będący dziś jedną z najulubieńszych

Whoever has found himself on one of those beautiful trips to the mountains organized by professor Chałubiński must have heard a march theme always played by the local "orchestra," which today has become one of the most liked of all Górale melodies. Its theme is

Figure 3.12. *Słodyczkowa* (Kleczyński 1888).

melodyj góralskich. Temat ten w swojej prostocie brzmi jak następuje: [fig. 3.12]. Jest on niezawodnie bardzo dawny; odkrytym on został jednak dopiero przez profesora Chałubińskiego zaraz w pierwszych latach jego bytności w Zakopanem. Grywa go Jędrzej Słodyczka, rozumny góral ze wsi Bystrego, który będąc małym chłopcem, nauczył się tej melodyi od swego dziadka; od niego melodya nazywa się "Słodyczkowa". [. . .]

Otóż Słodyczka grywał tę pieśń, ale nie była ona własnością ogółu, nie była popularną. Prof. Chałubiński zachęcił do jej grania, radził im, jak mają na swych instrumentach rozłożyć basy, i teraz jest ona jedną z najulubieńszych. (Kleczyński 1888, 52–53)

straightforward as in the following: [fig. 3.12]. This theme is certainly an old tune, however it was discovered by professor Chałubiński in his first years spent in Zakopane. This tune is played by Jędrzej Słodyczka, an intelligent Górale from the village of Bystre, who, when he was a little boy, learned this melody from his grandfather. After him this melody is named "Słodyczkowa." [. . .]

And so Słodyczka played this song, but at the time it was not a tune that belonged to everyone, it was not popularized. Professor Chałubiński encouraged the playing of this melody. He advised them how to play the bass on their instruments, and today it is one of the tunes most well liked. (Kleczyński 1888, 52–53)

Jan Kleczyński (1837–1895) was a younger contemporary of Kolberg and, like his colleague, a musicologist and composer. In 1882 and 1884 he visited Zakopane and toured the Tatras and Podhale with Dr. Tytus Chałubiński guided by Jan Sabała, the duo introduced at the beginning of this book. He published three articles about Zakopane and music (Kleczyński 1883, 1884a, 1884b) and a longer piece in 1888 that gathered together music transcriptions from his earlier publications. Kleczyński's articles provide clear accounts of how the popularization of Podhale among the

Polish inteligencja was influencing Górale music-culture and creating the conditions that define the second period of ethnographic literature on music in Podhale. In short, these conditions were caused by new music performance contexts created by the increasing number of tourists in Podhale; these contexts were brokered by outsiders who would begin to influence Górale musicians themselves. Chałubiński was what today we might call a "culture broker."

The excerpt that heads this section, taken from Kleczyński's 1888 annotated publication of seventy-four melodies from Podhale, is a telling account of the popularity of a tune then known as *Słodyczkowa*, named after Jędrzej Słodyczka, a Górale violinist who was apparently fond of playing the tune. We learn from Kleczyński that Tytus Chałubiński single-handedly increased the popularity of this tune, and that he even instructed Górale musicians on how they should play the *basy* part. Today, more than a century later, this same tune is known as "Marsz Chałubińskiego" (Chałubiński's march, see fig. 1.18) and is part of the popular *zbójnicki* dance cycle. With so few specific tunes (in contrast to tune families or *nuty*) documented prior to Chałubiński's time surviving in the current repertoire, it is reasonable to ask if "Marsz Chałubińskiego" would still be played today were it not for Chałubiński's active culture brokering.

Kleczyński's account also tells of Chałubiński's mountain outings with groups of Górale musicians and dancers. In the evenings, even after strenuous hikes, they would play music and would dance while Chałubiński himself called for certain tunes, effectively exercising some control over the music and dance played by Górale on his outings (Kleczyński 1888, 52–53; see also fig. 0.2). We are left with the picture of Kleczyński and other Polish elite visitors to Podhale being introduced to Górale music-culture through events arranged by the most popular promoter of the region, Dr. Tytus Chałubiński—a lover of Górale culture who had no qualms about suggesting ways to improve that culture. Kleczyński's writings about Górale music-culture, then, are writings about Górale music-culture as brokered by Chałubiński.

Even more profound than the active cultural brokering described by Kleczyński is the musical content of his transcriptions. After a century of descriptions and transcriptions that do suggest some stylistic continuity with twentieth century Górale music-culture, but very rarely include specific tunes still played, the brokered image presented by Kleczyński contains an amazing number of tunes also found in representations from the twentieth century and current in Górale repertoire. Of the seventy-four numbers transcribed and published in his 1888 article, I have traced twenty-one to twentieth-century sources (see Cooley 1999b, 150, for a table linking specific tunes in Kleczyński with twentieth-century sources). This contrasts with the single tune I was able to identify positively in Kolberg's roughly contemporary and much larger collection (excluding the transcriptions that Kolberg copied from Kleczyński's publications). An additional twenty-three items transcribed by Kleczyński fit models of muzyka Podhala as described in chapter 1. The collection also includes genres and examples not specific to Podhale today (at least nine tunes are identified with music from neighboring regions: Slovakia, Hungary, and elsewhere in Poland, for example), but much of the music is either current in the repertoire, documented in twentieth-century collections, or both—a dramatic shift from all earlier collections.

One reason for the discrepancy between Kolberg's and Kleczyński's representations of music in Podhale may be their different means of accessing music. By his own account, Kleczyński's access was brokered by Chałubiński who liked to keep company with musicians Sabała and Bartłomiej (Bartuś) Obrochta (1850–1926), the latter being the same musician mentioned by Gącienica-Giewont in the interview quoted at the head of this chapter (fig. 3.13; see fig. 2.4). Chałubiński also had his own ideas about what Górale music was and how it should be played, as illustrated in the above passage. Kolberg, on the other hand, was a seasoned fieldworker who probably had a knack for developing his own contacts. It is also known that at least some of the time when visiting Podhale Kolberg was the guest of the Hungarian Homolacs family, nobility who had a manor house on the edge of what is today Zakopane (Radwańska-Paryska and Paryski 1995, 534). It seems that his is a document of music experienced in the region regardless of who produced the music and under what circumstances. Kolberg showed little concern for distinguishing the music of Górale from any other music. Kleczyński, on the other hand, narrows the focus of his collecting to Górale of Podhale, and even more specifically to musicians from the village of Zakopane. When he includes music conceived of as being from elsewhere, this is clearly indicated. In these ways Kleczyński's work marks a sea change in the discourse on Górale and their cultural practices. His collection ushers in the

Figure 3.13. Bartuś Obrochta. Courtesy of Polskie Wydawnictwo Muzyczne, Kraków. *CD track 22*

second period of musical folklore, influenced by the promoting efforts of Dr. Chałubiński and by a growing *ruch regionalny* (regional movement).[9] His representation of Górale music reveals an emerging concept of muzyka Podhala that is carried into the twentieth century in the person of Bartuś Obrochta.

The next musical folklorists I consider are Stanisław Mierczyński (1894–1952) and Adolf Chybiński (1880–1952), both of whom were active in Podhale between the two world wars. I am leaping chronologically over several collectors of note (Kantor 1907, 1920; Matlakowski 1901; Stopka 1897, 1898) because their work is easy for modern scholars to locate relative to the first period of musical ethnographers, and because at least Stopka's and Kantor's musical transcriptions are notoriously inaccurate (Chybiński 1961, 183; Ćwiżewicz 2001, 23). Yet even with Stopka's inaccuracies one can make out a few *nuty* that are still performed today. Mierczyński and Chybiński, on the other hand, produced numerous transcriptions generally considered to be faithful by later scholars and by Górale musicians alike. They are also linked with Kleczyński through violinist Bartuś Obrochta, from whom all three collected *nuty*. Most important, Mierczyński and Chybiński established a record of repertoire that remains the standard today, a process that began, I argue, with Chałubiński and his active promotion and brokering of Górale cultural practices.

Adolf Chybiński was a musicologist with an interest in the music of Podhale, and in Polish folk music in general. He contrasts with Mierczyński in that his impact on Górale music today is abstract—through his scholarship rather than through the memory of his person. During my interviews with Górale musicians, Chybiński's name is rarely evoked, whereas Mierczyński's name is raised with some frequency as exemplified in the interview with Tadeusz Gąsienica-Giewont quoted at the head of this chapter. This is owing, I propose, to their different styles of research, especially their diverse attitudes toward the method we now call "fieldwork." Although he did spend time in the mountains, Chybiński was not particularly fond of fieldwork, and much of his scholarship is based on data collected by others (Bielawski 1961, 14). He was what Alan Merriam would have called an "armchair ethnomusicologist" (Merriam 1964, 38–39), and this is reflected in the posthumous collection of his writings on folk music, including some previously unpublished works, in the book *O polskiej muzyce ludowej* (On Polish folk music) (Chybiński 1961).

The final section of Chybiński's book is a collection of 281 melodies from Podhale, 222 of which include one verse of text. The vocal melodies are strongly suggestive of muzyka Podhala as described by musical folklorists of Chybiński's time and later. Of the 222 songs, 192 are in duple meter (all of them in 2/4 time). Of these, 114 fit the 6 + 6, 6 + 6 poetic meter form common in Podhale and in vast areas of southern Poland. Forty-nine tunes contain ten quarter-note pulses per phrase (or five-bar phrases), a rhythmic structure suggestive of *wierchowa* and *ozwodna* genres specific to Podhale and closely related regions.

Reflecting Chybiński's apparent preference for working with data rather than individuals, forty-eight of the instrumental melodies are transcriptions he produced in 1920 from wax cylinder recordings made by Juliusz Zborowski in 1914.[10] All these recordings were of the violin playing of Bartuś Obrochta, the same musician who traveled with Dr. Chałubiński and whose tunes were transcribed by Kleczyński in the 1880s (see fig. 3.13). Unfortunately, while making his transcriptions, Chybiński effectively wore out the cylinders, although one can still derive some sense of Obrochta's skill and style (CD track 22). With few exceptions, these and the remaining 11 instrumental tunes (a total of 59) fall squarely into the genres and styles of muzyka Podhala; that is, they are in duple meter, many emphasize a raised fourth scale degree, and descending melodic shapes are prevalent. Many are clearly in the *ozwodna/wierchowa* genres (often with distinctive ten-pulse phrase structures) and *krzesana/drobna* genres. Six tunes are from the *zbójnicki* cycle as still performed in the late twentieth century (nos. 239, 254, 258, 259, 263, 279). The clear exceptions are a triple-meter tune (no. 270) and a csárdás (no. 272). Variants of 24 of the instrumental tunes are included in Mierczyński's 1930 collection of 101 melodies from Podhale discussed next.

Chybiński's impact on Górale music-culture is indirect, via his contributions to scholarship on Górale music rather than through direct intervention with Górale musicians. Published posthumously, his collection and classification of melodies reveal a narrowing of the conception of what Górale music is: he moved toward the concept of muzyka Podhala. For example, he recognized the augmented fourth scale degree as a frequent pitch in Górale scales (Chybiński 1961, 167–169). His work is valuable for anyone interested in Górale music scholarship, but he is largely unknown to Górale musicians today. In this regard, he contrasts sharply with his younger contemporary Stanisław Mierczyński.

When Górale musicians speak with me about Mierczyński (fig. 3.14), their comments frequently focus on his activities in Podhale (what I consider his fieldwork method) and his transcriptions of Górale music. For example, Tadeusz Styrczula-Maśniak told me that Mierczyński wrote the best book of Górale music with the

Figure 3.14. Photograph of Mierczyński, reproduced by R. Bukowski. Courtesy of the Muzeum Tatrzańskie, Zakopane.

best melodies from the best violinist—once again, Bartuś Obrochta. He also talked about how Mierczyński learned these tunes
by living and working with Obrochta, chopping wood for him,
helping him operate a mountain shelter, and playing *sekund* violin
in his ensemble (personal conversation, 1 February 1995). Tadeusz
Gąsienica-Giewont also spoke of how Mierczyński played music
with Obrochta for two years, traveling with him to weddings where
a lot of music was played (ac16.v.95). Józef Leśniak also remembers
Mierczyński as a man who knew how to play violin and who wrote
down the music of Obrochta (ac3.viii.95). When his transcriptions
are praised or criticized, the critique is usually based on the methods he used to produce the transcriptions rather than on the music
notations themselves.[11]

Mierczyński used a fieldwork technique we now call
"participant-observation," a method pioneered and advocated by
fellow Pole and, in his youth, frequent visitor to Zakopane,
Bronisław Malinowski. By the second half of the twentieth century
the participant-observation fieldwork paradigm was well established in anthropology and in related disciplines that employ an
ethnographic method. Participant-observation is prized as an effective means to gather information and gain cultural understanding, but the flow of information goes both ways (Cooley 2003). As
a composer and violinist, Mierczyński presumably came to Podhale
as a fully formed musician, and when he played *sekund* in Obrochta's band, one can imagine that he influenced the Górale musicians around him. Were they curious about his bowing technique? Did he hold his violin vertically, as do Górale when playing
sekund, or did he retain the horizontal, under-the-chin technique
that he certainly would have learned as a student of classical music?
If a medical doctor (Chałubiński) felt free to instruct Górale in
how to play certain pieces, would not an accomplished musician
have been even more so inclined? Perhaps, but I have unearthed
no record of that sort of intervention. Like Chałubiński, Mierczyński was certainly a culture broker, but his brokering seems to
have been accomplished indirectly through the books he published
and by the tunes he included in, and excluded from, those books.

Mierczyński's two books of Górale tunes (1930) and songs
(1935) remain the standard works by which others are judged. I,
too, use them as a benchmark for several reasons. First, they are
respected by many Górale musicians, if not for the transcriptions

themselves then for the way they were made, and because of the individuals from whom many of the *nuty* were collected, for example, Górale violinist Bartuś Obrochta. Second, they were researched and published at a crucial time in the cultural history of Podhale, a time when the region was a popular resort among Polish inteligencja but was not yet experiencing the truly mass tourism that came after World War II. And perhaps most important, Mierczyński's 1930 collection of violin pieces is the first, and still the largest, containing *basy* and *sekund* violin parts, and thus provides a clear sonic image of Górale string bands from the early twentieth century.

Though music in Podhale continues to change, I believe that Mierczyński's work, in effect, canonized the concept of muzyka Podhala that developed during what Górale historian Thaddeus Gromada (1975) has called Zakopane's "Golden Age," a period extending from the late nineteenth century to the Second World War, synchronous with the second period of musical ethnography in Podhale as I have defined it here. During this age, Górale were valorized as unique Poles possessing a quality of independence rare at the time, and their music likewise was interpreted as unique and free of oppressive influences. For this reason the mazurkas, obereks, and waltzes documented fifty years earlier by Kolberg were no longer fashionable in Podhale; instead, what were fashionable were the stark tunes of Sabała and his protégé Obrochta, invested with value by notable non-Górale such as Chałubiński and composers Ignacy Paderewski and Karol Szymanowski. All these forces converged to help create a recognizable style of muzyka Podhala. By "create" I do not mean that a new music was invented; I have shown that musical styles and genre characteristics similar to what we now recognize as muzyka Podhala existed at least throughout the nineteenth century. But those styles and genres were not codified and identified as uniquely the cultural property of the Górale of Podhale. The paring away of styles from elsewhere and the amplification of what was unique in the spectrum of music played by Górale musicians seem to have occurred during this "Golden Age" with the active intervention of "visitors" such as Chałubiński and later Mierczyński. It was Mierczyński who captured this style in the early twentieth century, who consciously gave it authenticity by claiming its antiquity and links to old Sabała, and who then memorialized the style in an authoritative book.

Mierczyński's 1930 *Muzyka Podhala* was not only the first to include *sekund* and *basy* parts, it was also the first collection organized roughly according to genre names used by Górale themselves: *Sabałowa, ozwodna, drobna, krzesana, zielona, Janosikowa,* tunes for the *zbójnicki,* and *cepowiny nuty* (what Mierczyński labeled *Weselna. Do oczepin*). A few tunes are not given genre classifications. They include five tunes called *Czorsztyńska,* a term I have not heard used by Górale but that probably refers to the Czorsztyn area of Spisz, the region to the east of Podhale and on the east side of the Tatras. Three of the five fit well into the *ozwodna* genre (nos. 11, 12, and 13), a fourth I recognize as a *staroświecka* ("old-world" similar to a *Sabałowa*) still commonly played (no. 10), and the fifth is a march now associated with the *zbójnicki* (no. 14). Mierczyński names a few additional tunes by location rather than genre: tunes from Liptów (Luptów in dialect), the region in Slovakia south of the Tatras (*Luptowska* nos. 16, 19, and 95); Spisz (*Spiska* nos. 18, 20, and 21); tunes from Orawa, on the west side of the Tatras (*Orawska* nos. 25 and 27); and one tune from Czarna Góra (Black Mountain), a village in Spisz near the border with Podhale and today considered a Roma village (*Czarnogórska* no. 26). Both Orawa and Spisz are now divided between Poland and Slovakia but were formerly entirely in Slovakia. By including these tunes as part of his collection, Mierczyński is recognizing the porous cultural borders between Podhale and Slovakia as well as the historical importance of the southern, eastern, and western regions of the Tatras in the cultural history of Podhale. And, significantly, at least half these tunes marked as from neighboring regions are still actively played in Podhale today.

Mierczyński also includes three marches: "Marsz Chałubińskiego," the tune published as *Słodyczkowa* by Kleczyński in 1888 discussed above; "Hej Madziar Pije," the only tune in Kolberg that I recognize as still current, also discussed above; and "Marsz Jaworzyński." One curious tune in Mierczyński's collection is labeled "Zbójnicka (Walczaka)" (no. 62). *Walczaka* probably means "little" or "quick waltz" (Polish *walczyk*), although this tune is not a waltz but has triple meter in the melody against duple meter in the accompanying instruments, as transcribed by Mierczyński. I have not documented a tune like this in the current repertoire in Podhale.

The wedding dances included by Mierczyński are all still used today in Podhale. I have heard these "krakowiak-like" tunes performed with the accompanying violins playing on the upbeat and the *basy* playing on the beat. Mierczyński represented two of his wedding pieces in this way (Mierczyński nos. 65 and 67) although one (no. 65) he transcribed in 3/4 time.[12] The melodic phrasing and harmony suggest 2/4 time, however, and this is how I hear the tune. The *cepowiny* tunes are unique in Podhale for their krakowiak/polka-like rhythm suggesting that they originated outside Podhale. The reasons for Górale's consistent and long-standing use of tune types otherwise not considered Górale for such an important ritual needs further study.

Karol Szymanowski captured the spirit of Mierczyński's collection in the introduction he wrote for its first publication. He proclaimed that the music of Podhale is completely different from other music in the Polish nation. This contrasts with earlier collections that made links between music in Podhale and genres common throughout Poland. Mierczyński's collection, on the other hand, contains no true waltzes, no obereks, no mazurkas, and no true polkas or krakowiaks, with the possible exception of the wedding dances. Included is music in the core repertoire of muzyka Podhala, especially thirty-one *ozwodne* and two versions of "Zielona," twenty-seven *krzesane* and *drobne*, eight *Sabałowe* together with four other "old-world"–type tunes, nine tunes to the *zbójnicki* dance cycle, three marches, three wedding dances, and seven tunes from close neighbors with historical ties to Podhale. By the unscientific measure of my ear, I recognize specifically about forty tunes as still current in the repertoire, but I imagine a competent Górale musician would recognize many more. With the exception of the *walczaka* mentioned above, nothing in the collection seems at odds with contemporary musical practice. By what he includes and what he excludes, Mierczyński presents a musical interpretation of who Górale of Podhale are: a unique people in Poland, circumscribed by their mountain existence, isolated, exotic—the ethnic "Other" within his own nation. Fifty years after Kolberg documented a more integrated sonic image of Podhale, Mierczyński musically canonizes an image of an isolated Podhale and Górale, an image that became increasingly important as the region developed as a tourist destination—as the region became increasingly less isolated.

Third Period: Post–World War II

Kotoński wiele razy przych- odził do mnie. Siadał na krześle tam dalej, musiał nogi wyluzować, i ja jego nogami ruszałem i tań- czyłem. Tak żeby mógł zrozumieć jak opisać ten taniec w książce. Tak to razem studiowaliśmy ten góralski taniec. To nie było łatwe, bo mu musiałem pokazać każdy krok, każde obicie i zakrzesanie. Kotoński pisze, że byłem jego nauczycielem. Bo to nikt za bardzo nie chciał udzielać infor- macji, bo to było bezpłatne. A ja miałem inaczej w głowie, ja umiałem zarobić pieniądze, a myślałem o tym, żeby moje na- zwisko zapisali gdzieś, bo chociaż umrę to dalej będę żył. Zawsze ktoś przeczyta i wspomni, był taki Leśniak, żył i tańczył, bo jest opisane. Sabała jak by nie został opisany przez doktora Cha- łubińskiego, to nikt by o nim nie wiedział.

—Józef Leśniak

Kotoński came to me many times. He sat there on the bench, then he had to loosen his feet, and I moved his feet and danced. [*Grabbing my feet, Leśniak shows me how he demonstrated dance steps to Kotoński.*] So that he would under- stand how to describe the dance in a book. So together we studied góralski dance. It was not easy, I had to show him every step, chip, and strike. Kotoński writes that I was his teacher. No one wanted to give information very much be- cause it was without pay. But I had something else in my head. I knew how to make money, but I was thinking how my name would be written down so that when I died, I would yet live. Always when someone reads he will re- member that there was once a certain Leśniak, that he lived and danced, because it is written. If Sabała had not been written about by Dr. Chałubiński, we would know nothing about him.

—Józef Leśniak[13]

Approaching half a century after musical folklorist Włodzimierz Kotoński sat with Górale dancer Józef Leśniak in his log home in Kościelisko, I sat with him. Just as Leśniak grabbed Kotoński's feet and showed him dance steps, he grabbed mine— but this time he was showing me how he showed Kotoński many years earlier (fig. 3.15). In a very real sense I was transported back through time and was physically connected with Kotoński—not the senior professor of composition I had earlier visited in Warsaw but the young musical folklorist of the 1950s. I suspect that Leśniak, too, was carried back in time to his youth. Here he was again, sitting across the room from an academic interested in learning and writing about his dancing and music.

Figure 3.15. Kotoński with his Kościelisko troupe, ca. 1952.
Kotoński is at the left, kneeling and wearing a stocking cap.
Tadeusz Stryczula-Maśniak, with whom I lived in 1994–95, kneels
directly to the right and is also wearing a stocking cap. Józef
Leśniak is on the other side of Tadeusz, wearing a brimmed hat.
Courtesy of Tadeusz Stryczula-Maśniak.

Though connected across time through several individuals with
whom we both worked, and though I am personally acquainted
with Kotoński and other ethnographers active in what I am calling
the third period (post–World War II and before the 1980s), Kotoński and I experienced Podhale in fundamentally different eras.
In Poland the postwar period is marked by Soviet influence (the
communist era), and in Podhale it is marked by the development
of mass tourism. After the war government initiatives funded efforts to replenish musical archives destroyed during the war. Some
communist leaders also worked to mold a new national identity
based on "people's" culture. The results of centrally funded fieldwork projects in Podhale include several valuable studies published
beginning in the 1950s, and the creation of a large recording ar-
chive housed primarily in Warsaw's Polska Akademia Nauk, Instytut Sztuki (Polish Academy of Science, Institute of Art). The
publications considered here are by Kotoński (1953a, 1953b,
1953c, 1954, 1955, 1956), Sadownik (1971 [1957]), and Szurmiak-
Bogucka (1959, 1974).

Kotoński went to the village of Kościelisko from 1951 to 1953 with the sponsorship of the Akcja Zbierania Folkloru Muzycznego (Campaign to collect musical folklore) and the Państwowy Instytut Sztuki (State Institute of Art), under the Ministry of Culture. His assignment was to raise to semiprofessional status a Górale song-and-dance troupe, but, by his own admission, the results of his work were more academic than performative (interview, ac23.iii. 95). The troupe he worked with, Zespół Leśniaków, marks a banner moment for the deliberate socialization of cultural practices in the communist era, but it seems that the musicians and dancers remained too regional for national cultural policies, and government support was withdrawn. The individuals in the troupe were the key sources of data for Kotoński's scholarship, however, and his publications on Górale music remain some of the most authoritative and thorough; they are also decidedly ethnomusicological in that they are concerned with issues and concepts of music practice rather than with collecting and classifying as an end in itself. This is especially true in his series of four articles published in the Polish journal *Muzyka* in 1953 and 1954. The articles cover a range of musicological questions: the Górale concept of *nuta* (harmony/melody), their system of tune classification, and changes in ensemble style (1953a); an analysis of intervals, scales, tuning, and harmony (1953b); musical rhythm and meter, and their relationship to poetic meter (1953c); and organology and polyphonic singing styles (1954). He even touches on one of the themes of my research—the impact on Górale music of the increasing number of visitors to Podhale (Kotoński 1953a, 23–24).

Kotoński also published two books. The first (1955) is a small collection of thirty-eight Górale songs, with a short preface explaining Górale music-culture, singing style, and performance practice. The second (1956) is *Góralski i zbójnicki: Tańce górali podhalańskich* (Góralski and zbónicki: Podhalan Górale dance), which includes a small collection of fifteen instrumental tunes with accompanying violin and *basy* parts. Intended as a manual for amateur dance ensembles, and containing elaborate descriptions of the *góralski* and *zbójnicki* dance sequences, the book is an excellent musical ethnography of Podhale.

In all his articles and his two books, the repertoire Kotoński treats is squarely within the canon of muzyka Podhala. Even though his definition of the ethnographic region of Podhale includes villages and areas where, a century earlier, Gołaszcziński documented polkas, waltzes, or other popular dance types, Kotoński includes no such excursions beyond the canon. By the 1950s muzyka Podhala is a known, recognized, and well-defined folk music.

The largest published collection of Górale songs is *Pieśni Podhala: Antologia* (Songs from Podhale: An anthology), edited by Jan Sadownik, first published in 1957, and reprinted in 1971. With the goal of presenting living songs of the time, fieldworkers for the State Institute of Art collected approximately 20,000 songs from 1950 to 1955 (Sadownik 1971 [1957], 16). Included in this anthology are 1,250 song texts, most of them single four-line verses, arranged according to textual themes, and made exceptionally accessible with the aid of multiple indexes. Also included are 143 melodies in one or two voices. The melodies (*nuty*) were collected and transcribed by Aleksandra Szurmiak-Bogucka, and were arranged in the now familiar categories of the canon of muzyka Podhala: *Sabałowe*, marches, *wierchowe, ozwodne, krzesane, zielone*, and *cepowiny*.

In addition to providing the music examples for *Pieśni Podhala*, Aleksandra Szurmiak-Bogucka published two books about Górale music. The first, *Górole, Górole, Góralsko Musýka* (1959), is a songbook for the general public juxtaposing excellent black-and-white photographs and interesting graphics with song transcriptions, including forty-seven melodies in one and two voices. In the brief preface to that volume, she twice invokes the concept of an "authentic" Górale music (Szurmiak-Bogucka 1959, 5–6). The songs included are all muzyka Podhala, following the same classification system used in *Pieśni Podhala* with two additional related categories: marches to the *zbójnicki*, and *zbójnicki* itself.

The second book, *Wesele Góralskie* (Górale wedding), published in 1974, is a description of an actual wedding in the village of Bukowina Tatrzańska, from the official engagement to the wedding rituals and dance party. The small book contains beautiful black-and-white photographs, song texts, and some melodies for one to three voices (no instrumental ensemble parts). The twenty-seven melodic transcriptions in the book emphasize muzyka Podhala (wedding songs and dances: *wierchowe, ozwodne, krzesane*, and one *zielona*) but also include two polka tunes (Szurmiak-Bogucka 1974, 78, 113). The text also mentions the use of "common" (read "non-Górale") polkas and waltzes (75, 113), and there are several photographs of couples dancing waltzes or polkas (106–108, 116–117).

In other words, forty-four years after Mierczyński's canonizing publication of Górale tunes, when music from outside the canon is included in a monograph on Podhale, it is carefully marginalized with the label "common" (*ogólny*), a word emphasized with quotes in the first reference (75).

Of course, musical ethnographers and ethnomusicologists of the postwar third period who reified the canon of muzyka Podhala established during Podhale's "Golden Age" were not acting in a social vacuum. Much has been made of the communist government's varying ideas about folk culture and its uses during this period, but it is a mistake to assume that all scholars of the time were actively doing the government's bidding, even when employed by the government (as all Poles essentially were). Instead of being concerned about the micro-control of individuals, I find it more useful to interpret the general trends in government and society as a whole, within and outside Poland. At the time Poland was busy rebuilding a war-torn society, a task that involved creating new forms of public entertainment and leisure, including folkloric festivals. This was the real influence in Podhale at the time, and these trends were mirrored elsewhere in the world. The primary ethnographers in Podhale during this era, Kotoński and Szurmiak-Bogucka, were both actively involved with the increasing trend toward song-and-dance troupes that performed at public festivals. These contexts were not entirely new, as I explain in chapter 4, but they encouraged clearly defined music-cultural practices that unambiguously represented regional traditions. The canonized muzyka Podhala worked very well in these contexts for various groups: musicians and dancers who had new opportunities to use their skills to make money or even to tour the world, festival producers in search of talent, and scholars who were employed to rebuild the archives of folk materials that had been destroyed and to help preserve the cultural practices in fresh demand.

Fourth Period: Musical Ethnography since 1980

In this brief review of recent ethnographies, I focus on two ongoing trends: (1) ethnomusicological studies, and (2) ethnographies by Górale themselves. The list of ethnomusicologists who mention Górale music and culture within larger works or who publish occasional articles about Górale is long (e.g., Czekanowska 1990; Dahlig 1991; Kubik 1985; Noll 1986; and Stęszewski 1970, 1980), but I concentrate on those who focus specifically on this topic.[14] Of note is the continuing work of Szurmiak-Bogucka (1991). Recent research offering new interpretations includes Zbigniew Jerzy Przerembski's series of studies (1986, 1987, 1989) on particular elements of musical form and style in Podhale. In an earlier publication, he offered a sociological study of the musical preferences of Górale that went against the conventional wisdom that Górale prefer muzyka Podhala to all other music (Przerembski 1981). For example, earlier Kotoński (1953a, 24) wrote that Górale do not like to listen to the radio and do not like or understand other music. In contrast, Przerembski found that his respondents preferred "light" music introduced to Podhale by radio and television. In a recent dissertation on Górale string bands Krzysztof Ćwiżewicz (2001, 17–18) accepts the accuracy of Przerembski's quantitative conclusions but believes they tell us little about the significance of Górale music and its meaning for Górale. In accord with my theories, Ćwiżewicz's work rejects the ethnographic trope of mountain isolation as the primary explanation of Górale music-culture and recognizes the "invented" nature of cultural practices and ethnic groupings as a response to interaction with difference, including the musical difference that many Górale simultaneously embrace (Ćwiżewicz 2001, 65).

Other ethnomusicologists expand the traditional locus of study to include Górale diaspora groups. Louise Wrazen (1988) pioneered this area with her dissertation considering the effects of immigration on the musical practices of Górale primarily in Toronto but also in Chicago. She concludes that, in the New World, muzyka Podhala loses some of its significance in communicating personal and community relationships but that it retains strong symbolic value for Górale identity and for recalling an idealized past (303). In an article in the journal *Ethnomusicology* (Wrazen 1991), she develops some of these ideas to illustrate how performance practices from Podhale are adapted for festivals in Toronto and Chicago. The Chicago community in particular was the focus of a master's thesis by Sachiko Okamoto (2001). She compares the musical practices in Chicago to those in Podhale, and concludes that they differ by degree in style and function but that, in Chicago, music continues to function to create community cohesiveness.

The second trend in recent research—Górale studying Górale—may be the most significant phenomenon to contribute to our understanding of Podhalan music-culture. A strong literary movement emerged among Górale in the late nineteenth century, including isolated ethnographic studies,[15] but ethnographic studies by Górale educated as ethnographers exploded in the 1980s and 1990s. Here I concentrate on those that focus on music-culture, most of the substantial works being in the form of master's theses. Two Górale scholars produced theses on *Skalni*, a Górale song and dance troupe in Kraków populated for the most part by Górale who are university students there (Naglak 1981; Cebula 1992). A third, by Edward Styrczula-Maśniak (1991), is a historical ethnography of his extended family's song and dance troupe, *Kapela Maśniaków*. Included in his thesis is a section on the regional movement in Podhale and the influence of the *Związek Podhalan* on the representation of music. In 1993 Halina Maciata-Lassak completed her thesis on traditional flutes and whistles in Podhale, including transcriptions of muzyka Podhala played on those instruments. Senior community scholar Jan Gutt-Mostowy published a traveler's guide to Podhale in English that contains a brief descriptive section on music (Gutt-Mostowy 1998, 87–95). Stanisława Trebunia-Staszel does not write specifically about music, but her excellent work on costumes is frequently based in musical contexts (Trebunia-Staszel 1995, 1997, 2000). More specific to music-culture are two articles by Franciszek Bachleda-Księdzularz (1981, 1984) that look at meaning and change in Górale music and dance.

   These substantial studies by indigenous scholars attest to an ever-increasing self-awareness among educated Górale, and to a continued appreciation of the cultural practices considered their own. A striking feature of this new wave of works by Górale on Górale is that they include new performance contexts for muzyka Podhala, especially stage shows and song and dance troupes. By contrast, the second and third periods of ethnography in Podhale are marked by nostalgia, including the work of Mierczyński who was careful to point out that many of the tunes in his collection he learned from Bartuś Obrochta, "the last representative of old Podhalan music," who himself learned from Sabała, an even older musician (Mierczyński 1930, v). Recent ethnography by Górale scholars, on the other hand, tends to balance nostalgia with subjects grounded in contemporary Podhalan life. For example, the three master's theses mentioned above study song and dance troupes, a phenomenon that has roots in the late nineteenth century but that blossomed after World War II. All three of the authors were active performers in the troupes they studied. Bachleda-Księdzularz

(1984), on the other hand, also addresses the impact of stage performances and troupes, but he longs for a bygone era when Górale music-culture was more central to social life. Gutt-Mostowy (1998, 95) similarly decries what he interprets as the degeneration of musical practice among Górale. In general, however, recent ethnographic work in Podhale is grappling with music in the present, not from an idealized Podhale of the past.

Summary

Certain trends emerge in the long history of ethnography in Podhale that parallel the development of Podhale as a tourist destination, first by and for Polish inteligencja, and then for the masses after World War II. In the first period of ethnographic research, Górale are represented as a distinct group with interesting music. This music, however, is not represented as a codified canon but rather as diverse practices centering around relatively identifiable characteristics while also including popular and folk genres from lowland Poland, Hungary, and what is now the Slovak Republic, plus several German-language songs. Although examples of tunes and poetic styles recognized later as specifically Górale were documented, they constitute just a few songs and poems among many. During the second period, marked by Chałubiński's activities in Zakopane, and the founding of the Towarzystwo Tatrzańskie in 1873, ethnographic representations of Górale music shift to stress distinct styles and genres—the muzyka Podhala of today. This trend coincides with a regional movement when influential elite Polish musicians and artists were frequenting Podhale. The recognition and maintenance of distinct Górale cultural practices were part of that regional movement. Musical ethnographers in the third period, after World War II, concentrated on replenishing archives destroyed during the war. Their work reified the canon of muzyka Podhala established in the second period. The fourth period begins around 1980 and includes ethnomusicological studies that consider Górale music within cultural contexts, and a number of studies by Górale of their own music-culture. Though recent scholarship generally emphasizes a bounded canon of muzyka Podhala (as does this present book), the primacy of this tradition is beginning to be challenged (Przerembski 1981) as is the implication that this music is inseparably linked to the Polish Tatras (Okamoto 2001; Wrazen 1988, 1991).

My work continues this latter trend. The Polish Tatras did not make muzyka Podhala what it is; people made and make muzyka Podhala. This is illustrated in the two grand narratives presented here: the settlement history of Podhale and the history of musical ethnography in Podhale. My conclusion is that the making of the modern ethnicity "Górale" is intricately bound with the making of muzyka Podhala. In other words, the new migration of tourists (including ethnographers) flowing to Podhale in the nineteenth century established relations of inequality and put into relief social and cultural differences that encouraged the making of the ethnic identity "Górale." Part of this process included the definition and codification of music-cultural practices.

Suggesting that tourists and ethnographers helped to make Górale ethnicity and music-culture does not deny the importance or validity of Górale identity and cultural practices. Nor is it my intention to denigrate the legendary independence and creativity of Gorale. On the contrary, the autochthonous residents of Podhale are to be admired for adapting to the changing socioeconomic climate introduced by the new migration while simultaneously maintaining a sense of distinctiveness when it was to their advantage to do so. The balance of this book illustrates how some Górale have done just this, responding in dynamic ways to ethnographic representations of their own cultural practices from within and without, while holding on to a strong sense of Góraleness. In this way they are truly modern in their cultivation of cultural practices interpreted as "traditional."

4

Village on Stage

Some words are invested with particular power. "Village" is one such word. On the one hand, a village is conceived of as a major accomplishment of civilization. One might reasonably expect to find all that is necessary for human life and socialization within a village. The words "country," "hills," "outback," and "mountains" evoke isolation and removal, but "village" suggests commerce, the exchange of ideas, a place to seek a mate, and perhaps even a place to experience good music. All but the most determined recluse will venture to the village on occasion to fulfill social and material needs. On the other hand, a village does not offer the amenities of a town, has none of the urban intensity of a city, and is hardly evocative of sophistication or cosmopolitanism. We prefer the village doctor for some ailments, but we rush to the big city hospital for others. Stepping over the village drunk, switching to the other side of the street to avoid the village idiot, and averting one's gaze from the beckoning of the village harlot, we note that the village is pure, good, an extension of all the fine things we hope for in family life. As Hillary Clinton (1996) famously declared, "It takes a village" (to raise a child . . . to heal a society).

The concept of "village" has survived modernism and post-modernism as a locus of powerful longing. The village has become a metaphor for goodness and purity, the place where tradition (another evocative and problematic concept) thrives. Of course villages are concrete realities; much of my fieldwork in Podhale was in villages: Poronin, Kościelisko, Małe Ciche, and so on, but I also spent a fair amount of time in towns: Zakopane and Nowy Targ, in particular. In the course of the histories reviewed in the previous two chapters, Zakopane grew from a *wieś* (village) into a *miasto* (town, city), an important and clear distinction in Poland. In America, distinctions between hamlet, village, town, and city are less clearly defined, and the term "village" is more evocative than it is descriptive. Is Greenwich Village, New York, a village in any way other than name? And if yes, how much of that is owing to the name itself? Naming has power, after all. And if the name "village" cannot take Greenwich Village out of the city, it can at least dull the sharp edges of urbanization with its power to evoke nostalgia, to suggest something that isn't, to challenge the pervasiveness of modernity.

With Górale ethnicity and muzyka Podhala firmly established by the mid-twentieth century, the play of music-culture within and outside Podhale exploded with adaptations to changing socioeconomic and political realities in the second half of the twentieth and beginning of the twenty-first centuries. Playing with the concept of "village" in a number of ways, the remainder of this book considers muzyka Podhala in the ethnographic present, as I have experienced it since 1989. What happens when musical practices associated with Podhalan villages are brought to festival stages? As I mentioned in chapter 1, I first interpreted such adaptations as abominations, pale reflections of "true" village life. Now I understand the festival stage to be a continuation of the very phenomena that helped shape Górale as an ethnicity and helped define muzyka Podhala.

Festivals, Folklore, Fakelore, and zespoły

At the end of chapter 1 I described some of my experiences during the very first trip I made to a Podhalan village, the village of Poronin.[1] I had traveled to witness a folk music and dance festival at the invitation of Polish ethnomusicologist Aleksandra Szurmiak-Bogucka. The festival was instructive; Szurmiak-Bogucka was able to instruct me in the different music and dance genres, and to point out regional variances between performance troupes, and so forth. Yet, at that time in 1992, I was not prepared to accept tourist festival performances as an integral part of present-day music-culture in the Tatras. The true village, I felt, was not onstage but rather in the back regions, the back yards, the basement rooms of those impressive log homes that lined the village streets and fueled my orientalist imagination. I had seen stage shows in Chicago; now I was in a real village. Show me the peasants!

When, in the afternoon of my first day in Podhale, I was invited to join the festival jurors and other notable individuals for dinner in a guesthouse there in the village, I believed that I had found what I had come to experience. However, as described in chapter 1, the music performed around the dinner table after the meal wandered beyond the villages of Podhale and across political and cultural borders. Thus the context that fit my imagined requirements for an authentic village experience presented a far more ambiguous musical picture than did the performances on the festival stage, a setting I believed to be, a priori, inauthentic.

My better understanding of the history of Podhale and the defining role ethnography and tourism had in the formation of muzyka Podhala and even Górale ethnicity compels me to reassess my early orientalisms. To achieve any sort of understanding of muzyka Podhala in the lives of contemporary Górale, perhaps it is best to start with the ways they most often learn, remember, and use the music today, rather than in an exoticized time and place of my imagination. Where better to start than the tourist festival stage shows, one of the more prominent and public places where muzyka Podhala is found. After all, if tourism and its companion, ethnography, shaped muzyka Podhala in the past, might they not continue to be a shaping force?

My initial negative reactions to folklore festivals were predetermined to a great extent by scholarly and popular interpretations of folk music that tended to focus on in-group activities—in this case, music by Górale for Górale. These in-group performances are similar to what Erving Goffman (1956, 66–70) called "back region" events, in his early theorizing of presentation in twentieth-century Western life. For Goffman, "front region" performances are done for an audience, suppressing some aspects of the activity

and accenting others. In the "back region," the front region presentations can be directly contradicted, since the actors are free to
act "out of character." This raises interesting issues, however, when
the front region performances involve the presentation of cultural
practices considered to be representative of the ethnicity of the
very individuals doing the presentation. For example, at folk festivals in Podhale, front region (front stage) and back region (backstage) performances both involve Górale performing aspects of
themselves. I believe that this is one of the primary qualities of
folk festival performances in Podhale and elsewhere. The musicians
and dancers are performing a myth about themselves. They are
Górale performing ideas about Górale. With these qualifications,
I will adapt Goffman's categories of "front region" and "back region" in my theorizing of Górale performance.

Front-region displays of culture at folk festivals in Podhale fall
into a category variously called "folklorism" (Ceribašić 1998; Lenk
1999; Marošević 1998), "Folklorismus" (see Bendix 1997, 13), or
even "fakelore" (Dorson 1976, 28). The intention of these terms
is to make a distinction between what is considered authentic or
real and what is believed to have been sullied for commercial or
ideological purposes. In general, this "folklorism" is degraded as
unworthy of scholarly attention or, at best, as less valuable than in-
group, back-region performances.[2] Folklorist Richard Dorson was
the most influential promoter of the notion that front-region performances (fakelore) were to be shunned by the serious scholar.
My approach to Polish Górale music-culture was influenced by the
lingering effects of Dorson's ideas when I first began studying the
culture in Chicago, where I worked as a public sector ethnomusicologist for the state of Illinois. There my closest colleagues were
folklorists, many of whom had studied at Indiana University where
Dorson had been a professor. I viewed folk festivals as valuable
places to collect data, but ultimately as only stylized representations
of something more authentic—a fake representation of the real
thing. In this way I misprized the front region in Poronin, while
highly prizing the back region. I still react this way to the extent
that I sometimes find myself experiencing a strong urge to flee a
festival site in order to escape the endless procession of troupes of
smiling peasants. Yet I keep going back to the foot of the festival
stage, simultaneously attracted and repelled.

My research suggests that by the end of the twentieth century
most, if not all, accomplished Górale musicians had been actively

involved in song and dance troupes that performed on festival stages. It is clearly a valued aspect of their musical practice. In order to help me understand the attraction and importance of folklore festivals in Podhale, since 1992 I have formally and informally interviewed Górale actively engaged in festival productions and the song and dance troupes that perform at folk festivals. Practicing ethnography in the participant-observation style, I also rehearsed with a children's troupe led by Jan Fudala and Krzysztof Trebunia-Tutka when living in Poland. Although the perspectives of Górale involved with troupes were not uniform, two themes emerged as constant: preservation (Górale must learn and perform Górale music in order for it to survive) and identity (playing Górale music strengthens one's sense of Górale identity).

Here I use the phrase "song and dance troupe" or simply "troupe" in a specific way that corresponds to how the word *zespół* came to be used during and since the communist era. Although the word literally means "group," "troupe," "team," or "unit," state sponsorship of folkloric song and dance troupes by the Communist Party in the second half of the twentieth century resulted in widespread and specific connotations for the term *zespół*.[3] A *zespół* is not just any collection of singers, dancers, and musicians, nor does it refer to a band of instrumentalists alone (what Górale call a *muzyka*). A number of characteristics distinguish a troupe or *zespół*. First, a troupe is a relatively formal group, often with a hierarchy of leaders: artistic director, dance director, band leader, and so on. Second, a troupe is frequently sponsored by an organization: a school, church, or business, for example. Third, a troupe comprises an ensemble of singers, dancers, and instrumentalists who meet together regularly to rehearse. Finally, and related to the third characteristic, troupes have become teaching institutions where children and sometimes young adults learn music, song, and dance. Before the Communist Party lost hegemony in 1989, a troupe, or *zespół*, often carried the stigma of political propaganda, but this connotation faded quickly in the 1990s.

Song and dance troupes are found throughout Poland and surrounding nations (see Piotrowski 1986) and can be linked to the breakdown of older forms of village social structure caused by the advancing industrialism of the nineteenth and twentieth centuries. Linked with nationalism, troupes emerged with the very rise of the concept of "folk music" in Poland, as typically urban-based educated elites encouraged the preservation and promotion of peasant cultural practices (Noll 1986, 645; Konaszkiewicz 1987). These concepts and grand social changes are reflected in the rise of tourism in Podhale, in which the roots of song and dance troupes in this region of Poland are found. The rise of song and dance troupes are directly related to the ad hoc bands led by Sabała and later Bartłomiej (Bartuś) Obrochta, who would provide demonstration performances for tourist groups organized by the likes of Dr. Tytus Chałubinski. Obrochta was particularly significant partly because of his unique position in history (see figs. 2.4 and 3.13). He was an active musician (and mountain guide for tourists) from the late nineteenth century through the first quarter of the twentieth century, that is, from the era of Sabała, who represents old Górale music-culture to the interwar period when the first song and dance troupes were formed. Some consider his band to have been the first *zespół*-style troupe, although I believe it to have been a transitional-style band with one leg firmly in the Old World and the other in the new Podhale, where performing for the increasing numbers of tourists became a practice.

The rise of song and dance troupes in Podhale roughly parallels the rise of folklore festivals in the region, and the two can be seen as symbiotic cultural phenomena. One of the first troupes in Podhale was established in 1937 by Aniela Gut-Stapińska, an educated Górale from the neighboring region of Orawa who moved to Podhale and became fascinated by Podhalan folk culture. She published several ethnographic articles about Górale (1928, 1933a, 1933b, 1938). Her troupe satisfied at least three of the criteria for a *zespół* outlined above: the group was formally organized with a hierarchy (Gut-Stapińska was the leader); the troupe had a sponsor, the local rifle club, a paramilitary organization for youths similar to Scouts; and they rehearsed regularly and worked up presentations, apparently intended for festival stage shows. Franciszek Świder-Zbójnik was a member of Gut-Stapińska's troupe in 1937, and in an interview he informed me that the troupe performed "folklor, tylko góralski folklor" (folklore, only Górale folklore) and that they presented these performances at festivals (ac7.viii.95). One festival that Świder-Zbójnik mentioned in particular was called *Święto Gór* (Mountain holiday), which he attended in 1937 and again in 1938.

The Mountain Holiday festival was the first folklore festival in Podhale and reflected a relatively new context for presenting folk music and dance. Similar national and regional festivals were established across Europe beginning in the nineteenth century, but they reached Podhale only in the interwar period. This was a crucial period in Poland as Poles rebuilt the country as a new nation-state after more than a century of partition between Russia, Prussia, and Austria. Folk music was used deliberately to help reconstruct a sense of Polishness based on a collection of distinct regions (Brożek 1985, 19; Cooley and Spottswood 1997a; Wytrwal 1977, 316–317). Regionalism was a key theme of the Mountain Holiday festival, which was first held in Zakopane in 1935. The festival was sponsored by local governmental and regional organizations for the purpose of promoting the region—not just Podhale but the neighboring areas as well. In subsequent years the festival took place in other towns in and around Podhale, before the outbreak of World War II ended the festival. The regional emphasis of the festival and the novel idea of focusing on mountain folklore are themes continued in festivals in Podhale today.

The socialization of tourism, after communism became the official state ideology in 1948, impacted the development of folklore festivals in decided ways. Folklore festivals were typically expected to promote the ideology of a unified national "folk," contrasting with the regional emphasis during the interwar period. However, the idea of a unified national folk was never as thoroughly implemented in Poland as it was in other communist states such as Bulgaria (Rice 1994, 26–28). This appears to be especially true in and around Podhale where the most successful festivals celebrate regional folklore, not national. For example, to the west of Podhale in the Beskid Mountains exists an annual festival called *Tydzień kultury Beskidzkiej* (Beskid mountain culture week), and to the east the town of Nowy Sącz hosts a festival called *Święto Dzieci Gór* (Holiday of mountain children). As the name suggests, the director of this festival, Antoni Malczak (1992), cites the prewar Mountain Holiday (*Święto Gór*) festival as his inspiration.

The most successful festival of this sort, and certainly the most influential in Podhale, was Zakopane's *Jesień Tatrzańska* (Tatra Autumn), which began in 1962. This festival was the idea of Krzystyna Słobodzińska, a woman raised in Warsaw who married a man from Zakopane and who spent most of her adult life there. She explained to me in an interview that neither she nor her husband were Górale but that she admired Górale for their style (interview, 20 July 1995, Zakopane, ac20.vii.95). In fact, the first festivals were not primarily folklore festivals but events designed to attract more tourists to

Zakopane with whatever means possible. Display of local Górale music-culture was just one among many other attractions. The event was first and foremost a tourist event; concern for promoting and preserving mountain folklore performance was an afterthought that only later gained prominence. By 1968, however, folklore performance was clearly the focus of the event, which was renamed *Międzynarodowy Festiwal Folkloru Ziem Górskich* (International festival of mountain folklore) and was turned into a contest festival with twenty-four folklore song and dance troupes, six of them from abroad (Reinfuss 1971, 7). This annual festival continues today and is a focus of this chapter.

The International Festival of Mountain Folklore faltered somewhat after the end of communism in 1989. This was pointed out to me in 1992, the first time I experienced the festival in person, when individuals would comment on how few people were in attendance compared to during communist times. Although some individuals shunned folk music when they believed it was being co-opted by the communist government for propaganda (e.g., Włodzimierz Kleszcz, interview, Warsaw, ac22.iii.95), it was nevertheless entertainment when options were limited. Now government funding for the festival is no longer guaranteed, and it must seek new audiences and new sources of funding. The directors of the festival have generated impressive private sponsorship in recent years, but government support is still necessary. In 2003 there was some concern that the festival would be canceled for lack of public funds (but it was not).

Despite the challenges of Poland's financial situation, the Zakopane festival continues to emphasize the international quality initiated in the 1960s. For example, the main competition of the 1996 festival featured sixteen troupes, eleven from abroad. In 2000 eighteen groups were featured, fourteen from abroad. The premise of the festival is that all performing troupes should represent music-cultures from mountain regions. Underlying this theme is the widely held belief in Podhale that all indigenous mountain people are similar—a belief promoted by the Zakopane festival itself. Although claims for the universality of mountain people are dubious, the origins of the festival concept to promote the Tatra regions in the interwar period were grounded in the very real connections of music-cultures along the Carpathian Mountain chain—music from Podhale is more closely related to music from other Carpathian Mountain regions than to lowland Poland. The Zakopane International Festival of Mountain Folklore draws performers from around the world, but each year it includes a sizable delegation of troupes from the Carpathians.

When I spoke with Krzystyna Słobodzińska in 1995, she told me that her goal for the festival back in 1962 was to attract tourists to Zakopane. A secondary theme of promoting and preserving Górale culture emerged later in our conversation: "I tried to run the festival in a way that Górale would not forget about this, that they are Górale."[4] She believed that the festival was responsible for an increased interest in Górale song and dance troupes. The theme of preservation was echoed by Elżbieta Chodurska (1996, 1), the director of the festival for most of the 1990s, in an interview with me and in her "welcome" published in the 1996 festival program book. However, she interpreted the goals of the festival dramatically differently. Instead of stressing the increased tourism the festival might generate, she believed that the festival was an opportunity to show people how Górale from Podhale live, and for Górale from Podhale to see how mountaineers from other parts of the world live. Though both Słobodzińska and Chodurska saw good as well as bad effects of tourism in Zakopane, Chodurska was much more circumspect about the good that the tourist industry was bringing to the local residents. She said that tourists are necessary for *Zakopiańczycy* to make a living since there is no other industry in the area. I noted Chodurska's use of *Zakopiańczyk*, a term that literally means any resident of Zakopane. Although I have not located any reliable sources for demographic information about the ethnic composition of Zakopane, it was often repeated to me in conversations that Górale were the minority—that the "new migration" had overwhelmed old-family Górale at least in this town. Noting that she herself is Górale, Chodurska presented far more ambivalent views about the impact of tourism and the festival on Górale culture than did Słobodzińska (interviews, ac20.vii.95).

The story I relate about the International Festival of Mountain Folklore in this chapter, and about Podhale in this book, is in many ways strikingly similar to the history of the White Top Festival in 1930s Virginia as told by David Whisnant (1983) in his book *All That Is Native and Fine*. In tracing the history of the White Top Festival, he shows the impact of elite "cultural workers" on the mountainous southeastern region of America beginning in the 1890s—a process of cultural intervention that in various ways parallels the processes in the southern mountain regions of Poland. At around the turn of the century ethnographers such as Cecil Sharp believed that the Appalachian Mountains contained isolated pockets of racially pure Anglo stock with preserved old folk culture (Karpeles in Sharp 1954, viii). Similar views about mountain isolation and racial purity are part of the Tatra myth (see, for example, Ćwiżewicz and Ćwiżewicz 1995; Czekanowska 1990, 84; Kotoński 1956, 18; and Wrazen 1988, 48). The historical context for Whisnant's study is the industrial invasion of the Appalachian Mountains, a process of modernization that ultimately stripped many "indigenous" peoples (meaning "white Anglos" to these early cultural interventionists) of their land and often their means of a decent livelihood. At about the same time in Podhale, the mythical mountain region's isolation was also being invaded by many of the same industries: mining, logging, and tourism. Although the same modern industries took root in the Tatras and in the Appalachians, their impacts on the different mountain regions varied. In the Tatras, tourism has had the most pervasive and lasting impact while the impact of mining was relatively minimal. Tourism was also an industry in some areas of the Appalachian Mountains in the late nineteenth century—for example, the Luray Caverns in Page County, Virginia, was already a major tourist destination in the 1880s (Jeff Todd Titon, personal communication)—but coal mining was and continues to be a much greater threat to traditional lifeways. The White Top Festival in Virginia was originally thought of as a means of preserving the festival directors' image of the region's traditional folk music. The roughly contemporary (1935) Mountain Holiday festival in Podhale and the many festivals in the region since were first created to stimulate tourism. Concern for cultural preservation among the festival organizers in Poland came later but now survives as an important justification.

Ultimately Whisnant uses the White Top Festival to understand and illustrate the cultural politics of America. I, too, find festivals fertile ground for cultural politics, especially the politics of cultural, regional, and ethnic identity. With roots in precommunist Poland and continuing after the fall of communism, festivals in Podhale provide a type of symbolic continuity that spans at least a portion of the dramatic changes Poland experienced in the twentieth century. But festivals are not simply a cultural carryover from a previous era; they enter the twenty-first century as modern-day rituals not unlike other more traditionally recognized calendric rituals that define and reify a people's relationship to their universe and ensure their continued livelihood. Interpreting festivals as rituals also helps to reveal why they are important and interesting.

Festival as Modern Ritual of Regional Identity

"Ritual" can be applied to folklore festivals in the two fundamental ways that social scientists use the term. First, a ritual is a stylized symbolic representation of objects, beliefs, or truths of special significance to a group (see Connerton 1989, 44; Durkheim 1915; Lukes 1975, 291). These items of significance are usually in the realm of the unknowable and what I call the "super-rational," by which I mean concepts about which rational thought does not lead to conclusive results but that are not necessarily irrational. Often beliefs in the super-rational realm are simply taken for granted or require so-called leaps of faith. This is the essence of religion in which faith supplements reason, and religious objects, beliefs, and truths are reaffirmed by the faithful with ritual.

The second way social scientists use the term "ritual" is in reference to performances that are intended to be effective or transformative: a participant or participants are transformed, or a group's relationship to nature or other groups is transformed, and a means of living is preserved (see MacAloon 1984, 250; Pertierra 1987, 199–200; Schechner 1983, 131–158; Turner 1984, 21). For example, at a wedding two individuals are transformed from single folks into married folks. Many agricultural societies perform rituals to ensure successful crops, and pastoral societies have rituals to ensure the fertility of their herds. However, rituals and performances intended to entertain are not exclusive of each other. Instead, Schechner (1983, 137–138) proposes a continuum spanning the space between two motivations for performances: efficacy (a quality of ritual) and entertainment (a quality of theater). Like most performances, the tourist folk festivals in Podhale contain elements of both ritual and theater.

Interpreting tourist folk festival shows as ritual is appropriate and offers new understanding of Górale music-culture in several ways. First, although countless weddings and other life-cycle rituals are enacted on stage at folk festivals, this is not where the transformative power of these performances lies. No one believes, for example, that the couple married on the folk festival stage is actually married at that moment. However, the staged folklore shows for tourists do effect a transformation in the relationship of Górale to the international audience that attends festival shows: those performing onstage are marked as Górale via clothing, speech, song, music, and dance, while those offstage are symbolically not Górale—they are "other" for the moment, even if they are ethnically Górale. In this way festival performances produce and maintain aspects of Górale identity threatened by the very social arrangement the festival creates that now places a people, formerly described as isolated, in an increasingly international, multicultural environment. Festivals are places where, according to Ceribašić (1998, 42), groups can ritually legitimate and fix identities, even if only temporarily. Folk festivals in Podhale are rituals about the new globalizing social, political, and economic environment in which Górale now find themselves.

Second, interpreting folk festivals as rituals helps one to understand the position of muzyka Podhala in the context of all the other music that is performed and consumed in present-day Podhale, including Western pop, classical, disco, and jazz. By periodically performing muzyka Podhala, Górale (re)create and preserve it until the next performance. Once ritually preserved before the very audience that threatens to obliterate Górale cultural practices by absorbing them, Górale are free to go into the world and behave as Górale or as non-Górale as they please. And this is exactly what they do. For example, at the International Festival of Mountain Folklore in Zakopane, each evening, after the official festival stage is vacated, the festival performers congregate at a hall owned by a local Górale fraternal organization and sponsor of the festival. Here the former smiling peasants don street clothes, or stay in their regional costumes, and dance the night away to an eclectic mix of canned disco, techno-pop, and pickup bands—a wild mash of identities and traditions in a corporal, musical, sartorial enactment of a new global and cosmopolitan identity so studiously avoided on the front-region festival stage.

Third, interpreting folk festivals in Podhale as ritual provides a frame for understanding some of the changes traditional societies are experiencing in Europe. Folk festivals in Europe and in Podhale specifically emerged in response to the threat posed by large-scale social and economic changes to traditional lifeways, and to what Benedict Anderson calls "cultural systems" and "taken-for-granted frames of reference" (Anderson 1991 [1983], 12). In other words, traditional systems of belief and social organization with their inherent areas of the unknowable and the super-rational were being transformed and replaced. As this happened, new rituals were established to help legitimize the new and emerging systems.

One emerging system that employed folklore studies and later folk festivals is nationalism as theorized by Benedict Anderson. Festivals arose in Podhale at a time when a rapidly changing world needed to be organized and defined, and a place needed to be symbolically created in that world for Górale. The history of folklore studies is linked with that of nationalism and, as Regina Bendix (1997) has shown, is rife with the quest for the essence of things—for the "authentic." Issues of essence and authenticity are most clearly present at folklore festivals, the type of festivals celebrating a new awareness of regional and national folk and folklore that emerged in the nineteenth and twentieth centuries. Extreme examples include the state-managed folkloric song and dance troupes and national festivals favored by the ministers of culture in communist states after World War II. Lending credence to the claim that these festivals are best interpreted as new rituals, some state-managed festivals were deliberately intended to replace earlier calendric and agricultural rituals with new rituals confirming the authority of the state (for an example from communist Poland, see Dąbrowska 1995, 66).

To illustrate some of the ways that village life is represented onstage, I offer two case studies. The first, focusing on the International Festival of Mountain Folklore in Zakopane, analyzes folklore festivals not for their folkloric content but as meaningful rituals in the modern world. The second study is a microscopic consideration of some of the ideas and ideals ritually enacted at festivals with a specific and contested musical style.

Case Study 1: The International Festival of Mountain Folklore

The International Festival of Mountain Folklore, staged every autumn in the town of Zakopane, is the predominant folklore festival in Podhale. The following description and analysis is based on my experiences of the festival in 1992, 1993, 1995, and 2000, and on interviews with festival directors, participants, and audience members. The festival changes each year, and the following description does not necessarily reveal how the festival is organized today. My use of present tense is a narrative device to suggest the ethno-graphic present, although the events I describe are historical.

Like many modern-day festivals in Poland, the International Festival of Mountain Folklore in Zakopane features a contest. For this reason one particular type of authoritative influence of eth-nography and ethnographers is tangibly experienced at the festival by Górale musicians and by tourists (compare to Elschek's 2001 account of the role of ethnomusicologists in Slovak festivals). Con-test folklore festivals in Poland feature a panel of jurors who eval-uate stage performances using criteria heavily invested with notions of "authenticity." For example, at the Zakopane festival each troupe is judged in one of four categories arranged in an implied hierar-chy: (1) authentic troupes (*zespoły autentyczne*); (2) artistic elabora-tion (*zespoły artystycznie opracowane*); (3) stylized troupes (*zespoły sty-lizowane*); and (4) reconstructed troupes (*zespoły rekonstruowane*) (from the 1995 Zakopane Festival booklet). The jurors at this and other festivals are usually academically trained ethnographers of one sort or another—ethnomusicologists, ethnochoreologists, an-thropologists, or folklorists. In the past, members of the commu-nities and ethnic groups represented onstage were often not en-trusted with the responsibility of evaluating themselves, a value judgment reminiscent of the 1930s White Top Festival fiddle con-tests in Virginia at which fiddlers themselves were not allowed to judge contests in a top-down effort to ensure "standards" (Whis-nant 1983, 229). Whether active efforts were ever made to exclude Górale themselves from juries, the situation is slowly changing. Since 1994 the juries generally have at least one Górale member.

The relationship between tourists, ethnographers, and per-formers is ritually established each evening at the Zakopane festi-val. Before the troupes begin performing on the main festival stage, the emcees turn the attention of all present to a long row of tables directly in front of the stage about halfway across the spectators' seating area. Seated at these prominent tables is a panel of six or seven jurors who stand as they are introduced, and the audience claps. These high priests of the festival ceremony come from Po-land and other European nations represented by the festival per-formers. They are culture brokers who will judge each troupe per-forming at the Zakopane festival based on the jurors' collective notions of "authenticity." The recognition of the jury by the em-cees is an important part of the public ceremony but is not sym-bolic of anything particularly Górale. Instead, I interpret this daily

feature as symbolic of a value shared by the organizers and participants—a symbolic acknowledgment of a belief in the authentic.
With ritually actualized power and authority, the jurors (together
with the festival organizers) evaluate and ultimately control the
content of the festival performances.

Ethnographers and tourists alike value what is perceived as authentic rather than what is perceived as spurious. Historically the
industries of tourism and ethnography are linked in their quest for
authenticity, although the quest itself may take different paths. Musical folklore studies in Europe, folklore studies in Europe and
America, and to some extent European ethnomusicology today all
bear the mark of Johann Gottfried Herder's imperative to search
for national authenticity in folk poetry (see Bendix 1997, 16–17;
Suppan 1976, 117–120). The late-eighteenth- and nineteenth-
century Romanticists' fascination with the "folk" (associated in Europe with the peasant class, and in America with the concept of
the common man) as the locus of purity and authenticity in contrast to urban society has been repeated in different locations and
times, including in Poland since the late nineteenth century. In
academic ethnography the dichotomous view that cultural practice
is either authentic or its opposite, spurious, has been challenged in
recent decades, although it still permeates both scholarly and lay-
people's discussions of Górale music-culture and of folk culture in
general (Bendix 1997, 13). The promotional literature for festivals
in Poland is laced with evocations of authenticity. For example, a
flyer for the 1992 Beskid Mountain Culture Week promises to be
"an authentic celebration of tradition," and the stage performances
at the Zakopane festival are juried using authenticity as the main
criterion.

As I use the term here, "authenticity" is not something out
there to be discovered; rather, it is a concept that is made, constructed in a process of "authentication." Like music, it is a cultural
construct imbued with meaning. As Barbara Kirshenblatt-Gimblett
and Edward Bruner have written (1992, 304), the issue is "who has
the power to represent whom and to determine which representation is authoritative?" (see also Little 1991, 160). Similarly Regina Bendix (1997, 17), who has framed the study of the discipline
of folklore in terms of a quest for the authentic, deconstructs the
discursive formation of authenticity as an object while retain-
ing the inherent value of the quest for the authentic. She replaces
the question "What is authenticity?" with "Who needs authentic-

ity, and why?" and "How has authenticity been used?" (Bendix 1997, 21).

As Richard Peterson (1997, 209) has shown with a study of American country music, authenticity is ever changing and can accommodate seemingly contradictory concepts. With the popular country music he considers, authenticity is achieved through a delicate balance of tradition and originality. Similarly Jon Cruz (1999, 40–42), in his study of black spirituals, shows authenticity to be a conundrum, a concept that is always moving and changing in the face of sometimes conflicting ideologies. On the other hand, authenticity in Podhale seems to be generated by faithfully replicating past cultural practices, albeit in an innovative format. This opposition is mediated within the realm of "heritage," as theorized by Barbara Kirshenblatt-Gimblett. In her use, heritage is "the transvaluation of the obsolete, the mistaken, the outmoded, the dead, and the defunct. Heritage is created through a process of exhibition [... which ...] endows heritage [...] with a second life" (Kirshenblatt-Gimblett 1995, 369). I believe that the circular nature of her argument is intentional: heritage has recourse to the past (preservation) and creates a new cultural production in the present (invention); heritage is created in performance, and performance gives heritage new life. With more than a century of heritage exhibits for tourists in Podhale, one can observe the circular nature of heritage. Performed tradition becomes the tradition; the representation becomes the actuality. Heritage begins to reference heritage. I find Kirshenblatt-Gimblett's theorizing of heritage especially attractive, because she does not allow for the familiar dichotomies of history or fantasy, old or new, folklore or fakelore. Heritage is all these things or, rather, the negotiation of the false dichotomies they suggest.

Such a theorization of heritage and authenticity frees one to appreciate the folklore festival as a place where such false dichotomies are mediated. For example, the first festivals in Podhale in the 1930s were simultaneously innovative while deliberately preserving cultural practices interpreted as heritage. Festival directors and performers today often strive to preserve the past while transforming it for new performance contexts. But this is not unique to tourist festivals. Musicians reinvent music and make it live in the very act of performance. In contrast, Kirshenblatt-Gimblett's theorizing of heritage concentrates on physical objects and locations—

things that exist outside individual humans. Perhaps this accounts for her litany of the moribund characteristics of objects of heritage: "the obsolete, the mistaken, the outmoded, the dead, and the defunct" (ibid.). Here we are focused instead on objects of heritage that require warm bodies—music performances—in an effort to understand why the individuals who undertake the powerful act of performing heritage onstage do so.

The dynamic between preservation and invention at folklore festivals has become ritualized. Rituals are always a dynamic balance of preservation and invention—they are reinvented, performative acts with the intention of preserving a memory, a belief system, a way of life, and even an ethnicity. Annually marking autumn, the Zakopane festival joins other more commonly recognized calendric ceremonies such as harvest rituals and festivals of the church calendar. But unlike the ritual ceremonies it joins, and in some sense replaces, the Zakopane festival does not pretend to "influence preternatural entities or forces on behalf of the actors' goals and interests" (Turner 1973, 1100). Yet, like past calendric rituals performed to ensure the success of crops, this newly created public ceremony also works to ensure the continued livelihood of the performers. For example, few Górale in the late twentieth century make their living by means of highway robbery, a legendary Górale profession celebrated in the *zbójnicki* dance that I describe below, but many Górale do earn a living wage in the tourist industry of which this festival is no small part.

The Zakopane festival also ritually enacts ideas about localism and globalism. The festival hosts an international collection of performers who travel to Podhale bringing distinct music-cultures, yet symbolically the festival celebrates in striking ways the local Górale culture—a culture most often described in ethnographic literature as a product of mountain isolation. Although it is an international festival, little attempt is made to include symbols of identity from different cultures in the festival proceedings and ancillary productions. For example, one's first contact with the festival is likely to be some form of printed advertisement, such as a poster or calendar. The 1993 calendar features a photograph of the Górale music and dance troupe that will represent Zakopane at the festival that year (fig. 4.1). The troupe is in full regional costume, and the musicians are playing while a couple dances a *góralski*. Below the photograph is a calendar with months written in Polish and weeks

Figure 4.1. 1993 Zakopane festival calendar. Photograph by Stanisław Momot. Courtesy of the Biuro Promocji Zakopanego i Podtatrza.

going from Monday to Sunday in the Polish style even though the bold proclamation "XXV International Festival of Mountain Folklore" is spelled out in English. In the lower portion of the calendar is the festival logo, a stylized dancing Górale male complete with hat on head and *ciupaga* in hand raised overhead. One who has spent even a short amount of time in Podhale recognizes the logo figure as a male Górale dancing the *zbójnicki*. The international is boldly advertised with recognizably local images.

Figure 4.2. 1995 Zakopane festival calendar. Painting by J. Tycner. Courtesy of the Biuro Promocji Zakopanego i Podtatrza.

The 1995 festival calendar is peculiarly local, featuring caricatures of many local personalities, scenes, and situations. Significantly for the topic of this book, it also pokes fun at tourists and Górale's dealings with them. Suggesting the ambivalence many Górale hold for tourists, a wooden gate over the road proclaims *Witojcie* ("Welcome," in dialect), but it has been violently attacked with a *ciupaga* and several knives (fig. 4.2). Lurking behind the gate is a modern-day *zbójnik*, a highway robber, brandishing a pistol and updating his archetypal *zbójnicki* hat with a ski mask. As with the 1993 calendar, in the foreground are Górale (all caricatures of actual musicians) playing music and dancing. Similar to the festival logo image of a dancing Górale, this calendar is a symbolic representation of Górale identity: Górale are those Poles who play violin, dance their peculiar dance at the drop of a hat, and live off us tourists through various schemes from robbery to heritage.

Tensions between the local and the global, the traditional and the innovative, the spurious and the authentic, and between tourism and ethnography are played out in many ways with physical

Figure 4.3. Festival main stage under the tent, Zakopane, 1992, with the troupe "Miao" from China performing.

and enacted symbols under the large, round circus-style tent erected each year for the festival (fig. 4.3). For example, the physical arrangement of ceremonial space articulates the relationships between tourists, presenters, and jurors. Nestled within the round festival tent is a square formed by the four massive posts that lift the tent canvas (fig. 4.4). The large square area is dead center in the round tent. On the top side of the square is the performance stage, the ceremonial altar on which folklore performances are offered. Directly opposite, on the bottom side of the square, are the jurors seated behind their long table. Roll the circle around and they are on top, reversing positions exactly with the stage. Within the square, in the central space bridging the distance between performances and the official evaluators, is prime seating for the audience, and about half this seating is reserved for festival organizers, press, special guests, and others, including visiting ethnographers such as myself. Thus the jurors are separated from performers by a human buffer, half of them tourists and half officially attached to the festival ceremony itself. The area behind the jurors and the remaining two sides of the central square not occupied by the stage are all filled with tiered, curved bleachers adequate to seat several thousand guests—the public. Thus the jurors and three sides

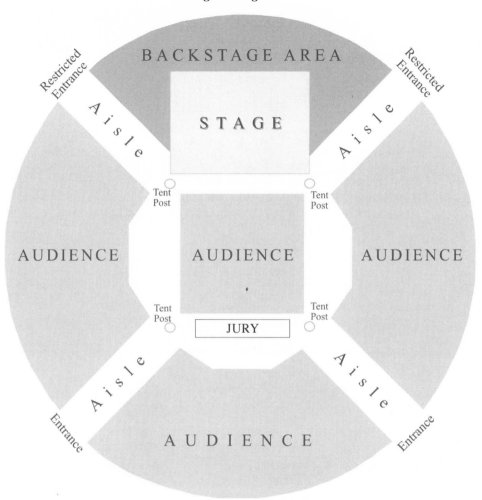

Figure 4.4. Diagram of space under the festival tent.

of the performance stage are surrounded by tourists, by the "public" of this public ceremony. The activities of the jury and the performing folklore troupes all take place "in public" although separated from the public through the ceremonial arrangement of space.

Each evening in this ceremonial space the festival begins as three men in Górale costume walk onstage and play a fanfare on long wooden alpine horns. The alpine horns are blaring examples of heritage as theorized by Barbara Kirshenblatt-Gimblett (1995, 369–370); new life is given to objects whose former use is no longer

Górole, górole

Górole, górole
góralsko muzyka
cały świat obyjdzies
nima takiej nika.

Zapraszamy na XXVI Międzynarodowy
Festiwal Folkloru Ziem Górskich
ZAKOPANE 1994
20-28 sierpnia

Figure 4.5. "Górole, górole," as it appeared on the back cover of the 1993 Zakopane festival booklet. Courtesy of the Biuro Promocji Zakopanego i Podtatrza.

viable. The horns' past function as instruments that shepherds used to signal their flocks is obsolete, but they now have new life, signaling flocks of tourists to the start of the festival.[5] As the men finish and carry their horns offstage, a man and woman also in Górale costume emerge singing "górole, górole." The song "Górole, górole" serves as a Podhalan national anthem and, at least during the 1990s, was published in the festival booklet (fig. 4.5). It translates:

Górale, Górale
Górale music
One can go around the whole world,
there is nothing like it anywhere.

This text can be interpreted in several ways. Perhaps those who traveled from other mountainous regions of the world for this festival of mountain folklore hear the song as an affirmation of some sort of link between all mountain people and between all mountain music. "Jesteś Górol tyz" (You are a mountaineer also), I have heard Górale say when meeting someone who comes from any hilly area. Other listeners may interpret the song as a claim for the superiority of Podhalan Górale's music. Each listener interprets the song in his or her own way, if the listener understands the text at all, that is; but to many Podhalan Górale who sing this song, it is an enacted symbol of the Tatras and the music from the Tatras (see also Wrazen 1988, 287).

The high descending melody, the rubato rhythm, and, when sung by Górale, the polyphony ending in unison with men and women singing in the same octave register all combine to make this enacted symbol of Górale heritage unmistakably Polish Górale from Podhale. During the 1992 festival, the anthem reemerged at a party for the international cast of festival participants on the last evening of the week-long event. In a humorous ritual transformation, each group was invited to perform "Górole, górole" and to dance a Podhalan-style dance in a final mock contest. In other words, each group was invited to try its hand at being a Górale from Podhale. Here the anthem was recognized as a specific example of the music-culture of the festival hosts.

The space within the confines of the festival tent is further marked as Górale by the emcees' consistent use of a linguistic code. They speak in the strong Górale dialect, which is almost incomprehensible to other Poles. Most Górale, and certainly the emcees of the Zakopane festival, are perfectly capable of speaking standard Polish, but they deliberately switch to dialect in settings where Górale identity is important. This deliberate switching of codes is used in the service of ethnic identity. The conscious use of dialect is an example of heritage "adding value" by using an aspect of Górale identity as a symbolic code (see Kirshenblatt-Gimblett 1995, 370–372). The alpine trumpets, the costumes of the emcees, the song that opens each concert, even the dialect used by the emcees all symbolically mark the festival as Górale.

Within this contextual frame of Góraleness, each troupe offers a version of heritage (national, regional, local) specific to an ethnic subgroup—authentic heritage onstage. Troupes that compete in the first category, "authentic," frequently present a staged version of a life-cycle, or calendric, ritual, such as a wedding, a Saint's day celebration, or a solstice ritual. One year I witnessed a Turkish troupe enact a circumcision rite complete with a squirming adolescent boy. This example highlights the assumption that, in so-called traditional societies, just about any occasion is pretext for song and dance. I do not believe that the Turkish youth was actually circumcised onstage any more than I believe that couples are actually married in the numerous wedding rituals presented on stage. However, these productions are self-conscious public statements of ideas and beliefs about heritage. The performances are complex creations reflecting complex histories, just as an actual wedding ritual enacts and references history.

Figure 4.6. Official pin for the 1995 Zakopane festival. Courtesy of the Biuro Promocji Zakopanego i Podtatrza.

Figure 4.7. Door detail carved by Józef Styrczula-Maśniak, Kościelisko.

When symbols or representations of other peoples appear, they are often domesticated into the context of Górale heritage. The official pin of the 1995 Zakopane festival is an example (fig. 4.6). The caricatures of guest performers are domesticated within a geometric motif from Górale material arts—within a symbol of Górale heritage. Although this particular design is common throughout Europe, the Zakopane festival pins are generally based on a Górale motif or a motif thought to symbolize Górale (fig. 4.7). I believe that within this context the design is recognized as specifically Górale.

One of the dances featured by the group from Zakopane at the 1992 International Festival of Mountain Folklore is also recognized as being specifically (and "authentically") Górale while simultaneously referencing a transnational and even multicultural heritage. I am referring to the dance called *zbójnicki*, part of the recognized canon of muzyka Podhala, as introduced in chapter 1. The legendary mountain robbers celebrated in the *zbójnicki* dance sequence are especially interesting as symbols of Górale identity since most *zbójniki* were from the Beskid mountains and the southern Tatras in what is today the Slovak Republic (Brzozowska 1965, 464–465). There is some question whether they were ever actually active in Podhale, and most were certainly Slovaks, not Poles. The legend of the *zbójniki* spans the multiple cultures that populate the regions surrounding the Tatra Mountains, and they embody the spirit of travel, a required activity if multiculturalism is to be achieved. Ironically the myth of the *zbójniki*, who once gave lowlanders and potential tourists reason to avoid the mountains, is now transformed into heritage that attracts tourists.

The multicultural quality of the *zbójnicki* dance is also evident in the music itself. In all other genres of instrumental music associated specifically with Podhale, the accompanying violins play only on the beat, bowing invariably on the quarter note, as this music is conventionally transcribed. The *zbójnicki* sequence, however, features tunes accompanied with a lilting pattern created by the accompanying violins who add an eighth note offbeat on the open A string. The A string is activated with a quick up-bow on the offbeat (see fig. 1.18, chapter 1, and CD track 11). The result is not a polka—the *zbójnicki* is too slow—but a sound more similar to a Carpathian Slovak version of the Hungarian csárdás that employs a double-pulse bowing technique for the first, slow half. Although produced with different bowing techniques, the result is a similar eighth-note accompaniment. Like the *zbójniki* legend, the music for the *zbójnicki* dance comes from across the border in Slovakia and what was Hungary before 1918. The closest precedent is probably Hungarian military recruiting dances (*verbunkos*) from the time of the Austro-Hungarian Empire.

The *zbójnicki* dance links the histories of tourism, ethnography, and Górale music-culture in an interesting way. As I explained in chapter 3, the tune now called "Chałubiński's March," closely associated with the *zbójnicki* dance, was first published in 1888 by musical ethnographer Jan Kleczyński. Now bearing his name, the tune was popularized by the Warsaw physician during the tourist outings that he arranged. I wonder if the tune would still be played today and the dance still danced if not for Chałubiński, Kleczyński, and their ethnographic and touristic interventions.

In any case, the *zbójnicki* dance is not just good theater; it is highly symbolic of ideas about Górale, especially Górale men. *Zbójniki* were independent, brave, strong, and loyal. When I asked

Stanisława Trebunia-Staszel and Paweł Staszel, two key performers in the Górale troupe that performed at the 1992 festival, why the *zbójniki* legend is important today, they explained that *zbójniki* did not allow the rich landowners to have control of them (personal conversation, 28 April 1995, Nowy Targ). *Zbójniki* embody an important historical myth about the settlement of the Tatras—the myth that people fled there to avoid becoming the servants of others. It is ironic, then, that the tourist industry, which created the modern context for this symbolic dance of independence, may have succeeded in subduing the legendary independence of Górale more thoroughly than any previous attempts.

The Zakopane festival is an international festival about a local people—a multicultural ritual celebrating one culture. I am reminded of the response of Elżbieta Chodurska, who was then festival director, when in 1995 I asked her about the goals of the festival: "The first goal is to show how Górale live. [...] The second goal is for tourists and Górale to see how others live," she replied (ac20.vii.95). In other words, the festival is an arena in which to compare and contrast lifeways, or cultural practices. The international quality of the festival provides an ideal platform on which Górale can symbolically perform their difference: see how the world sings—see how Górale sing; see how the world dances—see how Górale dance. Under the premise of gathering together people who share mountain living in common, Górale of Podhale then represent what is unique about their own brand of mountain culture. They ritually create for themselves a unique identity by referencing heritage through an elaborate framework of symbols, enacted and physical, in the face of a changing world.

The change to this world is globalization which enables, perhaps forces, many of the international performers and tourists at the festival to share certain cosmopolitan views of the world, and have similar life experiences (they live in market economies, wear similar "European" styles, listen to similar popular music made in Europe and America, have similar experiences watching television, etc.). In this context, it is imperative that the symbols of difference—of ethnicity—be increasingly formalized and stylized. Such formalization and stylization first drove me away from front-region stage performances of folklore, but when interpreted as ritual, they draw me back in. Ultimately it is formalization and stylization that make rituals recognizable as such. Likewise, the stylized manner in these front-region performances of referencing large ideologies (identity, or us, not them), place (region and village, not stage), and time (back then, not now) is consistent with other more traditionally recognized rituals. The staged presentations weekend after weekend, year after year, of music and dance once (presumably) found only in villages has resulted in new rules, new performance conventions, new arenas of musical meaning. The front-region festival shows of the late twentieth century referenced earlier festival performances as much as they referenced anything back-region. As Richard Schechner (1982, 46) has noted, "rituals disguise themselves as restorations of actual events when, in fact, they are restorations of earlier rituals." The classic example is the ritual of communion in the Christian mass. The priests and congregation reenact the last supper, but the gestures, clothing, and setting are not intended to replicate how Jews of two thousand years ago dined. In a similar way the stylized representation onstage of a courtship dance is not supposed to be about actual courtship; instead, it is the symbolic representation and abstraction of courtship as done by a particular people (Górale), in a particular place (Podhale).

Formalized, stylized symbolic abstractions of objects, historical facts, ideas, and beliefs are also qualities of rituals. Weddings enacted as stage shows are rife with such symbolic abstractions: bread, salt, and greenery to symbolize fertility and plenty, for example. Górale today abstract their own heritage into distinct symbolic makers of Góraleness—of identity—and perform or enact these symbols onstage before tourists in a deliberate ritual to ensure their place in today's world. In this way the tourist festival ritual joins other rituals used by people to symbolically represent what is important to them and to influence their environment so as to ensure their continued well-being. The survival of Górale as an ethnic group no longer depends first and foremost on successful crops and healthy livestock—frequently the concern of folk rituals in the past and now the topic of many stage presentations at tourist folk festivals. Today the tourist industry itself is a leading means of livelihood in Podhale, and folk festivals help to ensure that tourism continues. Such festivals also provide a venue where Górale can reaffirm their identity and their distinctive music-culture in the face of increasing globalization. Festivals emerged in Podhale when tourism was becoming a significant social and economic force in the region, a phenomenon that, both then and now, does much to put Górale in face-to-face contact with the rest of the world. The structures of tourism that transformed Podhale from a relatively isolated mountain region into a tourist destination at the same time provide Górale with a means for effectively preserving their music-culture and ethnic group. Not only does interpreting tourist folk festivals as rituals position them meaningfully in the present, but it also enables one to better understand the power and meaning of these festivals beyond their value as entertainment.

Case Study 2: Festivals and Contest Style

A theme throughout this book is that ethnographers, broadly defined, have had a hand in shaping Górale ethnicity and Górale music-culture. As illustrated above, one place ethnographers and Górale musicians regularly come face to face is at folklore festivals. However, in order to concentrate on festivals as rituals, I deliberately sidestepped the obvious questions about how the ethnographers on any given festival jury impact the music performed at the festival. In this second case study I attempt to redress this by considering how one particular performance practice became the center of a mild disagreement between ethnographers and Górale musicians at a festival.[6] Ultimately this controversy over a performance practice is interesting not just for what it reveals about historic narratives and musical practice but also for how it demonstrates the vitality of muzyka Podhala and its role in the discourses on Górale ethnicity.

The controversy concerns a type of ensemble violin playing called "double-lead" or "double-*prym*" that is emblematic of ideological differences between Górale musicians and those who would represent them. I illustrate this point with specific events that I documented at two different folkloric music festivals in Podhale. The first example is from the 1992 International Festival of Mountain Folklore which, as I explained above, features a contest judged primarily on notions of "authenticity" by a panel of jurors usually trained in some facet of ethnography. The second example comes from the 1995 Poronin Summer Festival, but it takes into account a post-festival, back-region celebration rather than the front-region stage performances.

Both examples involve a song and dance troupe called "Skalni" based in Kraków, well outside the region of *Skalne* Podhale. Even so, Skalni is the most influential *zespół* in Podhale. How can this be? Skalni is a singular and influential troupe for several reasons. Kraków is and has been for centuries a leading intellectual center in Poland with the prestigious Jagiellonian University, several colleges, and institutes. This reputation, combined with its proximity to Podhale, encourages many of the area's brightest and most talented young people to attend university there. For many of these students this is their first extended trip away from the Tatras, and they find themselves overwhelmed with homesickness, perhaps a universal phenomenon at all residential schools. Longing for the company of other Górale, some of these students join Skalni as both a place to socialize with other Górale students as well as to learn Górale music and dance. Numerous individuals told me that, before they left Podhale to attend university, they had expressed little interest in the music and dance of the Tatras and that they had learned muzyka Podhala for the first time in Kraków.[7] After they earn their degrees, many of these individuals return to Podhale and become community leaders. A vast majority of the song and dance leaders I interviewed in Podhale were alumni of Skalni.

During the weeklong 1992 Zakopane Festival I conducted a short interview with Krzysztof Trebunia-Tutka, one of the emcees of the festival as well as a *prym* violinist for Skalni, the featured Górale troupe at the festival that year. At the moment of our interview Krzysztof seemed mildly agitated. Earlier that same day he had performed in a band contest—part of the Zakopane Festival. Together with Paweł Staszel, he played in what he called a "double-*prym*" violin style wherein two violinists improvise melodic harmonic polyphony accompanied by several additional violins and a *basy*. Figure 4.8 is a transcription of a recording I made of that performance (CD track 23). The first *prym* (top line) begins the piece, followed by the *sekundy* and *basy*. With the second phrase (pick up to bar 6), the second *prym* is clearly audible. After the repeat of the second phrase, the tune is sung in harmonic polyphony followed by an instrumental repeat (not represented in the transcription) clearly played in double-*prym* polyphonic style. Note the similarities between the two *prym* melodies and the two vocal parts.

After this performance Krzysztof learned that one of the jurors believed that the double-*prym* style is not traditional and therefore was not acceptable for the contest. In my conversation with Krzysztof, he protested saying that his grandfather played with two lead violinists as early as 1925. Górale sing in two parts, Krzysztof ex-

Dolina, dolina, na dolinie szałas.
Ej, cemus mnie dziewczyno do niego nie
wołos.
Ej, cemus mnie dziewczyno do niego nie
wołos.

Valley, valley, hut in the valley.
Hey, girl why don't you call me into
it.
Hey, girl why don't you call me into
it.

Figure 4.8. "Dolina, dolina," played by Krzysztof Trebunia-Tutka and Paweł
Staszel, double-*prym* style. *CD track 23*

plained, so it is only natural that they play in two parts (fieldnotes, 19 August 1992). In subsequent performances on the Zakopane Festival main stage Paweł and Krzysztof alternated *prym*, never playing onstage together. I do not know if this was a deliberate strategy to please the jury or if it was built into the program they had already planned, but, in any case, for this second performance Skalni went on to win the coveted gold *ciupaga* in the first contest category, "authentic troupes."

Both these performances were front-region performances, that is, they were performed on stage for a public and panel of jurors, both of whom make certain demands on the performers. My next example is a back-region performance by and for Górale. I documented this example on video in 1995 in Poronin, a small village just six kilometers from Zakopane, at the *Poroniańskie Lato* (Poronin summer) festival. The final troupe to perform was Skalni, the same group in which Krzysztof Trebunia-Tutka and Paweł Staszel played in 1992, but now Paweł was the *prym* and Krzysztof no longer played with the troupe. After their stage performance Paweł invited me to join some of the troupe members for dinner at a nearby restaurant where I documented this next example.

As the eating waned, singing began and violins emerged. Paweł was joined by Krzysztof Trebunia-Tutka's father, Władysław (introduced at the end of chapter 1). Like the other musicians present, the senior Trebunia-Tutka had performed earlier onstage and was still in traditional costume. Although by far the most experienced and respected musician in the restaurant, Władysław has an amiable personality, and he freely yielded lead-violin (*prym*) to Paweł. Yet at a certain moment Władysław shifted into an authoritative stance and gave a brief and I believe masterful lesson about performance practice. The following descriptions and transcriptions of music and speech are derived from a video I made while sitting across the table from Władysław (v22.vii.95). Tracks 24–31 on the CD accompanying this book contain the audio from that video, and each track is detailed below.

In the middle of a song in the *wierchowa* genre with rubato singing in harmony, in this case accompanied by several violins and an *altówka* (3-string bowed lute adapted from a viola), Władysław suddenly stood, stopped the music, and described how he believed the three violins and one *altówka* should play together as an ensemble. He declared (CD track 24, beginning with a fragment of the *wierchowa*):

Cztery głosy: pierwszy prym, drugi prym, pierwszy sekund, drugi sekund. Nie może być jeden głos, że trzech gra na jeden głos. Tak jakby syćka górale grali na jeden głos, syćka na dół. Muszą być pierwszy, drugi—sopran, alt, tenor, bas. Był w chórze? Trzeba się było uczyć. Ja się uczyłem!

Four voices: first *prym*, second *prym*, first *sekund*, second *sekund*. It can't be one voice, that three play one part. It's as if all Górale played one part, everyone down low. There must be first, second—soprano, alto, tenor, bass. Have you been in a choir? If so, you should have learned. I did!

Taking his violin under his chin, he demonstrated the second *prym* (*prym* 2) part for a few bowings (fig. 4.9, CD track 25):

Figure 4.9. Władysław Trebunia-Tutka, second-*prym* part (v22.vii.95). *CD track 25*

Then he played two bars of the first *prym* part (fig. 4.10, CD track 26):

Figure 4.10. Władysław Trebunia-Tutka, first-*prym* part (v22.vii.95). *CD track 26*

followed immediately by the next phrase (bars 4–6) of the second *prym* part (fig. 4.11, CD track 27):

Figure 4.11. Władysław Trebunia-Tutka, second-*prym* part, continued (v22.vii.95). *CD track 27*

Verbally labeling each part, he then demonstrated the first *sekund* part (violin II). Note the unvarying bowing on the quarter-note beats with slurred ornaments in between (the *prym*, on the other hand, avoids slurs) (fig. 4.12, CD track 28):

Figure 4.12. Władysław Trebunia-Tutka, first *sekund* part
(v22.vii.95). *CD track 28*

Finally, he demonstrated five beats of the second *sekund* part (fig.
4.13, CD track 29):

Figure 4.13. Władysław Trebunia-Tutka, second *sekund* part
(v22.vii.95). *CD track 29*

After this short and virtuosic demonstration of four distinct
violin parts, Władysław launched into a historical explanation of
style (CD track 30):

Zapisował sto lat temu, sto
piętdziesiąt. Ja tego nie wymy-
śliłem. Zapisane jest w notatkach,
profesor Chybiński pisze: "Unisono grał skrzypce z gęslami." A
to było "unisono" bo to grał nisko
to samo.

It was written one hundred
years ago, one hundred and fifty. I
didn't make it up. In his notes,
Professor Chybiński writes: "The
violin played in unison with the
fiddle." That was "unison" because they played down low the
same.

Returning his violin to his chest, he improvised a variant of the
first *sekund* part for six bars (fig. 4.14, CD track 31):

Figure 4.14. Władysław Trebunia-Tutka, first *sekund* part variant
(v22.vii.95). *CD track 31*

While still playing the last few bars of the first *sekund* part, he
commented: "Bartek Obrochta miał taki skład . . ." (Bartek Obrochta had such a group . . .).

Władysław's short demonstration is packed with information
about playing styles, including a reference to an early-twentieth-

century musicologist's description of performance style. First, Władysław Trebunia-Tutka single-handedly demonstrates his concept of the ideal Górale ensemble playing style, lacking only the *basy*—an instrument not represented at this informal back-region gathering. Below is an ensemble score constructed from each part as played separately by Władysław (figs. 4.9–4.14, CD tracks 25–31). The second *prym* part is a combination of the first three bars with which he began his demonstration and what I believe are bars 4–6, played by Władysław after he demonstrated the first *prym* part. The first *sekund* part is a conflation of the two demonstrations played by Władysław. Combining Władysław's brief examples into an ensemble score creates a fair representation of the double-*prym* style, if only for a few complete bars (fig. 4.15).

Equally intriguing to Władysław's brilliant demonstration of violin parts was his reference to the ethnographic literature on Górale music: "It was written one hundred years ago. [. . .] Professor Chybiński writes: 'The violin played in unison with the fiddle.'" Although he ages Chybiński considerably, Władysław quotes reasonably accurately a 1926 publication by the professor: "Long ago the first violin was played by a fiddler (on a small folk-violin), sometimes playing unison with a first violinist" (Dawniej I skrzypce grywał gęślarz [na gęślikach], niekiedy grający unisono z I skrzypkiem) (republished in Chybiński 1961, 96).[8] Władysław said this with marked irony and then corrected the past ethnographer, saying that the violin and fiddle were playing close to the same thing. I believe he is suggesting that the early writer misunderstood what he was hearing. The musicians of a bygone era were not playing in unison but in tight harmony—as he demonstrated with the two *prym* parts transcribed above. Finally, by referring to legendary violinist Bartek (Bartuś) Obrochta, Władysław backs up his opinion that the double-*prym* style is a historic practice.

This case study focuses on two different instances where Górale musicians disagreed with statements made about muzyka Podhala by authoritative non-Górale, because the object of their disagreement—the double-*prym* style—is symbolic of opposing views of Górale identity. What is it about the single-*prym* style that attracts the festival jurors' seal of authenticity but arouses such animated disagreement from both the junior and the senior Trebunia-Tutkas? I have two ideas, one historical and the other ideological. First, the single-*prym* style is documented in the earliest authoritative descriptions of Górale music, giving it legitimacy. Second,

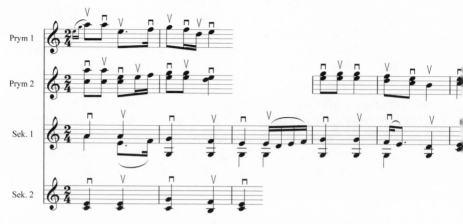

Figure 4.15. Ensemble score compilation of Władysław Trebunia-
Tutka's demonstrations.

this documented legacy of a single-*prym* style conforms to nostalgic
notions about a simpler, more pure (read "primitive") time in Podhale, notions that are ideologically important for ethnographers
and tourists but are interpreted differently by Górale musicians.
The double-*prym* style subtly subverts ideas of isolation and purity
by suggesting musical connections beyond Podhale.

As we have seen, the earliest reliable and substantive description of Górale music practice was Stanisław Mierczyński's *Muzyka
Podhala*. More than any other document, this book helped to can-
onize not only the repertoire of muzyka Podhala but also the style
and performance practice featuring a single *prym* responsible for
the highly ornamented melody and one or more accompanying
violins together with a *basy*. Figure 4.16 is reproduced from Mierczyński's book and illustrates this ensemble arrangement. The tune
is a version of the same *nuta* played by Władysław Trebunia-Tutka
(figs. 4.9–4.14, CD tracks 25–31).

The introductory pages to Mierczyński's book (1930, x) make
it clear that he was concerned about preserving old-style Górale
music. He is careful to note that his primary source of material,
Bartuś Obrochta, was the last representative of the *old* Górale style,
having learned to play violin in the nineteenth century. Like ethnographers, Górale also base their interpretations of their own music on perceived past practices. Both Krzysztof and Władysław
Trebunia-Tutka use historical narratives to defend their versions

Figure 4.16. "Czorsztyńska" (from Mierczyński 1930, no. 10).

of proper Górale music performance style. Krzysztof looks to his family history to defend the double-*prym* style. At the end of the video clip analyzed above, Władysław Trebunia-Tutka defended his interpretation of old Górale style by evoking the name of the same Bartuś Obrochta with whom Mierczyński as well as Chybiński worked to create their descriptions of Górale music. According to the historic ethnographic record, Obrochta's band and others played in a single-*prym* style. According to Władysław and Krzysztof, Obrochta and his contemporaries played in a double-*prym* style.

Here I do not attempt to determine how Górale musicians actually played in the first quarter of the twentieth century. Instead, I am interested in understanding how individual musicians and ethnographers today use the same music played by Obrochta and others nearly a century ago to tell different stories about Górale identity. This leads to my second idea about why some ethnographers continue to emphasize the single-*prym* style. I believe that the single-*prym* style reinforces nostalgia about an imagined simpler time in Podhale. Nostalgia is an occupational hazard for ethnographers, and not inconsequently a valuable commodity for the tourist industry (Kirshenblatt-Gimblett 1995). Reminiscent of periodic and nostalgic revivals of interest in American "hillbilly" string bands and "downhome" acoustic blues (Filene 2004), I propose that the single *prym* playing a strident melody accompanied by a harmonically sparse, strong steady pulsing rhythm sounds delightfully "primitive" to the cosmopolitan listener. It conjures notions of former times when village life was presumably pure and untainted by modern life. The willful *prymista* may also be emblematic of independence: the single violinist in control of his music's destiny. The sparse single-*prym* style conforms to the ethnographic trope about Górale and their legendary purity, independence, and distinctiveness resulting from mountain isolation.

However, it is my interpretation that Krzysztof, Paweł, Władysław, and other musicians use the same repertoire canonized by ethnographers to perform a contrasting history of themselves. They violate the code of purity when they perform in a double-*prym* style. They taint the canon of Górale music. They do so, at least in some cases, with full knowledge that they go against authoritative interpretations of their own culture by ethnographers past and present. Instead of celebrating isolation, the classic ethnographic trope, Górale musicians recognize connections when they make music—they perform a different story about Górale heritage. The double-*prym* style is a subtle stylistic step out of Podhale and west into the neighboring region of Żywiec or east into Piwniczna where musicians join melodic instruments in heterophony and polyphony. Double-*prym* is also a stylistic step toward Slovak and Hungarian music, which was very popular among Górale in the 1990s. In other words, Górale play themselves back along the Carpathian crescent—performing in the present the same history ethnographers relegate to the ancients. By using the double-*prym* style Górale musicians turn a canonized symbol of difference and isolation into a performed declaration of connectedness.

Musicologists, ethnomusicologists, and other students of music convincingly show how music is used to construct and maintain individual and group identities. A review of recent volumes of leading ethnomusicology journals, for example, reveals issues of identity to be ubiquitous. We know that music style is not only a matter of organized sound but may also be a clue to musicians' self-conceptions. As we have seen, the debate about an ensemble performance style references different histories of Górale, and suggests different interpretations of Górale identity. To answer questions about how Górale musicians played seventy-five or one hundred years ago is not the point here. Of greater interest are the ever changing meanings of musical style today. The challenge is to know not only the relationships of current musical style to historical styles but also to understand the varied and continually shifting cultural meanings of old and new musical practices. I have also shown how past ethnographic tropes are used, debated, and even discarded by the communities and individuals who were the objects of the ethnographer's research.

5

Global Village

In 1992 a cassette recording called *Twinkle Inna Polish Stylee: Higher Heights* was released, first in England and Western Europe and then in Poland (fig. 5.1). The cassette contained the musical results of a fusion between a Rastafarian reggae band based in London and a family band of Górale musicians from the Tatra village of Biały Dunajec. The recording extends the international quality of the festivals considered in the previous chapter and exemplifies what can happen when musicians go beyond observing a very different music from a very different place and try to blend that music with their own. The recording is also a tangible representation of the workings of globalization. The first part of this chapter traces the process of globalization by presenting a history of interaction between the Rasta reggae band and the Górale band, interaction both ideological and musical. The second part of the chapter focuses on the Górale musicians involved in this fusion project, and their innovative responses to the experience. I conclude by theorizing what I will call "globalism," a deliberate thought process behind the material workings of globalization, in an effort to un-

Figure 5.1. Cassette cover for *Twinkle Inna Polish Stylee: Higher Heights*. Painting by Władysław Trebunia-Tutka, and cover design graphic by Anna Baran.

derstand the local meanings of globalization. In other words, I consider some of the ways that the Górale musicians who took part in this fusion experiment are taking those experiences and reinterpreting them to create new expressions of Góraleness locally and globally.

At the heart of this study are tensions between the global and the local, between regionalism and globalism. In the Polish Tatras, as one might expect anywhere, this tension is manifest in society, in the production of music, and in musical form, thus reflecting the sort of homology between society and culture at the base of many theories in ethnomusicology and cultural anthropology (for a critique of similar homologies, see Wade 2000, 23). One of the ways I show that these tensions are realized in the Tatras is that ideas about the "global" are rendered musically as rather nondescript, sonic objects that we might interpret as "cultural grey-out." Fear of this so called cultural grey-out is an old trope in ethnomusicology, going back at least to Hornbostel in 1905 (1975 [1905], 263), and named sixty years later by Alan Lomax (1968, 4), but more recently sharply criticized by social and cultural theorists (see Appadurai 1996, 11, for example). The notion that the power and attractiveness of Western cultural forms will overrun all other "colorful" world cultures is itself a Western conceit and part of the discourse of globalization, but is not empirically founded. Here I revise the old apocalyptic idea with a twist and propose that there are instances of cultural grey-out but that they serve a function in the efforts of some who resist being co-opted by globalization. Cultural grey-out becomes a neutral background on which to display difference.

As in the previous chapter this book seeks to extend the notion of Góraleness beyond the politically laden and now traditional ethnographic interpretations of the Tatras as a *locus classicus* for the study of folk music in an ideal setting, and to present the region as a ground of contested and competing musical practices. The fusion of a well-established and respected Górale family band with a Rastafarian reggae band spotlights the extra-regional, transnational, global implications of what is happening in Podhale on the ground and in the airwaves. It reveals the region to be a field fraught with rival ideologies about what it means to be of the Tatras, of the mountains, to be a citizen of a modernizing European nation-state, and to be a player on the global music stage. These realities fly in the face of a tendency to deny modernity to the autochthonous residents of the Tatras and to require that they remain what Timothy Taylor has called in similar contexts "premodern" (1997, 126)—to remain isolated, ethnic, local, folk. Such imposed limits hinder not only this particular Polish demographic but also our ability as interested observers, scholars, and ethnographers to understand what appears to be happening in Podhale, in Poland, in Europe, and in the world. To recognize and reinforce the cultural borders drawn around the Tatra region would only make location a fetish which, to quote Veit Erlmann (1996, 479), "disguises the globally dispersed forces of production." To understand anything about Górale of the Tatras and their music, the nostalgic image of Górale appropriately dressed in regional costumes dancing *zbójnicki* or *po góralsku* must be reconciled with the world of today in which they live, make music, and dance.

The point is not to reject the folk heritage of Górale; I believe that the context of this book demonstrates that my affections lie there. And yet to understand the place of muzyka Podhala in a postmodern, postcolonial, post-communist world, one must recognize the interface of the old, the traditional, the reified, with the new, the modern, the global. That is why this chapter focuses on so-called worldbeat fusion. "Worldbeat" is the term used most commonly in America to refer to a commercial category of popular music that employs sounds not generally associated with American and Anglo-American popular music including the admittedly African roots of this genre and, in the case of reggae, African and Jamaican roots. Other terms used to refer to the same phenomena are "world music," "global music," and "global pop" (for discussions of these terms, see Taylor 1997, 1–3; Erlmann 1996, 467; and Feld 2001, 191). As used here, worldbeat music is almost always syncretic music—the sounds produced involve the combination of different forms of musical practice. The popular term for such syncretism is "fusion," another term with several viable alternatives ("hybrid" or "creole," for example; see Barber and Waterman 1995, 240–241), but "fusion" carries etymological and popular connotations that I find both appealing and appropriate. Whereas hybrids and creoles are genetic offspring created by the union of things or beings considered different in some significant way, fusion merges diverse elements usually through heat. Hybrids and creoles are a generation removed from the action that brought difference in contact; fusions emerge in the present at the moment of intense contact. Hybrids and creoles are the results of actions; fusions are the actions themselves.

In music, worldbeat fusions are created when individuals and small groups of people deliberately play with musically embodied representations of difference and sameness, with divisions and connections. It is this dynamic between difference and connection that motivates my interest in globalization and globalism, terms that scream sameness but may actually emphasize difference. The hopes and fears of unification implied by the twin concepts of fusion and globalization form one of the great myths of modernity, and negotiating the distance between homogeneity and heterogeneity is a point of hot debate in theories of globalization. Here I highlight a few approaches to this issue.

For Erlmann (1996, 470), world music is not about difference but is about the West remolding itself through association with otherness, and the very construction of the West has always re-

quired the "Orient" (Erlmann 1999, 175). Thus he rejects interpretations of "world music as an assertion of the politics of difference" and instead concentrates on "global aesthetics in the making"
(1996, 468). Erlmann ultimately arrives at a utopian vision of "a
world that is now truly one," to quote the final words of his more
recent book (1999, 282). Whether or not we agree with this view,
Erlmann's theorizing of globalization is compelling. At the center
of his argument is a view of the "global imagination" as an "epistemological symbiosis" of modernities, Western and otherwise
(1999, 4). The physical networks of exchange that make globalization a reality may have Western roots, but there are multiple
alternative histories that form global imaginations, even "antiglobalist interpellations" (Bohlman 2002b, 27). This active imaginative
response to the networks of globalization forms the basis of my
theorizing of globalism, a conceptual process that shares much with
Erlmann's emphasis on symbiosis.

Anthropologist Arjun Appadurai takes a different approach to
globalization, especially the issue of unification. For him, it is the
"contrastive" qualities of cultural activity that are meaningful,
rather than the substantive implications of culture itself (Appadurai
1996, 12–13). But in his recent call for "grassroots globalization,"
he moves closer to Erlmann's symbiotic interpretation. Writing
about ethnicity, anthropologist John Comaroff (1996) also stresses
the politics of difference in the wake of modernism, the ideological
engine of globalization. These ideas of contrast and performance
of difference are foregrounded in most theories of music and globalization, as well as in theories of identity and ethnicity, which, as
Mark Slobin (1992) has noted, are central themes throughout the
intellectual history of ethnomusicology.

My work suggests that the cultural processes of globalization
described by Bohlman and Erlmann as peculiarly Western actually
flow in many directions even within what is arguably a self-
constructed West, namely, Poland. This is where Slobin's (1992)
theorizing of micromusics within the West is helpful. Are Górale
marginal Westerners expressing this Westernness through worldbeat fusions, or are they the Other, a disenfranchised ethnic minority on the cultural fringe of the European West who reverse
Erlmann's process and remold themselves by taking part in worldbeat music? Globalization may be a Western conceit, but this does
not prevent anyone from adopting the technologies of globaliza-

tion and the ideas of globalism and using them for their own individual, local purposes.

Musical fusion is an ideal place to find the contrastive qualities of cultural expression so valued by Appadurai, although the point of some individuals engaged in worldbeat fusions may be to express difference within (not from outside) the hegemonic forces that make such media-driven musics possible. Leaning distinctly toward what Steven Feld (2001, 197) has criticized as "celebratory narratives of world music" that "tend to normalize and naturalize globalization," I find that Górale musicians are expressing distinction within the global, hegemonic, music industry. I will show here that at least one group of musicians in the Tatras have moved, over the course of a decade, from being defined musically as the exotic Other within global popular music to an implied understanding of a global aesthetic which I suggest they paste up as a grey background on which to simultaneously display their difference and their modernity. The cultural practice that results highlights difference both regional and historical, creating a pastiche in the sense of a hodgepodge, but also in the sense that Adorno (1973, 166–167 and 208) uses the idea of pastiche to describe how each performance deliberately evokes the past to give essence to a very present performance. In other words, each performance self-consciously engages in what Barbara Kirshenblatt-Gimblett (1995) calls the "heritage industry." Or as Fredric Jameson (2000, 202) wrote about postmodern pastiche, "producers of culture have nowhere to turn but to the past: the imitation of dead styles, speech through all the masks and voices stored up in the imaginary museum of a now global culture."

Jamaican Reggae and Górale Fiddling: Background

The fusion of Górale fiddling with Jamaican reggae was the result of deliberate, purposeful decisions and actions of known individuals at a particular moment in recent history. It was not, in other words, an organic merging of peoples and musics over time in an ostensibly anonymous folk process. Muzyka Podhala and reggae were brought together by a Warsaw-based radio producer shortly after the 1980s martial law period that led to the end of communist hegemony in Poland in 1989. It marks the beginning of a moment of popular reinterpretation of folk music within Poland, and a renegotiation of the politics of musical meaning in a reorganizing state.

Despite some official censure during the communist era, certain genres of popular music from the West, such as jazz and then rock, thrived in many Soviet bloc countries. This was especially true in Poland, where there was relatively free access to Western popular culture (Ryback 1990; Pekacz 1992). By "access" I mean that Poles were generally free to form rock bands, for example, and recordings of Western popular bands were usually restricted more by economic availability than by official policy. Though often interpreted as protest against communism, the actual use of Western forms of popular music varied from country to country, moment to moment, and between different groups and individuals. However, by the 1960s and 1970s, in Poland at least, general tendencies in the interpretation of certain music genres can be discerned: jazz was deemed by the cultural ministers to be "serious" music, and thus acceptable; other popular genres from the West, especially those associated with youth culture and falling under the rubric "rock," were associated with rebellion (as was the case in Western countries); village-based Polish folk music,[1] on the other hand, was popularly interpreted as having been appropriated by the Communist Party and was therefore rejected by some who resisted communist hegemony. It stands to reason that dramatic political change would result in a reinterpretation of the symbolic meaning of politically defined music genres.

With the 1989 collapse of the communist government there began a rapid stream of cultural events that led to the unlikely mix of Polish folk music and Jamaican reggae considered here, but the foundation for the fusion was laid earlier in the 1980s during the crucible of martial law. At this moment of intense political activity and grass-roots protest against the ruling communist government, Włodzimierz Kleszcz, a producer at Polish Radio in Warsaw, used his position and access to give political protest a musical soundtrack. His interest in protest music began earlier in the 1960s, when, along with others, he operated a "folk and protest song" fan club in Warsaw. As the linking of "folk" and "protest song" would indicate, I believe Kleszcz was referencing the sort of political protest music related to the 1950s "folk revival" in American popular culture that fed into the 1960s Civil Rights movement, not village-based "folk" musical practices in Poland. Extending the concept of "folk music" in ways that have become attractive to some scholars of Western vernacular music, Kleszcz was especially drawn to rhythm and blues, and rock primarily from Britain and America, genres that he came to realize were often versions by white performers of African American blues. This began his fascination with what he calls "black" music or "pan-African music," music genres of the African diaspora fusing with other music to make something different (Kleszcz, interview, Warsaw, ac22.iii.95). Thus what may have begun with youthful interest in popular music from the West developed into knowledge of and informed interest in musics that are transnational and expressions of a diasporic people's struggle against hegemonic powers of the West.

According to my conversations with Kleszcz (11 August 2000, Warsaw) and Norman Grant (30 August 2002, Santa Barbara, California), the radio producer and reggae band first met in 1986. Kleszcz began to bring Norman Grant and his band to Poland, sometimes paying them with studio time at the well-equipped radio station where he worked since hard currency was in short supply (Kleszcz interview [ac22.iii.95], confirmed by Grant in an informal conversation).[2] An important moment in the professional relationship between Kleszcz and the Twinkle Brothers was a concert Kleszcz helped to organize in 1989, just a few months after SOLIDARITY won the first free elections in Poland in more than forty years. The event was an anti-apartheid concert in Gdańsk, hosted by SOLIDARITY leader Lech Wałęsa,[3] to mark the ten-year anniversary of the shipyard strikes in that city. Norman "Twinkle" Grant and the Twinkle Brothers were featured, along with several other reggae bands known for relevant political messages (Larsen 1991; Morris 1990). The 1989 concert marked a watershed moment and a turning point for Kleszcz's musical political activism.

In 1989 a new flood of Western influence entered Poland. In a 1995 interview Kleszcz told me that as Western popular, and what he calls "roots," music became increasingly available in Poland, he grew concerned about roots music and culture from his own country. He began to fear that Polish youth were adapting Western music and culture wholesale with little depth of knowledge. His vision was to learn from "black" music how to preserve the very Polish folk music he earlier had shunned. "I'm treating my roots like black people are treating their own," he explained (ac22.iii.95). His idea was and is to combine popular music styles with Polish roots or folk music, creating something Polish that would draw the interest of Poland's youth.

Kleszcz found the Polish roots musicians he was looking for in the summer of 1991, when the Trebunia-Tutka family band "Tutki"[4] won a prestigious prize at a nationwide folk music contest in the Renaissance village Kazimierz nad Wisły (by the Vistula River). Kleszcz was impressed by the multigenerational family band and their traditional credentials: they were verifiable examples of "roots" musicians, and in his mind they were, on some basic level, similar to the traditional Rastafarian "roots" reggae preacher and musician Norman Twinkle Grant. In published descriptions of his fusion projects, and in his conversations with me, Kleszcz employs the language of globalization, but, with an interesting twist reminiscent of Appadurai's "grassroots globalization," he speaks of the unity of the world's oppressed peoples. When in 1995 I asked Kleszcz why he chose to fuse the musics of the Trebunia-Tutka Górale family with the reggae Twinkle Brothers, he explained: "Because [there is] a common vibe there, I tell you. [. . .] Our [Górale] from [the Tatras] are the same people in a cultural way [as Rastafarians]" (ac22.iii.95). Elsewhere Kleszcz draws a connection between Rastafarians' struggle against the psychological impact of a legacy of slavery and Górale's legendary struggles against serfdom (Kleszcz 1994).

The Trebunia-Tutka family that Kleszcz encountered in Kaszimierz nad Wisły is the same family I have mentioned on several occasions in this book (see discography, fig. 5.15). While there are many musicians in the extended family, the Twinkle/Tutki fusion performances feature three family members: Władysław Trebunia-Tutka, his son Krzysztof, and daughter Anna. Władysław has an advanced degree in the plastic arts from Kraków; his eldest son, Krzysztof, is an architect; and his daughter, Anna, has also been to college in Kraków since the production of the first recording I discuss here. That they retain a reputation for being a respected traditional music family is not inconsistent with their professional and academic achievements. In fact, Kleszcz was impressed that Krzysztof and Anna could speak English, something that certainly facilitated the fusion process with the English-speaking reggae musicians.

According to both Kleszcz and Krzysztof Trebunia-Tutka, the Twinkle reggae band and the Tutki Górale band were not organically drawn toward each other musically, but a third party outside both groups was necessary to make this fusion happen—Kleszcz himself. Simply placing musicians from different traditions together in a room, however, does not result in musical fusion. And since music is not merely sound but is driven by and carries ideas, some form of fusion of ideas within and about music must be achieved if a meeting between distant peoples and musics is to be successful. Indeed, the ideological justifications for this particular and admittedly artificial fusion are especially interesting.

The "Common Vibe": A Fusion of Ideas about Music

Two related ideas bind all three parties—Twinkle, Tutki, and Kleszcz: the idea of independence or freedom, and the idea of cultural identity. First, I address the perhaps universal human desire for independence that initially drew these distant musics and peoples together. The theme of freedom is overt in reggae music, especially when created by Rastafarians, believers in a religion that, in part, grew out of a struggle against colonialism and economic servitude (Hebdige 1979, 33–39). Norman Twinkle Grant is such a Rastaman with a track record of political protest songs, a quality that first attracted Kleszcz to the Twinkle Brothers. In the texts of Górale music, on the other hand, this theme is oblique with few direct references to *wolność* (freedom) or *niezależność* (independence) (see Sadownik 1971 [1957]). Yet historians of Górale society record centuries of struggle against serfdom; indeed, many of the settlers to the cold northern slopes of these mountains, the harshest in central Europe, moved there to avoid incorporation (e.g., Gromada 1982, 107). Musically this struggle is symbolized in the *zbójniki* legends that are celebrated in many Górale song texts, and were the theme of the first cassette produced by the Tutki/Twinkle fusion. In the legends of *zbójniki* and the human desire for independence and freedom, the Trebunia-Tutka family and Twinkle Brothers found an ideological theme that prepared the way for musical fusion.

Concern for cultural identity is the second idea that drew these Górale and reggae musicians together. Preservation of cultural identity is the motivation Kleszcz gives for his experiments and his creative promotions of Polish folk music. In a sense he is redressing a process of cultural colonialism that he had helped promote before the fall of communism in Poland. At that time he worked to promote Western popular music in Poland as a form of protest music. Now he is fighting to prevent the loss of Polish folk culture, the very cultural practices he previously avoided because of their associations with communist propaganda. When I asked Norman Grant if the music he made with Tutki had any particular message, he replied yes, they are Polish and we are Jamaican (conversation in Santa Barbara, California, 30 August 2002). In other words, their message was one of cultural identity in the context of perceived difference.

The issue of cultural identity as an idea that draws Jamaican Rastafarians and Polish Górale together, however, seems incongruous because of a third issue very often associated with cultural identity: race. Indeed, race may be *the* issue with this fusion project. The issue of race was raised by both Krzysztof Trebunia-Tutka and Włodzimierz Kleszcz during our separate interviews, but they approached the issue from very different perspectives. Kleszcz is concerned about the Jamaican musicians' perception of Poles, about their potential racism. Because of a legacy of slavery and Rastafarians' anti-slavery message, Kleszcz believes that he must explain the Poles' relative innocence on this matter: "If I'm going to talk with Rasta people, with roots reggae Jamaican artists, and if they don't know much about Poland, I have to explain all this, that we had no pirates" (ac22.iii.95); that is, Poland never engaged in the trade of African slaves. Krzysztof Trebunia-Tutka, on the other hand, is concerned with racism against blacks among Górale and among Poles in general. He equates this racism with chauvinism among Górale, some of whom, according to Krzysztof, think Górale are the most important people, after all (ac20.xi.94.1). In his musings about his family's collaboration with these musicians of different color, Krzysztof squarely confronts racism in his own culture, an action which I consider a positive step toward eradicating racism.

The Górale/reggae fusion project may inevitably be viewed through the lens of race by Poles, Górale, and Jamaicans, despite the liberal attitudes expressed by the actors in the project. Skin color was taken to outwardly manifest the cultural and geographical distance separating the icy Tatras from the tropical Jamaican island. Following what I suspect is a common urge among ethnomusicological fieldworkers to admire the people they study, during fieldwork I tried to explain (or justify) racism among Górale as a result of isolation, the very trope I elsewhere worked to debunk. But now I suspect that racism in Podhale, at least black/white racism, is a cultural import from America. The largest population of Górale outside Podhale is in Chicago, where many Górale retain regional and even village ties while engaging in Chicago's unique style of neighborhood politics fought in the language of race. Attitudes fostered in Chicago's Górale community may have returned to Podhale. America also exports ideas and attitudes about racism with its popular culture, especially in television programs widely viewed in Poland. Yet in the early morning hours after experiencing the first live performance ever by the Twinkle and Tutki bands in February 1995, I was shocked by what I perceived as racism. Hitching a ride home with an acquaintance connected with a local radio station, I was caught off-guard when he commented several times that it was interesting (or did he say "funny"?) to have Górale perform with black people (fieldnotes 25.ii.95). I tried to elicit an explanation, but none was forthcoming. While I wanted to talk about musical fusion and audience reaction, the person driving me home was fixated on skin color. Considering how rare it is to find a black or brown-skinned person in Podhale, maybe I was the one asking the less relevant questions.

Returning to the unifying quest for human independence, how is this theme manifested in the Twinkle/Tutki recordings? The first cassette produced by the fusion band *Twinkle Inna Polish Stylee: Higher Heights* traces the life and death of the legendary Janosik, the Robin Hood–like *zbójnik*. In the English portions of the recording, Janosik is translated as "Johnny the Outlaw." As Kleszcz wrote on the cassette j-card, "Twinkle takes us into the magic world of the mountains telling the story of their most famous son Johnny the Outlaw. [. . .] The story has grown over the years, nurtured by the ever-present new examples of stubborn defiance in the belief that it is a man's right to be free" (J. Kleszcz and W. Kleszcz 1992). I did not learn in my interviews if the telling of the Janosik legend was Kleszcz's idea or that of the Trebunia-Tutka family, or if it was something they all happened upon together. But I will note that Krzysztof Trebunia-Tutka recorded a straightforward Górale music version of the Janosik legend with another group of musicians at about the same time that the Twinkle/Tutki fusion recording was produced. Perhaps the Janosik theme was on his mind.

The Fusion of Musical Sounds

Once a common human desire for independence and freedom was established as grounds for ideological fusion, the Górale and Rastamen still faced the task of fusing their distant musics. This process began when Kleszcz approached the Trebunia-Tutka family and asked if they would be willing to welcome into their home in Biały Dunajec some Jamaican reggae musicians, and to see if they could make music together. They agreed, even though they were not particularly familiar with reggae music (interview with Krzysztof Trebunia-Tutka, Zakopane, ac20.xi.94.1). Under Kleszcz's guidance, Jamaican Rastamen Norman "Twinkle" Grant and his bass player Dub Judah visited the Trebunia-Tutka family in the autumn of 1991.

According to the j-card notes to the first cassette, they immediately achieved a spiritual union that allowed the practitioners of these distant musics to find their groove together. However, Krzysztof Trebunia-Tutka described to me a more tedious process into which his father, Władysław, entered with some reluctance. Krzysztof's explanation of the process of musical fusion can be illustrated in the music itself. He describes the first session as being awkward but eventually settling into a process in which the Górale musicians played one of their tunes while Norman Grant and Dub Judah tried to improvise something that fit. Then the Rastamen played some reggae while the Trebunia-Tutka band tried to improvise something. Norman Grant confirmed at least half of this account of the fusion process when I spoke with him in 2002, saying that the Trebunia-Tutka family band jammed while he and Judah added a rhythm for dancing. After experimenting in this fashion for a few days, the musicians traveled to Warsaw and recorded as much music as they could at the Polish Radio studios where Kleszcz is employed. The raw cuts were then taken to London and pieced together by Adrian Sherwood and Derek Fevrier, forming enough tracks to produce several commercial cassettes.

The first cassette, according to Krzysztof, is entirely traditional Górale music to which Norman Grant and Dub Judah improvised or composed reggae-style accompaniments and sang Jamaican-English paraphrases of the Górale texts. The second release, *Comeback Twinkle 2 Trebunia Family*, released in 1994, used raw material from the same 1991 recording sessions in Warsaw that had been used for the first fusion release but with new vocals by the Trebunia-Tutka family. To my ear, *Comeback Twinkle 2 Trebunia Family* represents the other half of the fusion process: a reggae basis with Górale-style improvisations. Here I focus on the first cassette, which was the most successful of the Twinkle and Tutki fusions, and a watershed moment for Górale music on the world-beat stage. I have selected two characteristic pieces from the cassette that clearly exhibit some of the processes with which the musical fusion was achieved for many of the thirteen cuts on the recording.

The second track on the cassette is called "Skanking on the Grass." It is based on a Górale tune introduced in chapter 1 called "wiecno," meaning "forever" or "eternally." As with many Górale tune titles, "wiecno" is a reference to the structure of the tune, specifically the phrase and harmonic/ostinato structure.[5] In my experience, phrase and harmonic/ostinato structures are important means for analyzing and understanding structure in Górale music. As such, any alteration to phrase and harmonic structure is noteworthy. The unique feature of "wiecno," a dance tune, is that it allows the *prymista* to play as long as he or she wishes on either half of the harmonically defined two-part tune, even eternally. Or maybe its name derives from the *sekund* and *basy* players who are relegated to playing a single chord forever until the lead violin changes parts.

The first transcription here (fig. 5.2) is a straightforward Górale version as sung and played by Władysław Trebunia-Tutka with a band made up of members of his extended family. This version has six bars for the first sung phrase, and seven for the second phrase. The instrumental repeat of the *nuta* (not transcribed here) that follows the sung verse stretches the first part into ten bars and the second part into fifteen bars, illustrating the variable phrase lengths that characterize this two-part *nuta*. For an additional example of the variable phrase lengths of "wiecno," see figure 1.13 (CD track 6). In that version the two-part tune is played through three times; the first time, the first part has ten bars and the second part has eleven bars, the second time it is ten and fifteen, and finally twelve and eleven for the third time through. In both examples the meter is in 2/4 time marked by the *basy* playing deliberate bow strokes on the quarter notes. The harmony changes only at the end of each part or phrase: D harmony for the first part, A for the second part, with a cadence back on D for the final bar of the second part.

In "Skanking on the Grass," the fusion version of "wiecno," the same two parts/phrases are used, and the same Górale dialect text is sung, followed by an English paraphrase sung by Twinkle

Jo se inom wiecnom drobiym,
pod zielonym trownicku.
Łociec krzycy, Matka krzycy,
zedres kiyrpce Janicku.

I dance the forever dance,
across the green grass.
Papa cries, Mama cries,
you will ruin your moccasins.

Note: This transcription is made from track 8 of the CD recording *Music of the Tatra Mountains: The Trebunia Family Band* (1995, Nimbus Records).

Figure 5.2. "Wiecno" transcribed from *The Trebunia Family Band.*

(fig. 5.3, CD track 32). The cadence on D in the second part, however, becomes the first beat of the repeat to the first part in this fusion version (mm 17, 33, 49).

In the fusion version, instead of the first and second parts being asymmetrical and variable as they are in the Górale version, they are both rendered as eight-bar phrases with no "eternal" extensions that characterize most Górale performances of "wiecno." Each eight-bar section is clearly marked by the electric bass which changes from an ostinato on pitches D and B for the first part, to an ostinato on A and F♯ for the second eight-bar part. In the fusion version the first line of Górale text is stretched into eight bars, and the second into nine bars—the ninth bar being the first bar in the next eight-bar section. The Górale text in the fusion version also follows the traditional arrangement of text with melodic section: the first half of the poetic verse with the first part of the music, the second half of the poetic verse with the second part of the music. The English paraphrase sung by Twinkle, however, is spread over several sets of the two eight-bar parts. It begins with a pickup to an eight-bar segment of part 2 (A-harmony, measure 25, in fig. 5.3).

Figure 5.3. "Skanking on the Grass" from *Twinkle Inna Polish Stylee*. By Norman Grant and Władysław Trebunia-Tutka based on traditional music and text. *CD track 32*

Figure 5.3. *Continued.*

Figure 5.4 is a composite transcription with a straightforward Górale version (top line, same as fig. 5.2) and the Górale text portion of the fusion version (from fig. 5.3). The gaps in the top line show where bars have been added in the fusion version to create two sections of eight bars.

"Skanking on the Grass/Wiecno" illustrates a relatively simple fusion process: an originally malleable phrase structure is standardized into eight-bar sections. Since it is the unique quality of this particular Górale *nuta* that the bar structure need not be any particular length, rendering both sections as eight-bar units does not necessarily challenge the integrity of the *nuta;* however, it does eliminate the improvised and playful variation of phrase lengths that adds interest to most performances of "wiecno."

The next example illustrates a more complex process of musical fusion. "Pod Jaworkem," the tune on which it is based, has an unusual phrase structure consisting of two parts of five and seven bars, respectively; the first part is subdivided into three- plus two-bar phrases, and the second into three- plus four-bar phrases. Figure 5.5 is a transcription of the first verse of text with tune. The audio example on track 33 of the CD accompanying this book is a version of the tune played by Krzysztof Trebunia-Tutka on a recording released in Poland about the same time as the reggae fusion recordings were released in England.

"Pod Jaworkem," called "Husband the Outlaw" in the fusion version, is dramatically altered. Like "Skanking on the Grass," this fusion tune is sung both in Górale dialect and in English, and, like the first example, the bar structure of this tune is altered to achieve symmetry. The Górale-dialect portion of the fusion version is stretched into a six-bar phrase plus a ten-bar phrase, totaling sixteen bars for the verse. The Jamaican-English verses present still a different poetic phrase structure: four, four, and eight bars. In both cases the sum total is sixteen bars. Track number 34 on the CD accompanying this book is the fusion version. First the Jamaican-English paraphrase is heard followed by the Górale-dialect version. Figure 5.6 compares the Jamaican-English verse (marked line 1) with the Górale verse (line 2). Beginning at 33 seconds into CD track 34, one can follow the transcription reading first line 1 all the way down, and then skipping up and reading line 2. The boxed-in measures in line 2, the Górale-dialect verse, show measures that have been added in the fusion version to make it fit a sixteen-bar structure.

Figure 5.4. "Wiecno," two versions.

Pod jaworkem, pod zelenym,
Hej, ore Andrzia wolkiem siwem.

Under the sycamore, under the green,
Hey, Andrzej plows with an ox.

Note: This transcription is made from the cassette "*Żywot* Janicka Zbójnika/The life story of Janicek Zbójnik," ca. 1992 Gamma, Kraków. The text is a phonetic spelling of the Slovak dialect.

Figure 5.5. "Pod Jaworkem" from *Żywot Janicka Zbójnika. CD track 33, transcription includes 0:15–0:27*

Many of the remaining twelve cuts on the first fusion cassette similarly take Górale tunes and fit them into reggae phrase structures. Krzysztof is correct when he claims that all the cuts on this cassette are formed around the music played by his family band. But the result of these fusions is a multivalent music that is heard and understood quite differently depending on whether the listener understands Górale dialect or English. For example, I imagine that the same music is experienced differently by listeners in London, where the cassette was first released, than it is by listeners in Poland's Tatra Mountains. This is especially true with "Husband the Outlaw," which retains an asymmetrical phrase structure for the Górale verses (six plus ten bars) but a symmetrical four-and-four-plus eight-bar structure in English. I suggest, however, that the musical language is universally understood as reggae. This may seem on the surface like a mundane observation, or a statement of the obvious, yet the essential aural quality of this music as reggae is central to its reception and function in the Górale community. And the reasons that the music sounds like reggae may not be the same for many American listeners as they are for most Górale listeners. I focus on two different reasons for why the music on the cassette *Twinkle Inna Polish Stylee: Higher Heights* sounds like reg-

Figure 5.6. "Husband the Outlaw" comparing the Reggae and Górale verses. By Norman Grant and Władysław Trebunia-Tutka based on traditional music and text. Twinkle Brothers and Tutki: *Twinkle Inna Polish Stylee: Higher Heights* (Twinkle Music 1992. Re-released in 1997 on CD by Twinkle Music and Kamahuk). *CD track 34*

gae: first, the phrase structures of the music and, second, the "beat."

The phrase structures of the two examples analyzed above demonstrate a process by which many of the Górale tunes featured on this cassette are made to sound like reggae. They are made to fit metrically into eight-bar patterns. Although some Górale tunes use four-bar patterns (such as *krzesana* "po dwa" [CD track 7] and the tunes to the *zbójnicki* [CD track 11]), many are less regular. The variety of phrase structures in muzyka Podhala is part of the richness of that music, and they organize the tunes into broad genres reflecting different functions in Górale's social use of music. On the *Twinkle Inna Polish Stylee* cassette all the tunes use eight-bar patterns, and all are one genre: reggae.

The second reason why the music on the cassette *Twinkle Inna Polish Stylee: Higher Heights* sounds like reggae concerns rhythmic structure—the beat. The beat, or what is colloquially termed the "dub," is a characteristic rhythmic texture provided entirely by the Jamaican reggae musicians and which consists of an ostinato played on an electric bass, a keyboard, and sometimes a guitar chording on the offbeat quarter notes, and a drum set that is more active in the first half of each bar and that accents the downbeats of the even-numbered bars when transcribed in 2/4 time. This is illustrated in figures 5.7 and 5.8, representing, respectively, the rhythm sections to "Skanking on the Grass" and "Husband the Outlaw."

Despite the relatively rapid tempo ($\quarternote$ = 130 or faster), the rhythmic textures, which are fundamentally similar in these two music transcriptions (figs. 5.7 and 5.8), provide a "laid-back" feel characteristic of reggae. This is achieved by a division of the rhythm into two distinct sections that alternate. In each 2/4 bar, the first quarter note is more active rhythmically, while the second quarter note is accented by the chording keyboard and guitar. By alternating the type of activity on every other quarter note, the feel of the tempo is effectively slowed by half. The Górale string trio and singing is considerably more active—compare the rapid text delivery of Tutki to the more relaxed singing of Norman Grant. This high-energy layer of sound over the laid-back rhythmic texture is comparable to the brass section in ska bands, a genre closely related to reggae.[6]

In summary, the music sound itself is dominated by the needs of reggae in two ways analyzed here: the phrase structure is reduced to eight- or sixteen-bar forms, and all music is accompanied

Figure 5.7. Rhythmic texture for "Skanking on the Grass." *CD track 32*

Figure 5.8. Rhythmic texture for "Husband the Outlaw." *CD track 34*

by a characteristic rhythmic texture. In other words, the Góraleness of the tunes around which this music is formed is subordinate to the rhythmic and phrasing needs of a different music—reggae.

Responses in Poland and Podhale

The Twinkle/Tutki fusion project was quite successful, reaching top spots on European charts. For example, the *Twinkle Inna Polish Stylee* cassette was number 9 on the World Music Charts Europe October 1993 ratings; and *Comeback Twinkle 2 Trebunia Family* made it to number 6 in November 1994 (Theurer 1993–94). Domestically the recordings were also a critical and popular success (Brzozowicz and Chmiel 1994), although the subject positions expressed to me by Górale lead me to conclude that the fusion recordings received mixed reviews in the Tatras. My interpretation suggests that this is so because the early fusion recordings employed Górale music in such a way that some of its qualities were overwhelmed by the reggae music; the resulting music was most likely heard as reggae with the Górale fiddling serving as ethnic "color." The music, however, remains multivalent and will be perceived quite differently by different individuals. For example, my myopic focus on muzyka Podhala rendered me deaf to the centrality of the reggae "dub" to the overall sound of the music until a fellow ethnomusicologist pointed out this characteristic to me. It stands to reason that some individuals might hear what is Górale in the music and suppress its reggaeness.[7] Nevertheless, at least some of the qualities valued in indigenous Górale analysis systems, such as a rich variety of phrase lengths, were the very qualities violated in the fusion projects.

This may be one of the reasons why, in my observations, the early reggae fusion projects were most successful outside Podhale, in Poland and in Europe as a whole. Some Górale tend to view the fusion as an anomaly that does not represent their interests. This fieldwork observation is supported by a survey conducted in the fall of 2000 by Polish ethnographers soliciting responses to a questionnaire.[8] In response to my questions about who among three separate fusion groups from the area best represents Poland as a nation, and Podhale as a region, a greater number of self-described Górale volunteered Tutki alone (playing traditional Górale music—not worldbeat) than chose the Tutki/Twinkle fusion band. The respondents apparently felt strongly about this choice because the Trebunia-Tutka family alone was not offered as an option on the questionnaire; many simply wrote it in. The sense that ethnic Górale had mixed feelings about the Tutki/Twinkle worldbeat fusion was amplified by my observations at their first live performance together in Zakopane. The theater was packed, not with Górale but with tourists. This is a casual observation, but I had lived in this region for some time and I had experience observing tourists and local Górale audiences. Certainly most of the individual Górale who regularly came to public events featuring muzyka Podhala were not there. Kleszcz and his reggae/Górale fusion project attracted large crowds of Poland's youth but did not

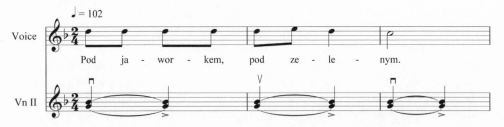

Figure 5.9. "Pod Jaworkem" with accompanying violin, Slovak style. *CD track 33*

attract Polish Górale. We are left with the spectacle of two distinct musics merging and attracting a listening audience different from the base audience for either music, namely, the European world-beat audience, who were for the most part neither Jamaican Rastafarians nor Polish Górale.

The challenge for acceptance that the Twinkle/Tutki fusion has among some Górale does not necessarily mean that Górale are intolerant of the fusion of distant musics; as detailed in chapter 3, Górale music is itself a distillation of distant musics into something unique to the Polish Tatra region. "Husband the Outlaw" is a good example of this distillation. It represents two layers of fusion and is illustrative of the history of Górale musicians adapting distant and not so distant musics for their own purposes. The song originates across the Tatras and a few kilometers east in Spisz, a region that today is mostly in the Slovak Republic but spans the Polish/Slovak border. This is not such a distant music, but it is not strictly muzyka Podhala. In fact, many tunes are shared on the north and south sides of the Tatra Mountains, but the style of this particular tune is distinctly Slovak. The clearest musical cue that this tune comes from Slovakia is the style of the accompaniment pattern. A careful audition of CD track 33 reveals two distinct pulses with each stroke of the bow by the accompanying violins, an *altówka*, and a *basy*. In my experience, whenever Górale musicians use such a double-pulse or düvö accompaniment, they are quite consciously playing in what they themselves interpret as a Slovak or Hungarian manner (fig. 5.9, CD track 33). However, in the Tutki/Twinkle fusion version of this tune, the accompaniment provided by Tutki uses a single-pulse bowing technique as is common in Górale music.

The tune is not the only borrowed element of this song. The

text of the song is in a Slovak dialect and speaks directly to the theme of the first Twinkle/Tutki cassette—Janosik, the *zbójnik* from Terchowa, Slovakia, who was captured and executed in 1713 (introduced in chapter 1). Whether he ever plied his trade on the Polish side of the Tatras is doubtful, but he remains a key figure today in Polish Górale ethnic identity. Thus "Husband the Outlaw" is a double fusion, first a Górale/Slovak fusion and then a Górale/reggae fusion.

From my perspective as a scholar of a regional music, the Górale/reggae fusion does not musically reflect an image entirely compatible with a more commonly held view of ethnic identity among Górale. I am referring to the stereotype of the ideal Górale who stubbornly resists servitude. This is the whole point of the Janosik legend retold on the Twinkle/Tutki cassette. Very similar to the co-option of the symbolic power of the *zbójnik*/Janosik legend at tourist festivals, perhaps a Warsaw radio producer and a band of Jamaican Rastafarians succeeded in doing what feudal lords never fully achieved in Podhale: they subdued musically the treasured independence of Górale. Musically the Górale material in the two 1992 recordings is ultimately subservient to the structural needs of reggae, the dominant identity in these fusion experiments. In 1995 this dominance was reinforced visually and spatially in the live stage performances of the Tutki and Twinkle bands: Twinkle and his reggae band took up most of the stage with the Tutki Górale band off to one side. It is not surprising that some Górale, especially those who are invested in traditional Górale music, are ambivalent about this Górale/reggae fusion.

Górale Globalism and the Appropriation of Worldbeat

The 1992 cassette releases and the subsequent 1995 stage performances by Twinkle and Tutki are not the end of the story. The Trebunia-Tutka Górale family members continue to use their experiences with distant musics to move their own local music in new directions (see discography, fig. 5.15). In a letter Krzysztof Trebunia-Tutka sent me in 1996, he explained that he believes it is important to continue experimenting with Górale music so that the tradition continues to grow and to interest each new generation. With the letter he sent what was, at the time, Tutki's most recent recording, *Trebunie-Tutki w Sherwood*. Although the recording still makes connections with the earlier reggae fusions, it marks a clear turning point by putting muzyka Podhala on center stage, compositionally and literally.

The evolution of the iconography on the cassette and CD covers of the fusion recordings mirrors the changes made to the music. The original cassette, *Twinkle Inna Polish Stylee: Higher Heights* features on the j-card cover a painting by Władysław Trebunia-Tutka (see fig. 5.1). At the base of the painting is a likeness of Giewont Mountain, a granite massif rising directly behind Zakopane and serving as a symbol of the town and the region. Above the mountain are the words "Higher Heights" and a green, red, and gold rosette based on the same common geometric design addressed in the previous chapter. Włodzimierz Kleszcz explained that this rosette design is a combination of a geometric symbol from Górale folk culture, with colors that unite Górale and Rastafarians: red and green are common colors in Górale costumes, and by adding the gold we have a palette with colors that symbolize Rastafarianism. The rosette, according to Kleszcz, became a symbol for the reggae/Górale fusion project (Warsaw, ac22.iii.95). On the binder edge of the cassette cover is the main title of the cassette, *Twinkle Inna Polish Stylee*. One can read this title in several ways. Perhaps it is in Jamaican-English patois and translates as "Twinkle in a Polish style." But a Polish reader might interpret the word "inna" as a Polish word that means "different" and thus read the title as "Twinkle's Different Polish Style." In any case, the cassette cover does not clearly indicate what is inside—it does not accurately describe the music on the cassette itself. The cover is dominated by images from Podhale and from Górale folklore. The music on the cassette is dominated by Jamaican reggae, though based on Górale themes.

The second release, *Comeback Twinkle 2 Trebunia Family*, this time in CD format and produced in 1994, marks a significant shift from the original fusion recording. When I interviewed Krzysztof Trebunia-Tutka in November 1994 he seemed eager to talk about this newest recording, noting how it differs from the previous fusion project. Norman Twinkle Grant singing in English is featured on only two tracks (2 and 5), and even these two tracks feature Górale dialect text. Tracks 7, 8, 10, and 12 are remakes of pieces on the earlier cassettes, but this time without the English texts. Most significant, the texts to half the songs are newly composed in Górale dialect by Anna Gąsienica-Czubernat, and express modern concerns of Górale. For example, one song laments the drying sources of traditional culture (track 3); another is about a Górale

Figure 5.10. CD cover for *Comeback Twinkle 2 Trebunia Family* (front). Painting by Władysław Trebunia-Tutka, and cover design graphic by Anna Baran.

who met his demise while seeking wealth in Chicago (track 12); a third warns about the influence of television (track 11). Three tracks (4, 6, and 14) are straightforward muzyka Podhala with no fusion component. In addition to these three tracks, however, only four tracks include traditional Górale music, and the "traditional" quality of all four is debatable. Track 10 is based on "Pod Jaworkem," the Slovak song that became "Husband the Outlaw" on the first fusion cassette. The remaining three tracks that use "traditional" material (3, 8, and 13) all use tunes generally attributed to Andrzej Knapczyk-Duch (1866–1946). As discussed in chapter 1, some do not consider these tunes to be traditional.

The dramatic shift in musical content on this second fusion recording is subtly represented on the CD cover. The front includes an enlarged version of the rosette from the first fusion cassette and the title *Comeback Twinkle 2 Trebunia Family* (figs. 5.10 and 5.11). I interpret this title to mean "Twinkle, come back *to* the

Figure 5.11. CD cover for *Comeback Twinkle 2 Trebunia Family* (back). Photograph by Włodzimierz Kleszcz, and cover design graphic by Anna Baran.

Trebunia (Tutki) family." This interpretation is reinforced by the first song on the CD "Normanie/Listen," based on "Góralu, czy ci nie żal," a romantic song well known among Poles about a Górale who was forced to leave his beloved mountains and travel to America to earn a living.[9] An English verse in the version on this CD calls for Twinkle to return to Podhale—by implication making him an honorary Górale. The back of the 1994 CD contains a photo of the Trebunia-Tutka family with Twinkle and bassist Dub Judah. This time the Rastamen are beginning to take on some of the trappings of Góraleness, specifically a Górale hat and sheepskin vest. Thus both in the content of the CD and on the cover, the Rastamen are being transformed into Górale rather than the other way around.

Our Twinkle Home, the third fusion release, came out in 1995 and was timed to complement the Twinkle Brothers' return to Poland. The cassette cover features Norman "Twinkle" Grant photographed in the home of Władysław Trebunia-Tutka (fig. 5.12).

Figure 5.12. Cassette cover for *Our Twinkle Home*. Photograph by Włodzimierz Kleszcz, and cover design graphic by Anna Baran.

Grant is clearly the main attraction, though he is set in an unusual environment. As the cover might suggest, Twinkle and reggae are the main attractions, though the setting contains elements from Górale cultural practices. On *Our Twinkle Home*, all the music is first reggae music to which the Tutki Górale band adds improvisations and compositions in a Górale style. The texts are clearly Rastafarian; for example, "Everything I Do—I Do It for Jah," "Don't Forget Africa," and "Jah Will Set You Free." None of the tracks includes Górale text. All three of the first worldbeat fusion recordings with Twinkle and Tutki used material recorded in Polish Radio studios in Warsaw in 1991.

The final CD with strong connections to Norman Grant and the Twinkle Brothers, *Trebunie-Tutki w Sherwood*, continues some of the innovative musical ideas begun in *Comeback Twinkle 2 Trebunia Family*, and it is also very Górale in spirit and content. On the surface this may not seem to be the case, since only five of the

sixteen tracks are based clearly on traditional Górale material
(tracks 3, 7, 10, 13, and 16) compared to all thirteen tracks on
Twinkle Inna Polish Stylee. A few of the tracks even appear to have
no involvement by the Tutki Górale band; tracks 2 and 5 are performed by a Polish group called "African Head Charge." Other
guests who perform with Tutki include "2 Bad Card" and "Kinior,"
a band led by Włodzimierz Kińiorski. The CD notes list the Twinkle brothers on two tracks: track 12 and track 3, which is a text
version of track 5 from the first cassette. Despite all this, the CD
is Górale in spirit and content, because most of the poetry is newly
composed in Górale dialect and is about issues concerning Górale
in the 1990s. Below are transcriptions and translations of the texts
of two such pieces: track 7, "Poniechane Podhale" by Władyslaw
Trebunia-Tutka; and track 11, "Kochaj a Buduj" by Krzysztof
Trebunia-Tutka. In addition to the five tracks based on traditional
Górale material are three tracks featuring newly composed texts
and tunes that employ five-bar phrase structures suggesting
Górale-style *wierchowe* or *ozwodne* (tracks 1, 14, and 15). Ultimately
the CD is eclectic with diverse styles, such as straightforward muzyka Podhala (track 13), stylized Górale music (tracks 1, 7, 9, 14,
15, and 16), Górale music with altered accompaniment styles (track
10), Górale/reggae fusion (track 3), rap (tracks 2, 5, and 12), jazz
and blues (track 6), and pop or disco (tracks 8 and 12).

"PONIECHANE PODHALE" (FORSAKEN PODHALE)
BY WŁADYSLAW TREBUNIA-TUTKA

Kieby nasi dziadkowie	If our grandfathers
Z grobu dziś powstajali	Could rise from their graves
Toby nad syćkimi nami	Then over all of us
I na calućkim Podholem	And in all of Podhale
Rzewnie se zapłakali.	They would mournfully cry.
Jako sie tyz miły Boze	How did, my dear God,
Selnijako zmieniło?	these things change for the worse?
Chałpy, sopy powolane	Homes, barns collapsed,
Drzewa stare wzścinane	Old trees cut down
Syćko sie dzis popśniyło.	Everything today has fallen apart.
Drzewiej dawniejsyk casak	Long ago in past times
Bywało u góroli	There were among the Górale
Bez calućkie seść sto roków	All over for hundreds of years
Bacoskowie i juhasi	Shepherds and shepherd boys
Gazdowali na holi.	Who farmed the mountain valleys.

Tajemice zbójnickie
Dziadkowie przekazowali
Bacowskie kotliki pełne
Z zbójnickimi talarami
Popod bucki chowali.

Drzewiej te gazdowskie dziewki
W skrzyniach miały przyodziewki
Dzisiok baby wielgie panie

Chodzom w śpilkach po dywanie
Syćko na sie powiesajom

Złoto srebło i pierzcionki.
Wto wie jaki rozum majom?!

Dolu, hore, calućkom wsiom

Murowanic nastawiali
Wysokik jako turnice
Pustyk jako siubienice
Z Polski powyjezdzali.

Dzisiok kozdy młody górol
Aut, masin mo bez liku
Kozdy goni za interesem
Za granicom za biznesem
Poniechali ojców zwyku.

Mrok ogarnon Podhole
Cepry zadeptujom hole
Wody, źródła i potoki
Zamieniły sie w rynśtoki
Ciemna kawa i herbata
Ciemna głowa puste słowa
Nastały se dziwne lata.

Cos my teroz pocniemy
My biydni Podholanie?
Dymby, bucki wyścinane

Puste chałpy poniechane
Co se po nos ostanie.

Hej coz my se pocniemy
Biedni Podholanie

The secrets of the brigands
That our forefathers passed on,
Baca caldrons full
With brigands' money
Hidden under the beech trees.

Long ago those farm girls
Had clothes in their dowry chest.
Today women go about like no-
    bility,
Walking in high heels on carpet,
They drape everything on them-
    selves,
Gold, silver, and rings.
What sort of understanding do
    they have?!

Up, down, throughout the vil-
    lages
Stone buildings have been put up
Like tall mountains,
Empty like gallows.
They've left Poland.

Today every young highlander
Has cars, machines without end.
Everyone chases interests
Abroad for business,
Forsaking our fathers' ways.

Darkness seizes Podhale.
Tourists trample the mountains,
Water, springs, and rivers
Have changed into gutters.
Black coffee and tea,
Black head, empty words.
These are strange times.

What will we do now,
Us poor Górale?
The oak and beech trees'
    strength is sapped,
Empty houses, abandoned.
What will be left of us?

What will we do,
Us poor Górale?

Hej sycko poniechane	Everything shamelessly disregarded,
Lasy wyrubane.	Forests cut away.

"KOCHAJ A BUDUJ" (LOVE AND BUILD)
BY KRZYSZTOF TREBUNIA-TUTKA

Refrain 1: Rżnij, rżnij, rżnij, rżnij . . .	*Refrain 1:* Saw, saw, saw, saw . . .
Przykozoł mi dziadek	Grandfather passed on the tradition
Jak chałpe budować	Of how to build a house.
Coby starym zwykom	So our old ways
Wierności dochować	Are loyally preserved.
Trza pierse z potoka	First, from the creek
Tulać wielkie wanty	You must hoist stones
Dobrze wypodpierać	So that they will hold steady
Syćkie śtyry kąty	All four corners.
Refrain 1: Rżnij, rżnij, rżnij, rżnij . . .	*Refrain 1:* Saw, saw, saw, saw . . .
Pote musis chłopce	Afterwards, boy, you must
Drzewa naryktować	Prepare the wood.
I wiekowe smreki	Aged spruce trees
Na węgły powiązać	Must be joined together.
Dach scytem ku drodze	The roof peak toward the road
Wielgi, ozłozysty	Huge and slanted
Będzie zochylina	Will lean
Kie bee dysc siarcysty	When the rain pours.
Refrain 1: Rżnij, rżnij, rżnij, rżnij . . .	*Refrain 1:* Saw, saw, saw, saw . . .
Gontów trya nascypać	To shave insulation
Z drzewa słoistego	From wood,
Piły ani gwoździę	Neither a saw or nails
Nie trza ci do tego	Are needed.
Piec ulepis z gliny	You will make an oven of clay,
Ku połedniu okna	Windows on the south side,
Nie będzie brakować	You will not lack
W twojej chałpie ciepła	Warmth in your home.
Refrain 2: Kochaj a buduj . . .	*Refrain 2:* Love and build . . .
W kozdym kącie pełno	Every corner is filled
Miłości i światła	With love and light.
Zycie ozgoreje	Life will warm you
Lepiej jako watra	Better than any fire.
Jak nos kiedy Pan Bóg	When the Lord will
Z tego świata weźnie	Take us from this world,

Będzie gniozdem dzieciom	There will be a nest for our children
A i wnukom pewnie.	And the grandchildren too.
Refrain 2: Kochaj a buduj . . .	*Refrain 2:* Love and build . . .

One track on the CD is an especially revealing illustration of the ways that the Trebunia-Tutka family is responding to globalization as represented by the relatively international Twinkle reggae band. In this example the Trebunia-Tutka family turns the tables, challenging reggae on its home turf by recording a version of a 1976 Bob Marley reggae classic, "Roots, Rock, Reggae" from *Rastaman Vibrations* (Island LPS 9383, 1976). Four years after a reggae band turned Górale tunes into reggae, we have a version of a reggae classic that does the reverse: it takes control of the text and thwarts the dub to make a commentary on the Trebunia-Tutka family's experience with the Rastamen, with reggae, and with globalization.

Track 4 on *Trebunie-Tutki w Sherwood* is titled "Nasze Reggae" (Our reggae) (book CD, track 35). It is a cover of Marley's reggae hit, but I do not hear it as reggae—it lacks the reggae/ska dub. A violin does mark the offbeat, but a second violin marks the beat, effectively canceling out the offbeat punctuation characteristic of reggae. The text is not a translation of the Vincent Ford reggae poem but rather a meditation by producer Włodzimierz Kleszcz on Górale music with the summary chorus "Our reggae is Górale music" (reproduced below). If the 1992 fusions turned Górale music into reggae, the creators of "Nasze Reggae" exercise the type of aesthetic reversal that Simon Frith (1996, 18) finds so compelling in his book *Performing Rites*, and they make a reggae standard not reggae (although also not muzyka Podhala by musicological standards). They use a de-reggaed reggae song to sing about their own music.

"NASZE REGGAE" BY WŁODZIMIERZ KLESZCZ (CD TRACK 35)

Rus sie i odzyj, nie dej sie pytać	Move and revive, don't make them ask
Hej, nase reggae obudzi cie	Hey, our reggae will wake you up
Serce zabije, nie godoj nie	The heart will beat, don't say no
Ze nigdy do dziś i cosi zrób	You have done nothing until now, so do something
Ukochoj jom od rania juz	Love her since dawn
Kołysoj jom ku świtaniu	Rock her till dawn
Nase reggae—góralsko muzyka	Our reggae—Górale music
Nase reggae—nuta miłosno	Our reggae—tune of love

Słonko za górom, koło nos mgła	The sun is behind the mountain, around us mist
Wiem co ty robis, zabijos cas	I know what you are doing, you are killing time
Dziwujes sie, jako to jest	You wonder how it is
Ze dajem więcej, a bierem mniej	That I give more and take less
Góralsko śpiewka to nase reggae	A Górale song is our reggae
Chodź se po chmurak jak ci tu źle	Walk in the clouds if you don't like it here
Nase reggae—góralsko muzyka	Our reggae—Górale music
Nase reggae—nuta wierchowo	Our reggae—mountain peak tune
Zyj, worce zyć nasom tradycjom	Live, it is worth living with our tradition
Zwady juz dość, cierta wygnoj	Enough quarreling, drive the devil away
Nie godoj nie samemu sobie	Don't say no to yourself
I ośmej sie—i o to chodzi	And laugh at yourself, that is the point
Tak witoj dzień coby dobry był	Welcome the day so that it will be good
Idzie nowy dzień i nowy cas	A new day is coming and the new time
Hej! Idzie miłość, to jej znak	Hey, love is coming and this is its sign.
Nase reggae—góralsko muzyka	Our reggae—Górale music
Nase reggae—nuta krzesano	Our reggae—krzesana tune

The most recent worldbeat fusion CD recorded by Tutki is provocatively titled *Etno-Techno*, released in 2000.[10] It is significant that much of the music on this CD is credited as "traditional" and is identifiable with the dance and song repertoire of the Polish Tatras. Without exception, however, all the tracks include a bass, drum, and keyboard rhythm mix, the "techno" response to the "etno" material. This CD is also a response to the Polish version of Euro-pop called "Disco-Polo," a trend popular in the 1990s that I have often heard Krzysztof criticize as being banal, without poetic sophistication, and sapping youth's interest in their own folklore. Krzysztof is hoping to draw that same youthful audience back into what he calls "their own" folklore. I will illustrate, with one example, how he goes about doing this.

"Nie patrzcie przez lupy" (Don't look through the magnifying glass), the first track on the *Etno-Techno* CD, is an example of a tune that suggests a traditional *nuta* but is substantially different

```
Voice (spoken):                                                _____
Violin solo:                                              _____
Chorus:                                            _____
Violins and basy:                         _____
Drum, bass, synth:  _____
                    1   5   9   13  17  21  25  29  33  37  41  45
```

```
Voice (spoken):                                          _____ etc.
Violin solo:            _____
Chorus:                                      _____   _____
Violins and basy:       _____
Drum, bass, synth:      _____ etc.
                    49  53  57  61  65  69  73  77  81  85  89  93 etc.
```

Figure 5.13. "Nie patrzcie przez lupy" layers analysis. *CD 36, transcription includes 0:00–1:18*

so that any Górale musician would recognize it as an evocation of traditional music and not a quote (book CD track 36). I hear the piece as constructed with five distinct layers that are stacked above the one constant: the drum, bass, synthesizer rhythmic foundation that introduces the piece (and introduces the CD, for that matter). In figure 5.13 this is represented as the lowest line, just above the sequence of numbers representing measures counted in 2/4 time. At measure 17 a string ensemble of two violins and a *basy* enter. This is a traditional Górale *muzyka*, as they call such an ensemble, minus the lead violin. The next layer added is a chorus of two voices at measure 33 and then a lead violin solo beginning in measure 41. At measure 81 the texture is paired down to the drum, bass, synthesizer rhythmic foundation with the introduction of a spoken, perhaps rapped, line.

Figure 5.14 is a transcription of measures 33–64 of "Nie patrzcie przez lupy," lacking the techno rhythmic foundation. Based on the sounds represented in this transcription, I first interpreted this piece as a "po dwa" or "in two" dance piece, a category of Górale dance music defined by two beats per harmonic change, usually on the chords DDAA. But here we find an unusual progression: the *basy* plays DD EE DD CC while the two violins play an A chord, followed by an E-major chord, then D to C major—not a common harmonic progression in muzyka Podhala. Note also that the voice part sets up an interesting harmonic and rhythmic tension: a G-natural and B against the E-major chord in the violins in bar 2, and a D chord against the C chord in bar 4. The voice part also suggests a five-bar phase over the repeating four-bar ostinato. This skewed phrasing is repeated by the lead violinist who begins with

Figure 5.14. "Nie patrzcie przez lupy" music notation. *CD track 36*

a version of the five-bar vocal melody in very characteristic Górale lead violin style, followed, however, by seven bars of much less characteristic playing. I hear this seven-bar second phrase as five bars, extended to seven by holding the last note. A two-bar sustain at the end of a phrase is very common in traditional Górale tunes, whereas a four-bar sustain, in my experience, never occurs. The result is twelve bars, although they are asymmetrically subdivided. I interpret "Nie patrzcie przez lupy" to once again be a juxtaposition of what are for Westerners, including in this postmodern context the Jamaican reggae musicians, an odd or musically "Other" five-bar phrase with a four-bar macro structure. These five-bar phrases were spaced over the ostinato to create eight- and twelve-bar units—both divisible by 4, the preferred phrase length of popular dance music.

It is precisely this sort of tyranny of the square meter which led me to conclude that the original 1992 fusions privileged reggae music over muzyka Podhala: they took Górale fiddling and used it as exotic color for a reggae album. Why, then, is this recording any different? The *Etno-Techno* recording subtly shifts the balance toward "etno," or Polish Górale music, primarily by fielding no strong counter-identity. The techno contribution is a nondescript background on which Górale music and poetic ideas are presented. The techno—the electronic drum and bass mix—in "Nie patrzcie przez lupy" forms the "greyed-out" background that is a realization of a "global aesthetic," though not what Erlmann had in mind when he used the concept. Contrasted with the violin and vocal parts, the techno mix evokes no location, no ethnicity, no nationality. Instead, it references modernity; it is the sound of globalization. What about the spoken or "rapped" text in "Nie Patrzcie"? Does this not suggest urban black America? Perhaps this is the intended reference, but what is actually being referenced? At least since Robert Walser's 1995 article "Rhythm, Rhyme, and Rhetoric" it has been clear that rap was originally a classic counter-hegemonic expression against the forces of globalization, although at the same time it requires the global reality of an African diaspora. Second, the type of poetic recitation Krzysztof Trebunia-Tutka performs in "Nie Patrzcie" is, by his own claims to me, a traditional form of Górale verbal expression. The violin and vocal chorus parts, on the other hand, are unambiguous sonic symbols of a locality (the Tatras) and of a people (Górale). The Górale performing for "Nie patrzcie przez lupy" project their "etno" difference on a grey screen of techno sameness.

Two quotes from the Tutki webpage description of this CD are telling (www.trebunie.pl/dysko_etno.htm). Krzysztof is quoted as saying: "We derive from the highlanders' tradition elements which are not very clear for people today: characteristic singing, very special highlander diapason, the way of performing each note, the way of improvisation and traditional instruments." On the other hand, Włodzimierz Kiniorski, the musician from central Poland who is responsible for the "techno" sounds on the CD, says: "I am searching for a color. That is what I am fascinated by and either I create it in a traditional way or by knob manipulating. It does not make any difference for me." He is interested in timbre, and he does not care how he gets it. He champions unattached sounds, global in their lack of reference to any location or even to any acoustic instrument. In stark contrast, using terms like "tradition," "characteristic," and "special," Krzysztof attaches his contribution to a people located in a specific region.

Globalization and Globalism in and of the Village

The Jamaican reggae and Górale fiddling fusions, followed by the continuing responses to these experiences by the Trebunia-Tutka family musicians, are examples of both globalization and globalism in the villages of the Polish Tatras. What distinguishes globalization from globalism? Sociologist Roland Robertson (1992, 58–59) outlines a history of globalization from the early fifteenth century but concentrates on the 1870s to the 1920s as the crucial "take-off phase," a period that, as I documented elsewhere (2000) and in chapter 2, was when the idea of Górale ethnicity was solidified. This was also the period when Polish symphonic composers began to use muzyka Podhala in fusion projects that share many of the qualities of the worldbeat fusions considered here. For example, Władysław Żeleński's interest in Górale music is heard in his circa 1870 composition *W Tatrach*. Perhaps the most prominent example that uses direct quotes of Górale tunes is Karol Szymanowski's ballet *Harnasie* (1923–31). These works compare favorably with the first Tutki/Twinkle fusion cassette in that Górale music is subservient to the needs and aesthetic demands of a very different music system. For Szymanowski, the use of Górale music in his ballet was intentionally "universal" (Szymanowski 1999, 131, 245–246), a conception that, despite the name, was narrowly inclusive of European elite society and therefore was international but not truly global. More important, Szymanowski and other composers in the "take-off phase" period of globalization provided no real opportunity for Górale musicians to respond to their compositions in a similar genre. Therefore they do not demonstrate the rising concept of world society and a more unified conception of humankind that characterizes Robertson's later stages of globalization. From this point I move away from Robertson's model and make a distinction between "globalization" as the mechanics of the widespread exchange of resources, capital, and information, and "globalism" as an ideology, a thought process, a conception, an idea.

"Globalism," as I am using the term, includes the multifarious ideological and conceptual motivations behind, and responses to, the mechanics of globalization by individuals and by groups. Globalism drives globalization, yet it can also be the coping strategies of those caught up in globalization. Globalism encompasses the economic and political motivations of multinational corporations and of governments, and includes as well the motivations of individuals who live far from metropolitan centers of globalizing power. Globalism also includes their works of imagination that engage new vistas made available to them through new networks of exchange—their motivations for becoming involved in a globally imagined world, for example. Globalism is how people are reacting to globalization, how they are renegotiating their own local meanings, re-imagining identities, musics, and communities. Globalism includes Appadurai's "work of the imagination" that enables one to imagine that she is a citizen of the world as well as of a family, tribe, community, nation, and nation-state. Globalism is when people begin to rethink their music and engage in this thing called worldbeat. The mechanics of globalization are unidirectional and flow from the metropole to the corners of the world where the infrastructure for creating and distributing capital, resources, information, and so on, may not exist. Globalism, on the other hand, requires no physical structures of production, only the idea of global identity, and therefore may flow from any location in any direction. In a self-perpetuating circle, globalism creates globalization which then re-energizes globalism. Yet globalism, as an idea and motivation, is not controlled by the workings of globalization; it is controlled by individuals and groups who are free to imagine globalization in new and different ways.

Parallels between nationalism and globalism are significant. Both are-isms, thought processes, and systems of beliefs or held truths. Nationalism is about creating a group of people who recognize themselves as a nation and as a state, who imagine themselves as related in some tangible way. Globalism is the new scope of self and community imagination, not yet replacing nationalism but adding a layer, a larger circle. Both-isms are discourses, yet globalism is an ever more polyglot discourse. Both discourses give voice to unity while thriving on heterogeneity (see Wade 2000). Thus both are balanced by the dynamic tension between sameness and difference.

Globalization and globalism are best understood locally. For this case study of globalization and globalism, I have focused my attention on a single family band, and often more narrowly on the person of Krzysztof Trebunia-Tutka. Individuals have a curious effect on cultural studies. While they are much less predictable and

F = fusion/worldbeat

r = rereleased materials or versions of previously released materials

F cd, ac: Twinkle Brothers & Tutki: *Twinkle Inna Polish Stylee: Higher Heights*, Twinkle Music 1992

ac: Kapela Krzysztofa Trebuni-Tutki: *Żywot Janicka Zbójnika* Gamma 1992

ac: Trebunie-Tutki: *Baciarujciez chłopcy* Stebo 1993

ac: Trebunie-Tutki: *Zagrojcie dudzicki* Stebo 1993

cd: Tutki: *Kolędy góralskie* Folk 1993

ac: Tutki: *Ballada o śmierci Janosika* Folk 1993

ac: Tutki: *Folk karnawał I* Folk 1993

ac: Tutki: *Folk karnawał II* Folk 1994

ac: Tutki: *Górale na wesoło* Folk 1994

F cd: Twinkle Brothers & Tutki: *Come Back Twinkle 2 Trebunia Family* Kamahuk 1994

cd: Trebunie-Tutki: *Śpiewki i nuty* Folk 1994

F ac: Twinkle Brothers & Tutki: *Our Twinkle Home* Kamahuk 1995

cd: Trebunie-Tutki: *Music of the Tatra Mountains—The Trebunia Family* Nimbus Records 1995

cd: Trebunie-Tutki: *Saga* Folk 1996

F cd: Trebunie-Tutki: *Trebunie-Tutki w Sherwood* Kamahuk 1996

F r cd: Twinkle Brothers & Trebunie-Tutki: *Greatest Hits* Kamahuk 1997

F cd: Trebunie-Tutki & Orkiestra Kiniora: *Góral-ska Apo-Calypso* Folk 1998

F cd: Trebunie-Tutki & Przyjaciele: *Podniesienie* Kamahuk 1998

F r cd: Warszawski Chór Międzyuczelniany & Trebunie-Tutki: *Jubileusz* Cantica ca. 1999

F cd: Trebunie-Tutki & Kinior Future Sound: *Etno-Techno* Folk 2000

F r cd: Twinkle Brothers & Trebunie-Tutki: *Best Dub* Kamahuk 2000

cd, ac: Trebunie-Tutki: *Folk Karnawał* Folk 2000.

F r cd: Trebunie-Tutki: *Jo ciek wolny* Pomaton 2000

Figure 5.15. Trebunia-Tutka Family discography

are more free to change location, expressive style, languages, professions, opinions, and so forth, than the amorphous "culture group" which they supposedly represent, individuals are also anchoring. Krzysztof Trebunia-Tutka is an example. I met him in 1992, a decade ago, and have observed his consistency even as the music he plays has changed dramatically. Krzysztof clearly sees himself in a global context, as a product of globalization. He recognizes the tension between family, ethnic, and regional tradition, and popular culture, including worldbeat music. As the bearer of a family music tradition, he demands the individual agency to adapt that tradition to the context in which he finds himself. He demands the privilege of lending his voice to the discourse of globalism when it suits his need to express his imagination as a child of the Tatras and as a citizen of the world.

6

Village for Hire

Fall 1994, afternoon, any day of the week. *Walking up Krupówki street from the bottom of the hill where the street ends at Kościeliska Street, I am bombarded with sounds. Closed to vehicles except horse-drawn carriages, so-called Górale taxis, the street is crowded with people (fig. 6.1). I start my journey as I exit the old log restaurant Redykołka, where Górale musicians play in the evening and tapes of muzyka Podhala are played during the day. Immediately on my left, a late-nineteenth-century stone church dominates the lower end of Krupówki. Inside this church, I once attended the memorial service for Tadeusz Sztromajer, the founder and longtime director of the song and dance troupe named after Bartuś Obrochta. Included in the music for the service were* wierchowe *played by Górale musicians, and the church organist played a few arrangements of Górale* nuty. *Back on the street I greet acquaintances, stop and talk with Andrzej, a young Górale taxi driver by day and Górale dancer at Redykołka by evening. Five young men in high spirits make their way down the street as I walk up it. They break into singing a* wierchowa. *Music cassette vendors, some in small booths set up on the edge of the street and some with stores, flood the street with recorded*

Figure 6.1. Looking up Krupówki Street across the intersection
with Tadeusza Kościuszki Street, Zakopane, summer 1997.

*music to attract customers. One vendor constantly plays tapes by the local
group Krywań, which specializes in plugged-in versions of muzyka Podhala. Others play more traditional muzyka Podhala or Polish, American,
and Western European pop music.*

*Crossing the intersection at Tadeusza Kościuszki Street, I hear mu-
zyka Podhala emanating from the offices of the Związek Podhalan a few
doors down on the left. Continuing up Krupówki I encounter a Roma
ensemble with violin, accordion, and guitar. A man who appears to be
getting a head start on the evening's revelry requests a tune* po góralsku

and sings a przyśpiewka. *The violinist obliges with a short* ozwodna, *but he "swings" the tune with a fluid bowing style favored by Roma musicians (and American swing-style fiddlers, among others). At least three Roma bands are active in Zakopane. One plays weekly at an old inn on the road to Kościelisko, another moves between two restaurants on Krupówki Street in the evenings, and the third plays in one of the many dining rooms in the hotel "Morskie Oko." This newly renovated historic hotel—a showpiece halfway up Krupówki—is an interesting study. In the evenings during high-tourist season, one has a choice of three different musics under the same roof. On the lower floor are two dining and dance areas: one is decorated like a posh 1950s nightclub and is for "Roma music"; the second features a rustic Górale-style interior with several open fireplaces. Górale ensembles are hired to play in this area, and they provide a few examples of muzyka Podhala usually with a pair of dancers, followed by polkas and waltzes for multiple-couple dancing. On the floor above, an old theater has been turned into a large techno disco with throbbing music and pulsating light shows.*

The festival stage and the fusion CD are not the only ways to experience music in Podhale. A walk up Krupówki Street any day of the week reveals an astonishing cornucopia of available musics, and the possibilities only multiply as one explores Zakopane's other streets. Classical music recital series are offered at a number of venues, including a villa once occupied by the composer Karol Szymanowski.[1] In addition to the Morskie Oko hotel, Zakopane boasts several discos, a jazz piano lounge, and an increasing number of "regional restaurants" that hire Górale ensembles. If isolation ever was the shaping force behind music in Podhale, it no longer is. Clearly the activities of Górale song and dance troupes, and the particular ceremonial representations on folk festival stages, are specialized corners of music-culture in Podhale. And it is too simple to conclude that the concert series and discos exist solely to cater to tourists, while Górale satisfy themselves with muzyka Podhala. In a large survey study of musical preferences in Podhale, Zbigniew Przerembski (1981) discovered that even Górale generally prefer music other than muzyka Podhala. Yet regardless of whether any individual Górale prefers muzyka Podhala, listens to it often or never, participates in a *góralska muzyka* (band), or sings in the Kraków opera, muzyka Podhala remains the primary musical marker of the people Górale and of the place Podhale. Muzyka

Podhala is to Podhale and Górale as *mariachi* is to Jalisco in Mexico, *flamenco* to Giatano of Andalusia, and *joik* to Sami of Finland.

Restaurant Music

No dyć kie łostatki,	Well, here is the last day before Lent,
to łostatki, to pódźme chłopcy	this last day, let's go boys
do karcmy popijemy se gorzołki.	to the tavern and drink a little vodka.
Moze tam bedom jakie dziywki,	Maybe there will be girls,
to se potońcyme,	so we can dance.
pozdejcie struny, posmarujcie smycki,	Tune the strings, rosin the bows,
i pudziyme se grajency i spiywajency.	and we will go play and sing.

—Song text performed by the Karol Stoch band,
Chicago, 15 July 1929

Despite the visibility of festivals and concerts, tourist restaurants may be the most common, pervasive, and most lucrative places for Górale musicians and dancers to perform. Playing for tourists may have displaced the internal social function of tavern/restaurant music celebrated in old songs, but this does not reduce the significance of restaurant music for other forms of socializing. In restaurants, tourists come in direct contact with Górale musicians and dancers. Their interactions are mediated by the individuals who run the restaurants and who make arrangements for tourist groups, but they are not mediated by ethnographers, concert producers, festival juries, and so on. The Górale musicians and dancers, restaurateurs, and tour organizers considered here all share the objective of earning money; they are also Górale who use their ethnicity to achieve this objective. Tourists provide money in exchange for food, drink, and entertainment, and Górale accommodate by inventing a representation of their heritage including food, drink, music, and dance (see Bendix 1989; Kirshenblatt-Gimblett 1988; Hagedorn 2001, 44–72, for comparable interpretations of cultural "inventions" for tourists). Ultimately these restaurants are part of society in Podhale; they are arenas for cultural exchange, and the musical practices therein are part of the region's music-culture.

I was introduced to the restaurant Redykołka during the sum-

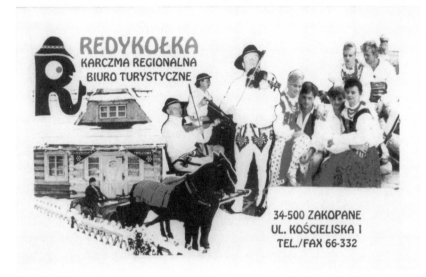

Figure 6.2. Postcard advertisement from Redykołka restaurant and tourist bureau, ca. 1994. Józef Styrczula-Maśniak is seated and playing the violin.

mer of 1992 by members of the extended Styrczula-Maśniak family, the family of the first Górale musician that I met in Chicago several years earlier, and the family with whom I most often live when in Podhale. That summer I stayed in the Kościelisko home of Józef Styrczula-Maśniak, and Józef played violin regularly at Redykołka. Józef's nephew, indigenous ethnographer Edward Styrczula-Maśniak, at whose house I lived during the summer of 1993 and in 1994–95, worked in a tourist bureau that shared the name Redykołka and was located in an adjoining building. Edward occasionally danced in the restaurant. Thus I was connected with the institution by the company I kept.

Redykołka is located just off the lower end of Krupówki, the main street in Zakopane. The facility is constructed of unusually large antique logs lovingly refitted into a beautiful and striking structure in the regional style (fig. 6.2). The emphasis on regional style is repeated in the interior which is decorated with glass paintings, wood carvings, and wooden furniture, all by local artists and craftspeople. The floors are unfinished wood, except for a flat stone floor in the roughly ten-by-ten-foot entrance area that serves as the dance floor. Crossing the threshold, one has the feeling that one is entering an old Górale roadhouse or *karcma*. The Redykołka is not unique in this sense; there are numerous restaurants in Zakopane, Nowy Targ, and in larger villages that emphasize regional style including regional music. However, the combination of restaurant and tourist bureau is unusual, allowing for more elaborate events than many of their counterparts could stage. The Redykołka tourist bureau claims to be the first dedicated to folklore tourism in Zakopane (Krystyna Bochenkowa, interview, ac13.i.95), and it hires musicians and dancers when a good number of tourists are assured—generally when a significant portion of the popular restaurant has been reserved. Offering architecture that is distinctly Górale, staffed by Górale wearing traditional costumes, serving distinctly regional fare, and presenting music and dance that (at least in my interpretation) is Górale, the Redykołka restaurant and tourist bureau trade in Górale folklore, offering paying customers their interpretation of Górale cultural practices.

The format of music events at Redykołka is relatively fixed regardless of the band providing the music (see Cooley 1999b, 329–331). Usually starting at 7:00 P.M. and ending around 10:30, the events alternate between *góralski* dance sequences and group couples dances, with a *zbójnicki* dance sequence toward the end of the evening. The *góralski* and *zbójnicki* dance sequences are demonstrations danced by a group of approximately eight young Górale men and women hired for the evening (fig. 6.3). Probably because of the low ceiling and overall lack of space, the male dancers do not use *ciupagi* during the *zbójnicki* dances (fig. 6.4). Although Poland is spared the quick leaps to litigation that have redefined public spaces in America, one's imagination need not dwell long on the implications of swinging axes about in a crowded restaurant before the idea is abandoned. During the last dance in the *zbójnicki* sequence, the Górale women join the men and they finish dancing in several couples in the *góralski* style.

During the *góralski* and *zbójnicki* demonstration dances, a clear division between performers and audience is established: Górale in their distinctive outfits are acting out the folklore of this corner of Poland for tourists in their store-bought "normal" clothes who have paid for the privilege of enjoying the show. Even for Polish tourists from other regions of the country (*cepry*), these strange dances and costumes are exotic. During group dances the division is mitigated, and restaurant guests are encouraged to join in by the Górale dancers who go into the din-

Figure 6.3. *Góralski* dance, Redykołka restaurant, Zakopane, 1994. Andrzej Stopka, male dancer with back to audience; female dancers: Urszula Król, Małgorzata Papież, and Teresa Zwijacz; musicians: Józef Styrczula-Maśniak, *prym;* Bronisław Styrczula-Maśniak.

Figure 6.4. *Zbójnicki* dance, Redykołka restaurant, Zakopane, 1994. Dancers from left: Tomasz Kułach, Józef Kułach, Edward Styrczula-Maśniak, Andrzej Stopka.

Figure 6.5. Hired Górale dancing with restaurant guests, Redykołka restaurant, Zakopane, 1994. Dancer Tomasz Kułach, center.

ing area and invite individuals to dance with them. Other couples from among the restaurant guests join the Górale/*ceper* couples and crowd into the small dance area or dance down the aisle between dining tables (fig. 6.5). The group dances usually begin with a waltz and, after four to eight minutes, move into a polka for two to four minutes. Occasionally a two-step, tango, or csárdás is played as well.

A few words about the differences between how the group social dances (polkas and waltzes) are danced in America and in Podhale are necessary to clarify the image of an evening in Redykołka that I am creating. The way waltzes and especially polkas are danced in Podhale has very little in common with how these social dances are danced by Polish Americans and other Eastern and Central European immigrants and their descendants in America, as described by Charles and Angeliki Keil in *Polka Happiness* (1992). In America polka dancers move around the dance floor in a counterclockwise direction, sometimes with large, energetic steps. Similarly ballroom waltzes move rapidly around the dance floor counterclockwise with relatively large spinning steps. In Podhale, on the other hand, each couple is an independent unit dancing in place, moving about the dance floor at will, or alternating between stationary dancing and bursts of movement about the floor. There is no dominant direction of movement around the floor, as there is in many ballroom-derived dance traditions. In Podhale the dance steps are small, especially compared to ballroom waltzes. The eloquent and almost delicate style in which Górale dance polkas and waltzes contrasts dramatically with the vigorous footwork of male dancers for the *góralski* and *zbójnicki* dances.

Experiencing Redykołka

My own experiences in Redykołka were many and varied, although probably not typical of tourists who might visit a few times and then move on, nor of the locals who worked in the restaurant or just stopped by on occasion for a drink or a meal. Visiting the establishment over the course of a decade, my stance, role, and identity (Titon 1985) were constantly shifting between tourist, ethnographer, guest, friend, musician, dancer, local, and outsider. These different facets of my identity in Redykołka help me appreciate the place of this restaurant and other tourist restaurants in Podhalan society.

One of my first lessons concerned gendered roles in dance. When first visiting the restaurant as a tourist in 1992, the female dancers, hired to wear Górale costumes and to dance with guests, would ask me to dance during the group couples or social dances just as they would invite other tourists. Since I was not part of a tourist group that had reserved a portion of the restaurant, I suspect that I was singled out because I was the guest of my new friend and Redykołka employee Edward Styrczula-Maśniak. At any rate, I distinctly recall not being allowed to refuse a dance, and being led around the dance floor to a series of waltzes and polkas. In a music-culture where gender roles are clearly defined, everything was on its head. In a *góralski* dance sequence, men choose the women they will dance with, and the women have no real opportunity to refuse. Such gendered roles carry over into non-Górale social dances where a man generally invites a woman to dance, and then leads her in the dance. As an outsider, a foreigner, and someone who spoke rudimentary Polish, the cultural distance between myself and the Górale women, it seems, allowed for more commonly prescribed gender roles to be reversed.

In subsequent years when I was well known to the dancers and

their employer, Krystyna Bochenkowa, they no longer felt obli-
gated to ask me to dance (to treat me like a tourist or guest).
Instead, Krystyna occasionally asked me to join the hired Górale
dancers in inviting the tourists/guests to dance during the social
dances. At one time she even suggested that I don a Górale costume, but for better or worse, no suitable pants were found. She
was more prone to ask me to dance with restaurant guests if they
were English-speaking. This role was for me the most unusual as
I became a bridge between Górale and tourists. When dancing
with English-speaking tourists, they would be curious how I
learned to speak English so well, and when they learned I was
American, their curiosity would shift to what had brought me to
Podhale. These tourists, it seems, had assumed that I was Polish
Górale because I sat with, spoke with, and drank with the Górale
dancers and musicians in the restaurant. I am not ethnic Górale,
nor am I even of Polish heritage, but in Redykołka I "put on"
Górale ethnic identity.[2] I enjoyed playing this role and moving
between identities, some mistaken and some real. The Górale
dancers, on the other hand, did not have this option, at least not
in this setting. They *were* Górale as advertised. They might speak
French, German, or English in addition to Polish and Górale, but
they remained what their costumes suggested. I could not fully
share their identity, and they could not fully share mine.

My occasional role in Redykołka as a violinist also suggested
to the uninitiated that I was Górale. I first played with the house
band one evening after I had been rehearsing with a local song and
dance troupe. I had my violin with me in the restaurant, and Andrzej Karpiel-Replon, the *prymista*, invited me to join in. Local
musicians passing by the restaurant occasionally came in and sat in
with the band for a few numbers, so my appearance with the band,
even without costume, was not unusual. When playing in the band
or joining the Górale dancers in recruiting dance partners from
among the guests, I experienced a certain feeling of ownership of
place. Even though it was a ruse, I felt a bit as if I were *of* this
place—of Podhale. This was amplified by my ability to get by with
my limited violin-playing abilities during the *góralski* dance sequences, yet I had more trouble playing the polkas and waltzes. In
other words, I could play the music specific to Górale and used in
this setting to demonstrate Góraleness, but I could not play with
equal skill the more generic and cosmopolitan music. My American
identity was masked by the lack of physical traits to distinguish me

from Górale, and my behavior suggested to some that I was Górale. Relative to the (other) tourists in the restaurant, I was more of Podhale than they were. I was not, however, of Podhale to the extent of true Górale. I was bridging an identity space—a space that is very important to many Górale—the space that separates Górale from *cepry*. Although we all shared the same physical space, I was inhabiting a unique identity space, unlike the Górale in costume and unlike the other restaurant guests. I was inhabiting a phenomenological space where the reality I experienced was dependent upon the interactions between myself, Górale, and tourists (see Titon 1985, 21).

The liminal space that I occupied in Redykołka offers insights into the relationships between tourists, and Górale dancers and musicians. The economic structure of this relationship is basic. Górale dancers and musicians dance and play for hire. At Redykołka, this means periods of playing and dancing over the course of three-and-a-half to four hours. For musicians like Józef Styrczula-Maśniak this came after a long day working his farm, but there is not much money in small farms and the cash he earned at the restaurant was an important part of his livelihood. At the time, Edward Styrczula-Maśniak earned his living working in the Redykołka tourist bureau during the day and occasionally dancing in the restaurant in the evenings. They, together with the people who run Redykołka, were all Górale who chose to exploit their identity in order to earn a living. They were musicians (and dancers and cooks) for hire.

Being a musician-for-hire is not unusual and is familiar to musicians. In many situations in many societies, being a musician is to be in what is unglamorously called the "service industry." In the service of others (although it may also serve the goals of the musicians), musicians-for-hire play at their employers' or customers' whim, fulfill their desires, and generally accommodate their sense of musically articulated aesthetics. Perhaps this is why some Górale speak disparagingly about music in restaurants. However, simple economics cannot explain what happens when village musicians-for-hire are employed to represent their village, their region, their own ethnicity. Although I have never had a Górale musician tell me that a tourist restaurant is the ideal place to perform or experience muzyka Podhala (that honor is usually given to weddings), the musicians and dancers at Redykołka did exercise great control over their self-representation. In fact, they had more control in restaurants than they did at juried festivals and more than when performing for fusion concerts controlled by non-Górale producers. Just as I controlled how I represented myself and was perceived by others at Redykołka, the Górale dancers, musicians, restaurateurs, waiters, and cooks, cooked up, served up, danced up, and played up an image of Górale that they chose to present to tourists. Of course, their choices were mediated by an imperative to give the tourists what they wanted and expected, but this is the very image of Podhale and Górale negotiated between Górale and others since the nineteenth century. And clearly the music, costume, and dance are different today because of touristic interest, but Dr. Chałubiński is no longer needed to tell the musicians how to play the *basy* parts (Kleczyński 1888, 53; see chapter 3 in this book); Górale do that themselves. And they also exercise great control over individuals among the tourists. I experienced this when I first went to Redykołka and was asked to dance. I suppose I could have refused, but it would have taken some effort. Górale controlled the space; I was in their space. When I later took on some of the identity of a Górale, I felt that sense of control from the other side when I invited restaurant guests to dance. Beware of the hired help; they forever want to do things their own way.

Yet control does not necessarily mean that the Górale at Redykołka present the optimum image of Góraleness for tourists to consume. Józef Styrczula-Maśniak told me that he played differently for tourists than he did at weddings. At Górale weddings the clientele understood the traditional style of playing but tourists did not, and he played to be understood (Fieldnotes IV, 1992, 24). Even in subsequent conversations I was never able to satisfy my desire to know what exactly was different about the way he played at the restaurant and at weddings, other than the suggestion that the dancers in the restaurant sometimes dance the wrong steps to particular tunes. Weddings tend to be the mean by which Górale measure other music-events in Podhale, but my analyses show that, at the Redykołka and at weddings, the repertoire performed is essentially the same, with the exception that the *zbójnicki* is not danced at weddings. The repertoire played at Redykołka, I find, also compares favorably to the festival performances considered earlier. The main difference is the high-profile presence of polkas, waltzes, and other non–muzyka Podhala social dance forms. Polkas are performed on festival stages, but they are relatively rare, and rarer still are waltzes, tangos, and two-steps. In Redykołka the majority of the music was non–muzyka Podhala group dances. Not only do they make up the majority of the dances played but each waltz/polka set is also longer, lasting about ten minutes, when the *góralski* sequences were only five to seven minutes on average. But these proportions are roughly equivalent to what the proportions are at weddings. It is not the repertoire that distinguishes weddings from restaurants.

It is true that the performers in restaurants for tourists can sometimes be loose with their interpretation of Górale music and dance, but it is also true that exceptionally good dancing and playing does happen at Redykołka on occasion. One such occasion was 14 November 1994. I wrote in my field journal when I arrived home in the early hours of the morning that the music that night was for the tourist group but was played from the heart as well. A spirit of joy in the music and dance pervaded the *góralski* and *zbójnicki* sequences. Edward Styrczula-Maśniak, who was one of the hired dancers that evening, agreed that it was a special night and that the music and dance was from the heart, especially for the "demonstration" *góralski* and *zbójnicki* dances. Playing the Redykołka is a job, but the musicians and dancers are also old friends with a love for their shared music-cultural practices. Sometimes, for no apparent reason, doing one's job can become an act of celebration. I wonder if the tourists noticed? At least some of the Górale did notice, and this, together with the internal critique of evenings that are not as fine, suggest that more is at stake here than entertaining and making money.

My interpretation of restaurant performances at Redykołka and the handful of other regional-style restaurants in Zakopane and Kościelisko is that the repertoire performed is a fair representation by Górale of Górale music of the late twentieth and early twenty-first centuries. Muzyka Podhala is a specialized portion of that repertoire but not its limits. Just as the styles of music and dance that make up muzyka Podhala were carried to Podhale by migrant workers and settlers from many directions and from as far away as the Balkans, it is also true that polkas, waltzes, reggae, rock, hip-hop, and other musics are carried to Podhale by radio, television, and recordings, by tourists, and by Górale who travel outside Podhale for employment and pleasure. Górale, then, play polkas and waltzes for the next wave of visitors who do not know how to dance *góralski* but who have the desire and social need to dance nonetheless. Górale give back to tourists what tourists have, in part, given to them: new forms of social dance. Whereas the *góralski* and *zbójnicki* dances clearly separate the performers (Górale) from the audience (*cepry*), the group dances bring the two groups together in space, music, and movement. Finally, the mix of muzyka Podhala with polkas and other social dances represents more faithfully what Górale musicians play for themselves at weddings, name-day parties, impromptu gatherings, and so on, than does the exclusive presentation of muzyka Podhala featured on the festival stage. The one exception to this is the Górale funeral, a particular semipublic performance event which I consider in the following chapter. The tourists at Redykołka are experiencing Górale music-culture even when they may think they are just dancing a polka.

7

Back to the Village

About 1:30 A.M., 16 January 1995, on Gubałówka Mountain above Zakopane. *For two consecutive nights I have been at the restaurant on this mountain ridge documenting the wedding of Katarzyna Słodyczka and Adam Lassak. This is a traditional Górale-style wedding complete with musicians to accompany all aspects of the ritual. The festivities have been blessed with crisp, cold weather and deep snow, brightened by the sun during the day and the full moon at night. Several horse-drawn sleighs taxied the wedding party, including musicians, between the chapel and banquet hall. A perfect winter wedding in the Tatras.*

On this, the second night of the wedding festivities, I have videotaped some exceptionally energetic dancing po góralsku *by a man who appears to be in his late twenties. As I prepare to leave the party I compliment the gentleman on his dancing and ask him where he gained his skill, expecting a reference to deep family roots in Górale tradition or to a father or grandfather who loved to dance. I am caught off guard, however, when instead he refers me to a* zespół *(song and dance troupe) named after Klimens Bachleda. There I can learn everything about Górale dance, he informs me.*

Weddings and Funerals

One reason that I remember this brief encounter with Jan Gutt, the skilled dancer in the Górale tradition, is the way he directed my attention away from the nostalgic and toward the obvious with a simple reference to a *zespół*, a song and dance troupe. He reminded me that while weddings may bring one back to the village—off the festival stage, away from "worldbeat" fusions, out of the tourist restaurant—one carries a bit of the festival, the experience with the world encouraged by fusions, and some notions of service and entertainment perfected in restaurants back into that village. One always brings souvenirs of one's travels home to the village. Folklore festivals return to the village in the form of the song and dance troupes that taught the generation now being married how to dance *po góralsku*. Muzyka Podhala and dance *po góralsku* mark the wedding as Górale, but most of the time on the dance floor is given over to more cosmopolitan dances such as foxtrots (United States), tangos (Argentina), polkas (Czech Republic), and waltzes (Austria). Finally, restaurant culture finds its way into weddings as they move out of the home and into public spaces, such as the wedding considered in detail below, which happened to take place in a tourist restaurant. I may have been blinded by nostalgia, and nostalgia is an important player at weddings and other village rituals, but Jan Gutt reminded me that nostalgia requires a modern world in which to reside.

That mid-January wedding was a nostalgic event in many ways: the bride, groom, and their parties wore traditional Górale costumes, as did many of the guests; Górale musicians were on hand to accompany every event in the wedding sequence; fine horses with specially adorned harnesses drew sleighs over the packed, deep snow. In one sense this wedding was a conscious nostalgic act reminiscent of (imagined) weddings of a bygone era. But in another sense this was a thoroughly modern affair that drew on the past for symbolic power and relied on the present to make it all happen. The same musicians who accompanied the bridal party in their own horse-drawn sleigh as they traveled between chapel and banquet hall later played into microphones to ensure they would be heard for the dances. During a section of the ceremony when guests present the newlyweds with gifts, traditional items like bread and vodka were exchanged, as was an automatic electric laundry machine. In the evenings the horse-drawn sleighs were replaced by automobiles. Future nostalgic trips back to this wedding were guaranteed by the smattering of video and still cameras at every turn. The archaic and the modern mixed freely.

The context—ancient and modern props—repeated in the content. Yes, fine *góralski* dancing took place at this wedding just as I imagine it did at the weddings of this young couple's grandparents, but we also danced the same cosmopolitan couples' dances found around the European inflected world. And as dancer Jan Gutt reminded me, even one of the most traditional activities of the wedding celebration, the *góralski* dancing, is now most often learned in the relatively modern institution of song and dance troupes. The slippery concepts (even ideologies) of ancient and modern, of tradition and modernity, are concepts about time. Tradition encodes a cyclical conception of time, modernity a linear conception. Life-cycle rituals mark a change in time for individuals but within the context of an unending cycle, thus obtaining "timelessness" (for a critique of this anthropological trope, see Borneman 1996, 220). Modernity is a moment on a linear projection—the present is valued and the return to something past is considered a regression, or at best a parody. Weddings, like all rituals, are also about time. They are rituals of hope for the future grounded in the past.

At every turn, weddings are distillations of deeply held ideas about identities, localities, histories, and the present. Better yet for scholars of cultural practices, these ideas are *performed* at weddings, enacted on a series of community stages for the community, by the community. So potent is the distillation of meaning in weddings that ersatz weddings are an intoxicating staple on festival stages—in my estimation performances by the community, about the community, for the community, *and* for outsiders. So evocative is the symbolic power of the wedding that the International Festival of Mountain Folklore in Zakopane opens each year with a contest of *pytace* (askers, announcers, criers) followed by a staged wedding including a procession of the wedding party led by *pytace* along Krupówki Street in Zakopane. Later the *pytace* return and lead not a bride and groom through the village but, instead, all the song and dance troupes featured at the festival that year (figs. 7.1 and 7.2). Weddings in festivals; festivals in weddings.

The second return to the village considered in this chapter is funerals. Funerals pose an emotional contrast to weddings, and yet they share much in common with weddings. Both are rituals that dramatically transform individuals from one state of existence into

Figure 7.1. *Pytace* leading festival participants along Krupówki Street in Zakopane, 1992.

Figure 7.2. *Pytace* Stanisław Krupa and Jan Krzeptowski-Sabata leading a wedding procession, Olcza, 1995.

another: from the realm of maidens to matrons, of bachelors to husbands, of the living to the dead. Challenging my claim of the emotional contrast of weddings and funerals, but strengthening their ties, is the tradition of wedding laments found in many parts of Eastern and Central Europe (Alexiou ca. 1974; Čiurlionytė 1980, 373; Holst-Warhaft 1992; Kaufman 1988; Lloyd 1980, 309; Nevskaia 1993; Tolbert 1988; Warner 1990, 38–41). However, wedding laments and funeral laments are conspicuously absent in Podhale. Both rituals also involve highly stylized movements between the private and public realms—between the home and the Church, for example—and both require the ritualized extraction of individuals from their homes. Movement between ritualized spaces (home, church, cemetery, reception or banquet hall) is most often accomplished with a procession through the village. These processions constitute the most public performances at funerals and weddings. Processions begin and end in enclosed ritual spaces that encircle a subgroup within the village community—self-selected in the case of funerals but selected via invitation at weddings.

The performative qualities of funerals and weddings are what draw me to consider these life-cycle rituals side by side, for both are occasions in which people break from their daily routines and literally or imaginatively return to the village to perform ideas about what is most meaningful to them as individuals, family, and community. They are heightened moments of social negotiation: a Górale wedding negotiates and constructs meanings between two individuals, between two families, and between community and Church; a Górale funeral emphasizes the negotiations between family and their deceased, and between community and Church. Weddings and funerals are ritual performances about the things held most dear to those involved, and I propose that the music performed at these events reveals much about how people may conceive of themselves. Funerals and weddings are a deliberate return to the village and to classic notions of ritual as active recreations of the communal self.

A thorough study of the construction, negotiation, and maintenance of identities, genders, and so on, at weddings and funerals in Podhale could easily fill a book or two (for examples from different communities, see Sugarman 1997; Kligman 1988). Here my interest is simultaneously more general and specific. I am interested in how music is used at weddings and funerals as self-representations and as community representations by the actors involved. Specifically I am interested in how they enact and construct representations of Górale ethnicity. I am less concerned about constructions of, for example, genders and gender relationships (an important feature of weddings) or the expression of mystical beliefs (an important feature of funerals). Here my concern is the performative representation of self and community as compared to the other performance practices in Podhale presented in this book.

Weddings and Ritual Nostalgia

What better place to indulge a "romance with one's own fantasy," one of the ways Boym (2001, xiii) defines nostalgia, than at a wedding. I accept Boym's argument that nostalgia is a condition of modernity and of radically new ways of engaging with notions of the past. Weddings, like most rituals, tend toward the "traditional" by which I mean cultural practices that deliberately attempt to repeat old cultural practices. This helps to explain the great care given to symbolic objects and gestures that are meaningful in the context of the wedding but that may lose meaning beyond that context. For example, what place does modern obstetrics leave for the symbols of fertility that abound in wedding rituals? Would those young people who chose a "traditional" Górale wedding opt to continue getting about the village via horse and carriage the week after their marriage? Why does the bride, who has her beauty symbolically covered with a headscarf during the wedding, continue to show herself in public without a head covering after the wedding? Exemplifying Boym's description of modern nostalgia as "a mourning for the impossibility of mythical return, for the loss of an enchanted world with clear borders and values" (8), Górale weddings lack the laments familiar in other European folk practices but nonetheless are a joyful lament for archaic lifeways. Instead of ritually ensuring fertility, the bride's virginity, and the couple's prosperity, might late-twentieth-century Górale weddings ritually ensure the continuation of Górale ethnicity with all its attendant cultural practices? In this way weddings accomplish for the village what folkloric festivals accomplish for an extended, even global, conception of place.

In a gesture that illustrates Kirshenblatt-Gimblett's (1995) theorizing of heritage, one's first encounter with a Górale wedding is likely to be a printed invitation that simultaneously promises a wedding in the future while referencing weddings of the past. Printed on special white card stock, folded once to create a single folio, the invitation to Katarzyna Słodyczka and Adam Lassak's wedding contained the following:

On the front side, a line drawing of *pytace* on horses with the following dialect verse in the lower right corner:

Otwiyrojcie wrota	Open the gate
nasi przyjociele,	our friends,
przyśli my Wos pytać	we came to invite you
Przydźcie na wesele.	come to the wedding.

On the left-hand side of the opened card, the verse continues:

A kiedy wybije	And when
—godzina	—our hour rings
przydzie nom cało	our entire family
na nas ślub rodzina.	will come to our wedding.
Momy gorzałecki	We have spirits
dwie becki kopiate	two barrels heaped with
piecone indyki	baked turkey
i kury cubate.	and crested chicken.
Bedziemy sie ciesyć	We will rejoice
mocno przycupkować	wildly dance
muzyka Tutków	the Tutki band
bedzie nom przygrywać	will play for us
Pytomy Was piknie	We ask you dearly
przydźcie na wesele	come to our wedding
Bedziemy Wos witać	we will welcome you
w Gubałowskim siele.	in the hamlet of Gubałówka.

And on the right-hand side of the open folio:

Katarzyna Słodyczka	Katarzyna Słodyczka
i	and
Adam Lassak	Adam Lassak
Barzo Piyknie Pytomy, przydźcie na nas Ślub	We very warmly ask you, come to our wedding
dnia 14 stycznia 1995 o godz.1300	on the day of 14 January 1995 at 13:00

do kościółka na Gubałówce	at the church on Gubałówka
i na wesele, a bedzie ono	and to the celebration, which will be
w Restauracyji na Gubałówce.	in the restaurant on Gubałówka.
—*Ojcowie i Młodzi*	—Parents and the Young Couple

On the back cover is an additional line drawing of *pytace* on horses leading the bride and groom who are riding in a sleigh pulled by two horses.

According to descriptions of Górale weddings provided to me personally by Górale and found in published descriptions (Szurmiak-Bogucka 1974, 19–22; Gutt-Mostowy 1998, 78), the *pytace*, two young men hired for their strong voices and horse-riding skills, would publicly announce the wedding and personally deliver oral invitations on horseback several weeks before the wedding (see fig. 7.2). The *pytace* deliver their information with a formalized series of songs and speeches. In my experience with Górale weddings in Chicago and in Podhale, printed invitations such as the one reproduced above replace the first duty of the *pytace:* to personally invite guests to the wedding in song. However, the invitations are still delivered personally by the young couple. As Stanisława Trebunia-Staszel stated succinctly when writing to me about this custom, "one should give, not send, the invitation." The *pytace* are nevertheless rendered iconographically on the invitations. Printed invitations are therefore a material break with ideal traditional wedding practices and a concession to modern conventions ushered in by nearly universal literacy, yet they mark the wedding as "traditional" by nostalgically evoking what the invitation is not (not *pytace* singing while riding horses but instead words printed on paper). The above invitation is also marked as "Górale" with the use of dialect (the pronoun *Wos* [you, plural] instead of *Was*, for example). For the Gubałówka wedding of Katarzyna and Adam, the representation of *pytace* on the invitations can be seen as accurate advertising since *pytace* on horses did lead the several wedding processions (described below). The printed invitations for the wedding of Halina Maciata and Thomasz Lassak in Chicago in September 1993 were more overtly nostalgic. The front of the invitation featured a line drawing of *pytace* singing on horses leading the bride and groom pulled through the snow in a sleigh (fig. 7.3). *Pytace* did fulfill some of the traditional ceremonial roles at their wedding, but understandably absent on that summer day in the near south side of urban Chicago were horses, sleigh, and snow.

Figure 7.3. Front of the wedding invitation of Halina Maciata and Tomasz Lassak, Chicago, 1993.

These wedding invitations reference an ideal model, in this case based on a fairly fixed notion of what a traditional Górale wedding is, and they embody the first adjustment to that model in order to accommodate the realities of the times and the desires of those immediately involved. In Podhale and elsewhere where Górale live in critical numbers, one ideal with which to begin is what has been described to me as a "traditional," "old-fashioned," or simply "Górale" wedding. Based on my interviews with individual Górale, Gutt-Mostowy's (1998, 77–81) brief description of Górale weddings, and Szurmiak-Bogucka's (1974) short but authoritative book *Wesele Góralskie* (Górale wedding celebration), I summarize the many stages of such an ideal Górale wedding as follows (cf. Noll 1991, 360):

1. *Pytace* with groomsmen and bridesmaids gather at the groom's house, eventually traveling with the groom and his parents and relatives to the bride's house.
2. At the bride's house the bride is dressed by the wedding hostesses in a white dress decorated with myrtle. The bride also presents the groom with a new shirt. Following the dressing of the bride and groom, both kneel for a blessing by the wed-

ding host, a senior male usually related to the bride or groom. This is accompanied by solemn music played by a Górale string band.

3. Wedding mass at a church is preceded by a procession to the church, led by singing *pytace* on horses and followed by the wedding party in horse-drawn carriages or sleighs. Provided with their own large carriage or sleigh, the musicians play music during the procession.

4. Procession back to the bride's house, led by singing *pytace*. The procession is halted by one or more "gates" erected by local villagers posing as "Gypsies" who demand a ransom. *Pytace* sing, and the band plays. At the door to the bride's house, the bride and groom are presented with bread and salt. All are greeted with music, provided by the string band, as they enter the house.

5. *Wesele* proper, or celebration, including copious amounts of food, special homemade wedding vodka, music, and dancing.

6. *Cepowiny*, an elaborate capping ceremony late in the evening when the bride's garland (a symbol of maidenhood and virginity) is replaced by a scarf (a symbol of a married woman).

Wedding on Gubałówka Mountain: A Case Study

On the fourteenth and fifteenth of January 1995 I had the pleasure of attending and documenting the wedding of Katarzyna Słodyczka and Adam Lassak by virtue of the fact that the Maśniak family with whom I was living was invited. My immediate experience with the wedding began with stage 2, the gathering at the bride's house. This was the first public phase of the wedding now that publicly performed announcements by the *pytace* have been largely replaced by printed invitations delivered by the young couple (Andrzej Tokarz and Stanisława Trebunia-Staszel, personal communication). If printed invitations are the first accommodation of tradition to modernity, the second is the replacing of the bride's house with a relatively large public meeting place for stages 4 through 6 and sometimes stage 2 as well. This was the case for the Słodyczka and Lassak wedding, for which a large restaurant on top of Gubałówka Mountain overlooking Zakopane served as the location of all the wedding ceremonies traditionally associated with the bride's house.

The band arrived at the restaurant before noon and serenaded the bride, her family and party, and guests as they prepared for the arrival of the groom and his party. In this case the band was led by Władysław Trebunia-Tutka (already known to readers of this book), as promised in the wedding invitation, and consisted of the typical instruments (three violins and a *basy*) with the somewhat unusual addition of an accordion, and later a double-bass and an electric guitar. Although I did not record all the music played at this second stage of the wedding, nor during the arrival of the groom, I recall that the tunes were typically *wierchowe* and marches, including "Marsz Madziarski" (see fig. 1.17). When the groom and his party arrived just past noon, the band was positioned outside, next to the door where they serenaded the wedding party and guests as they entered. Supplementing any fee the band may have received from the families of the bride and groom, many individuals slipped money into an f-hole of the *basy* as they filed by.[1]

After the bride and groom were publicly and ceremonially dressed in their wedding best, the band played and sang another *wierchowa* or two while all gathered for the solemn blessing of and charge to the young couple by the wedding host, in this case the local scholar and author Jan Gutt-Mostowy (see Gutt-Mostowy 1998). Even here the modern world asserted itself when Gutt-Mostowy relayed salutations from Chicago. After the blessing, as the parents of the young couple kissed the bride and groom, the band led in the singing of a hymn, followed immediately by the *pytace* singing a special wedding song with a *wierchowa*-like melody (fig. 7.4, CD track 37). Then as the wedding party and guests began to leave and move toward the church, the *pytace*, Andrzej Słodyczka and Stanisław Lasak, accompanied by the band, sang a song with a tune called "wybodną" (see Szurmiak-Bogucka 1974, 44, for a version of this same song and tune).

The wedding party proceeded to the church (stage 3) in horse-drawn sleighs, led by the *pytace* riding horses and singing (same tune as that shown in fig. 7.4). The band played while riding together in a single sleigh that followed the two sleighs carrying, respectively, the bride and groomsmen, and the groom with the bridesmaids. Behind the band, several additional sleighs ferried members of the immediate family while the rest of us followed on foot. In this case the chapel was a short distance away, about three-quarters of a kilometer along the mountain ridge. When I arrived at the chapel (at about 1:00 P.M.) the band was greeting people outside, playing a six-bar *Czorsztyńska* (see Mierczyński 1930, #10). Inside the chapel and accompanied by an organ, the wedding guests

Figure 7.4. *Pytace* song (v14.i.95.1). *CD track 37*

sang hymns, *kolędy* (carols), and other church music. At one point, during communion, the Górale band played a *kolęda* while the congregation sang. At a different wedding that I documented in Podhale (v25.ii.95.1–2), the organist played her own arrangements of a few Górale tunes, and friends of the bride and groom sang a *wierchowa* with texts appropriate for the wedding mass. For the most part, however, the music in the church or chapel is Roman Catholic liturgical music with no particular connection to Podhale or Górale.

Outside the chapel just past 2:00 P.M. Trebunia-Tutka and his band played *wierchowe* as the wedding party returned to their sleighs and the *pytace* mounted their horses for stage 4, the procession back to the restaurant (again symbolically representing the bride's house). As the procession formed, the *pytace*, joined by the band members and others, sang, again using the same tune represented in figure 7.4 (*nuta* 1). This time the bride and groom rode together on the first sleigh pulled by white horses (all other horses in the procession were dark), followed immediately by the band. Between the chapel and the restaurant the procession was stopped by two "gates" with presumably local villagers posing as "Gypsies" who demanded payment in vodka and other gifts before they would allow the party to pass. The *pytace* commented on the situation with a *wierchowa*, using a variation of the first *nuta* shown in figure 7.4.

The fifth stage of the wedding was the feast with merrymaking, including singing and dancing. This part of the wedding is called the *wesele*, related to the adjective *wesoły* (joyful, cheerful, mirthful), the term is also used to refer to the wedding as a whole. It is not unusual for a *wesele* to last for several days, with breaks from the early morning to late afternoon. The Słodyczka and Lassak wedding went for two days at the Gubałówka restaurant with literally hours of music. The music for this extended stage of the wedding began with the *pytace* and band serenading the bride, groom, family, and guests as they once again entered the restaurant.

Just past 3:30 P.M., the dancing began when a man called a *góralski* dance. The *góralski* sequence was followed by a waltz to which several couples dance. During the group dances the *basy* was often replaced by a double-bass, and Anna Trebunia-Tutka would sometimes trade her violin for an electric guitar. As it did throughout the wedding, the accordion played for muzyka Podhala and for the group dances. Moving from *góralski* dance sequences, with primarily one man dancing with one woman, to group dances consisting, for the most part, of polkas, waltzes, fox-trots, and csárdáses, the band played with only short breaks for two nights running. I recorded approximately five hours of video at the wedding and enjoyed many more hours without running the camera. My observations are that dance floor usage was roughly equivalent to that at the tourist restaurant Redykołka considered in chapter 6, with the exception that no *zbójnicki* dances were danced at the wedding. A different yet nonconflicting way to interpret the use of the dance floor is to consider the negotiated balance of group social dances and *góralski* dances at weddings. Group dances are desired and needed because they provide all who are present the opportunity to dance. The *góralski* sequences, on the other hand, had a certain focused intensity, directing the attentions of all those assembled toward the dance space, toward the band and the music, and toward seeing who was dancing with whom and how they were dancing. In other words, although the *góralski* dance sequences demanded much less time during the *wesele*, they exerted much greater power in defining the event and the individuals for whom the event was staged.

Co wy starościny jesce tu robicie,   Hostesses what are you still doing here,
Co naśą rózycke [jesce] nie cepicie?   That our little rose you do not "cap"?

Figure 7.5. *Cepowiny: pytace* song beginning the *cepowiny* (v14.i.95.2). *CD track 38*

The central moment of the wedding celebration, however, began a few minutes past 9:00 P.M. when the *pytace* approached the
band and called for a dance *po góralsku*, at which time one of the
men turned the bride out to the dance floor and the other proceeded to dance two *ozwodne* with her. This was followed immediately by two krakowiak-like songs sung by the *pytace* while dancing together with the bride, one on either side (fig. 7.5, CD track
38), thus beginning stage 6 of the wedding: the *cepowiny* or capping
ceremony (also called *oczepiny*). In my conversations with individual
Górale I was told that this ritual is the most significant moment
of a wedding, perhaps even more important than the church ceremony. Defining a single moment as the most important in a wedding celebration that spans hours, even days, is not as helpful as
considering the celebration as a whole, but certainly the *cepowiny*
is invested with great symbolic weight. Descriptions of the capping
ceremony in the literature are fundamentally consistent with the

weddings I experienced and documented, including the wedding on Gubałówka Mountain.

The bride is the center of attention during the Górale *cepowiny*, not unlike other wedding practices in Central Europe, and it has been interpreted as a reflection of the fact that the bride bears the brunt of social transformation brought on by marriage. Her virginity is celebrated, not the groom's, presumably because it is her purity that guarantees the family's honor and the family name. Around the bride, social norms and values are reified in the symbolic language and gestures of the wedding (Kligman 1988, 74–76). Accordingly this central ritual publicly enacts the bride's transformation from a maiden (in the company of her maidenly friends and potential male suitors) into a wife (in the company of matrons and removed from the ranks of young women whom a young man may pursue). The most symbolic moment of the ritual is the replacing of the bride's wreath or garland with a headscarf.

Emphasizing the centrality of the bride, the groom has no active role in the *cepowiny* until the very end. Yet some symbolic parity is achieved when the groom's headgear, before he is allowed to dance with the bride, is also altered, although in a much abbreviated sequence of negotiations.[2] Whereas the bride's wreath is replaced with a headscarf, the groom's hat loses its feather, a symbol of the man's freedom (and phallus, individual Górale have suggested to me), which is presented to the wedding hostesses. However, in the weddings I have documented, there is little consistency in how a groom's hat and feather are treated, suggesting that such practices are not essential to the success of the ritual.

The wedding on Gubałówka illustrates the key components of the *cepowiny* ritual. Once the *cepowiny* began, the *pytace* continued dancing and singing with the bride between them, performing couplets about their unwillingness to surrender the bride to the wedding hostesses who represent married women. The wedding hostesses responded with sung couplets offering gifts in exchange for the bride. The content of the songs was jocular and teasing, and rife with double entendre. When not singing, the *pytace* and bride formed a basket circle, arms at one another's waists or shoulders, and danced with a polka step as the band continued playing variations on the same set of *nuty* that was used by the *pytace* and wedding hostesses to sing their couplets.

Almost the entire *cepowiny* was performed to four krakowiak-

type *nuty*, and these same *nuty* were used for the *cepowiny* at every
Górale wedding I have documented. The *pytace* most often sang to
the *nuta* represented in figure 7.5 (CD tracks 38 and 39) and occasionally to the *nuta* in figure 7.7 (CD track 41). The wedding
hostesses also used the *nuta* in figure 7.5 but also employed the
nuta represented in figure 7.6, and occasionally added versions of
the *nuta* represented in figure 1.20 in chapter 1. Below is a transcription of a brief section of the *cepowiny* from the wedding on
Gubałówka indicating which *nuta* was used for each couplet. This
sequence of couplets can be heard on the CD tracks 39–44. Versions of these same tunes were documented by Szurmiak-Bogucka
in 1974, and three were transcribed by Mierczyński (1930, nos. 65,
66, 67) in the early part of the twentieth century. However, wedding tunes from Podhale documented in the nineteenth century
by Gołaszcziński (1851) and Kolberg (1968b) are no longer used,
suggesting that the current wedding repertoire was established only
in the late nineteenth or early twentieth century.

The following sequence of sung exchanges between the *pytace*
(Andrzej Słodyczka and Stanisław Lasak) and hostesses (Anna Gąsienica-Roj, and Helios and Maria Stopka) at the wedding on
Gubałówka is representative of the current repertoire and of the
nature of the poetic content of *cepowiny* couplets. The sample begins with the *pytace* singing to the hostesses (CD track 39), using
a version of the *nuta* represented in figure 7.5:

Nase starościny maja pikne cycki,	Our hostesses have fine boobs,
Bo se z oscypkami chodzą do Wielicki.	Because they take the sheep's cheese to Wieliczka.

After the *pytace* finish singing, the band continues playing the same
tune while the *pytace* dance with the bride, and the hostesses con-
sult one another before singing the following reply to a different
nuta (fig. 7.6, CD track 40):

Nasi starostowie śpiewać nie umieją	Our hosts do not know how to sing
Bo sie w nase cycki głuptoki wpieprzają.	Because these fools reach for our boobs.

The *pytace* reply immediately with this demand for sausages in
exchange for the bride, sung to yet a different *nuta* (fig. 7.7, CD
track 41):

Ej nie wydom młodej pani,	I will not give the bride away,
Ej nie wydom, nie wydom,	I will not, I will not
Poki nase starościny	Until our hostesses
Z kiełbasecom nie przy- dom.	Come here with little sausages.

The hostesses give the *pytace* both sausages and sheep's cheese, but after a few moments the *pytace* demand wine as well with the following couplet (CD track 42) sung to a variation of the *nuta* represented in figure 7.6:

Ej nie wydom młodej pani,	I will not give the bride away,
Ej nie wydom, nie wydom,	I will not, I will not,
Poki starse starościny	Until the elder hostesses
Z wineckiem nie przydom.	Come here with wine.

The hostesses respond, using a variation of the *nuta* represented in figure 1.20 (CD track 43, the beginning of the hostesses' singing is not audible on this recording):

_____?	_____?
Hej pijcie wode, pijcie wode,	Hey, drink water, drink water,
Zeby . . . aby woda nie starcyła.	What's wrong with you that water is not enough?

They then give the *pytace* a bottle of sweet red wine. The *pytace* drink from the bottle and offer some to the bride who declines. The band plays a medley of several *cepowiny nute* while the *pytace* dance with the bride and eventually make a request for an orange, a traditionally rare fruit in the inclement Tatras (CD track 44, the *nuta* is the same as in fig. 7.7):

Ej nie wydom młodej pani,	I will not give the bride away,
Ej nie wydom, nie wydom	I will not, I will not,
Poki nase starościny	Until our hostesses
Z pomarancem nie psy- dom.	Come here with an orange.

After nearly half an hour of exchanges similar to those sampled above, the women succeeded in winning the bride from the *pytace*. Then they sat her on a chair, took the two meter-long broad, white ribbons decorated with myrtle and fern, all part of her wreath, wrapped them around her hair bun, and covered it all with a scarf. At other weddings that I attended, the wreath was removed from the bride's head before the scarf was tied. At one wedding that I

Figure 7.6. *Cepowiny:* hostesses singing to the *pytace* (v14.i.95.2). *CD track 40*

documented in Chicago, the wreath itself was simply wrapped around the bride's hair bun and pinned in place. No headscarf was employed. At the Gubałówka wedding, as at others I have documented, once the bride was "capped" the wedding hostesses sat on chairs placed on the dance floor and prepared to receive gifts for the bride and groom. What followed was a series of group and individual dances with the bride, beginning with the bridesmaids who sing farewell to the bride, noting that she has her man and now they must go and find theirs. They were followed by the groomsmen, and then guests, generally starting with family members. After singing and dancing with the bride, each individual embraced her and kissed her on the cheeks before presenting their gifts to the wedding hostesses. Immediately after giving their gifts, each guest was offered a shot of wedding vodka and a piece of sheep's cheese or sausage. At the Gubałówka wedding, this exchange of greetings and gifts went on for an hour, all accompanied by music.

Figure 7.7. *Cepowiny: pytace* singing to the hostesses (v14.i.95.2). *CD track 41*

In general, guests sang and danced to the same special four *cepowiny* tunes introduced above, but I noted at this wedding and at others that additional *nuty* were occasionally inserted, including a song using a *Janosikowa nuta* and *wierchowe*, some of them the same *nuty* that I documented at funerals, described below. At this particular wedding, some family members were from Slovakia, and they sang *wierchowe* for the bride that were closely related to Podhalan *wierchowe*, except that the band accompanied them with a double-pulse *düvö* style associated with Carpathian regions to the south.

The groom was not actively involved in the *cepowiny* ritual until about 10:30 P.M. When he appeared, he was greeted by the bridesmaids who then reformed a semicircle and danced with the bride, one of them holding the groom's hat adorned with a long eagle feather. After about five minutes of exchanges sung between the bridesmaids and groom, during which time he tried to buy his hat back, the groom simply grabbed his hat away while the bridesmaids were dancing. The bridesmaids, however, retained the long feather from his hat and thus achieved a symbolic alteration of his head-dress parallel to the bride's. After regaining his de-feathered cap, the groom called a dance *po góralsku* and danced a *góralski* sequence with the bride, signaling the end of the *cepowiny* and effectively the completion of the wedding, although the *wesele* continued for another day or two.

In all, the band played for about ninety minutes with only very brief pauses and only exceptionally varying from the four *cepowiny nuty*. The *cepowiny* was the longest single ritual event within the various wedding stages; the church ritual, for example, lasted only about one hour. And, of course, the *cepowiny* was preceded and succeeded by hours of social dancing. Weddings are indeed an excellent place to experience muzyka Podhala and more.

Weddings and the Musical Return to the Village

One quality of nostalgia is a longing for that which is unattainable. Although the village does not exist where everyone dresses in costumes that identify them as Górale from Podhale, where everyone speaks in a dialect heard as Górale, dances with steps and to tunes recognized as Górale, and drinks wedding vodka made from recipes guarded by Górale (one can never actually return to the village of one's nostalgic longings), the sense of identity and Górale ethnicity ritually enacted at weddings does exist. It exists in the performed reification of social norms and values that constitute a wedding ceremony. One can claim, then, that the village as an idea does exist in the act of performing the village. Perhaps for a moment one can return to the location of one's nostalgic longings after all.

The villages imagined in weddings such as the one considered above are Górale villages. Processions through the community, the village, are essential displays of this Górale identity. The wedding mass in a church or chapel displays and reifies these norms and values before God and gathered community, and the procession back to the bride's house (or banquet hall/restaurant) confirms Góraleness as the norm by means of contrast with the ersatz "Gypsies" who block their passage with gates and demand bribes. The most intimate transformation of social and sexual relationships is enacted during the *cepowiny* ritual during which the bride moves away from the company of maidens to the company of matrons. This is played out almost entirely between the bride and her community, with the bride's and groom's immediate family having no prominent role. Perhaps the assurance of the survival of Górale identity overshadows the survival of, for example, the Słodyczka or the Lassak family name.

A basic premise of many ethnomusicological theories is that the music people engage in and create informs us about their identity. A wedding may be the best place to experience real Górale music, but the experience of "Górale music" encountered at weddings is complex. Take the *cepowiny* ritual, for example, a heightened moment during the long first day of the wedding celebration. The capping ceremony may begin, and certainly will end, with a *góralski* dance sequence—what I have defined as core repertoire— but almost everything in between points beyond Podhale. This central ritual is accompanied by krakowiak-like tunes distinguished from other muzyka Podhala by rhythm and form. After the actual capping of the bride, but during the end of the *cepowiny*, I have documented at several weddings the insertion of *Janosikowa* tunes— tunes that Wrazen (1988, 105) includes in her category of "tunes of foreign origin." Can one express Góraleness with "foreign" tunes and tunes associated with the foothills of Kraków? The music at the church ceremony, also a heightened ritual moment, may employ melodic material considered uniquely Górale, but the poetic content and much of the music is linked with the Roman Catholic Church. The Roman Catholic faith, of course, is an important component to many Górale's self-conception, a substantial connection to a large international body of like-minded believers. Even a majority of the dance music, then, is not *góralski* but dances and music that boast worldwide currency.

Muzyka Podhala does retain prominent places in weddings, however. The entrances to ritual spaces are typically accompanied by a band playing core muzyka Podhala repertoire. The transitional and public processions employ singing by the *pytace* using their characteristic Górale-style tune with its raised fourth scale degree (see fig. 7.4). The band is given a special carriage or sleigh, and they play muzyka Podhala as they process. Further, muzyka Podhala and *góralski* dancing are intense and defining moments of heightened attention at the wedding feasts, even if they do not consume most of the time spent on the dance floor.

If it ever did exist, the isolated mountain village in Podhale no longer exists. As the music Górale play, sing, and dance to confirms, the people of Podhale are also citizens of Poland, Central Europe, and the world. Górale identity is complicated, and one performs Góraleness with competent steps and singing *po góralsku*, not with the inability to dance a polka, waltz, or even a krakowiak.

Funeral in Kościelsko: A Contrasting Case Study?

28 September 1994, Zakopane. *I am taking a break from the funeral of Maria Chałubińska, the granddaughter-in-law of Dr. Tytus Chałubiński. She fell and died in the mountains last week. She was a mountain guide. There are lots of folks here wearing knickers and red sweaters—the outfit of fellow guides. The gist of the sermon was, don't think "poor" Maria; she had a very rich life. (Fieldnotes, 28 September 1994)*

My first experience with a funeral in Poland was a photocopied sign posted at a bus stop in Zakopane. What caught my eye was the name, Maria *Chałubińska*, the feminine form of Chałubiński, the surname of the physician from the nineteenth century introduced at the beginning of this book. It had never occurred to me that his descendants might still populate Podhale; perhaps I would learn something by attending this funeral.

One is not generally invited to a funeral like one is invited to a wedding; instead, word is spread mouth to ear and via public postings, such as the one that caught my attention as I waited for a bus. People do not plan on falling in the mountains and perishing when they set out for a hike. Deaths happen when they do, and the living adjust their schedules around them. While funerals rarely allow the sort of planning invested in weddings, they are nonetheless like weddings in that they are deliberate rituals marking a life-cycle transition. I believe that the spontaneous and profoundly introspective qualities of funerals make them significant places to seek enacted representations of identity symbols. For example, although by this time the Chałubiński family had lived in or been associated with Podhale for more than a century and were highly regarded by Górale, they were not Górale. At Maria Chałubińska's funeral, sartorial symbols connected her to the Tatras (many in attendance wore their mountain guide outfits in solidarity) but not to Górale. I jotted in my fieldnotes that there was no muzyka Podhala, but I could be wrong here since I did not witness the procession to the church nor the graveside service, where I have since learned that muzyka Podhala is played at Górale funerals.

In studies of European music-cultures, laments are an important genre (e.g., Alexiou ca. 1974; Holst-Warhaft 1992; Kaufman 1988; Nevskaia 1993; Suliteanu 1971; Tolbert 1988), but Górale have no special repertoire for mourning—they have no laments. In fact, muzyka Podhala performed at funerals includes some of the same tunes played at other events, including dances. Perhaps for this reason funerals tend to be overlooked in the literature on Górale music-culture. Yet the music at funerals is distinguished by the repertoire it emphasizes, and the types of tunes lacking, rather than by a separate special repertoire. And more significant, muzyka Podhala is a powerful presence in the funeral rites of Górale, at least at the funerals of those who emphasized Góraleness in their lives as an important part of their identities. Like weddings, funerals are moments for family and community to reflect on deeply held beliefs and ideals. Funerals are also the one type of community event in present-day Podhale least mediated by outside pressures unless one considers the Catholic Church to be "outside." I argue, however, that the Church has been incorporated into the local sense of Góraleness for several centuries and that the Church is better considered a gateway to the outside—to the wider world outside Podhale and, for believers, to an afterlife. With that caveat, I propose that funerals are the most inwardly "backstage" events in the community, almost completely oblivious to outside intervention (with the possible exception of the village priest who may or may not be Górale). Funerals are the ultimate return to the village.

The differences inherent in the musical practices of funerals and at other performative events considered in this book are obvious: funeral performances lack the spectacle of festival performances, there are no prizes to win, and they are not intended to entertain and to sell recordings as are worldbeat fusion projects. Of course, funerals and weddings also differ on many key points in addition to their assumed (if problematized) emotional contrast. Whereas staged weddings are a mainstay of festival performances, I have never seen a Górale song and dance troupe enact a funeral onstage. Still, the music I have experienced at funerals is often exquisitely beautiful and would surely move an audience. The differences in how the Górale string-band music is practiced at funerals as opposed to weddings is reflected in how such ensembles are achieved. For a wedding, a band (or two) is hired to play for the enjoyment of all present. In the case of the wedding on Gubałowka Mountain described above, we saw that the band was mentioned by name in the wedding invitations, presumably to promote the grandeur of the celebration and to encourage those invited to attend. In contrast, at a funeral, an ad hoc string band forms on the spot as musicians volunteer their services and talents to pay homage musically to the deceased and his or her family. The ensembles that form at funerals are often musicians who may have never played together before, whereas at weddings the ensembles are usually a more or less distinct group of musicians who frequently play together. But the musical practices specific to weddings and funerals exhibit significant commonalities that warrant consideration. One similarity has already been stressed: both are moments of collective self-reflection and are therefore significant locations for considering the relationships between musical-practice and the self-conceptions of individuals and communities. Another gives structure to the first: both weddings and funerals use muzyka Podhala for specific rites, but clearly marked off from muzyka Podhala at both rituals are significant music events that link participants to the wider world beyond Podhale (and to an afterlife beyond this world, in the case of funerals). I propose, then, a musically articulated divide between ideas about Górale's relationships to things and people beyond Podhale, and sometimes to contrasting ideas about life and people firmly grounded in the local.

To illustrate these points I will describe one of several funerals for old family Górale that I documented in Podhale: the funeral of Józef Karpiel on 1 December 1994. I was asked to videotape this funeral by Wojtech Styrczula-Maśniak, one of the sons from the house where I lived in Kościelisko at the time, and a son-in-law of the deceased. Although I was saddened by the grief experienced by Wojtech, his wife Ewa, and their family, I was pleased to have an opportunity to use my skills and equipment to aid the Styrczula-Maśniak family after they had given so much to me during my continuing residence in Podhale.

This funeral, like the other Górale funerals I documented, consisted of five distinct stages: (1) viewing of the body in the home of the deceased;[3] (2) procession from the home to the church; (3) mass in the church; (4) procession from the church to the cemetery; and (5) graveside eulogies and burial. Muzyka Podhala is played in stages 2 and 5, during the procession and in the cemetery. At one funeral I attended the church was some distance from the cemetery, and the string band also played muzyka Podhala during stage 4 (v18.ii.95). Muzyka Podhala may occur in the church as well, played by a Górale string band or by the church organist or by both. In my musical analysis I focus on the use of muzyka Podhala, with some attention to the specifically religious music that follows the rites of the Roman Catholic Church as locally practiced.

Józef Karpiel's home was in Polana Biały Potok (White stream glade), a remote corner of Kościelisko Village. Many of us who had gathered for the funeral did not enter the house but waited outside on this sunny but bitterly cold day, brightened by a fresh coat of snow. A carriage with two white horses stood in the driveway before the house, and off to one side a row of twelve men in green hunting outfits stood, holding double-barrel shotguns. Mourners began to emerge from the home a little after 1:00 P.M., led by the village priest, the cantor (church organist), and two men in traditional Górale costume bearing a cross and church banner. The priest wore black robes, and the cantor wore a special clerical hat. Four pallbearers in Górale costume with formal brown coats (of the same distinct style as those worn by the *pytace* at weddings) carried the casket from the house and loaded it onto the carriage as the cantor chanted and the riflemen shot off two rounds—a twelve-gun salute. Józef Karpiel was a sportsman, a hunter and skier, and had served in the military. The gunfire salutes by fellow hunters at this funeral were unique among the four that I documented.

When the casket was positioned on the carriage, the procession to the village church began, a trek of about four kilometers on hilly snow and ice-covered roads. The procession was led by the two men in Górale costume walking one behind the other, the first bearing the cross and the second the church banner. They were followed by two of the men with shotguns flanking about six boys carrying wreaths of flowers, and then three men abreast in military uniforms, the center man carrying a Polish flag. Next in the procession were thirteen children and one woman, most with arrangements of flowers, followed by seven Górale musicians, all in costume. The musicians were Stanisław Michałczek, first *prym;* Marek (Maja) Łabunowicz, second *prym;* Stanisław Styrczula-Maśniak, second *prym* and *sekund;* Bronisław Styrczula-Maśniak, *sękund;*

Józef Styrczula-Maśniak, *sekund;* Zdzisław Styrczula-Maśniak, *se-kund;* and Tadeusz Styrczula-Maśniak, *basy.*[4] As is the custom with *basy* players, Tadeusz hung his instrument by a strap over his left shoulder so that it could be played while walking. The musicians were followed by the cantor, the priest, and an acolyte, all three walking side by side, right before the carriage, driven by a man in Górale costume, and with a pallbearer walking at each corner. Following the carriage were members of the immediate family, flanked by several of the men with guns, and finally the remaining mourners.

I counted approximately one hundred mourners, including the priest and his entourage, the three men in military uniforms, and the musicians. About forty-five were women or girls, and about fifty-five men or boys. Twenty of the men were dressed in Górale costume, including the musicians, the pallbearers, the men with the cross and church banner, the carriage driver, and three others. In other words, traditional Górale costumes were worn to the funeral by men with special ceremonial roles, plus a few others. At least ten women were wearing traditional Górale clothing, perhaps more, but it is much more difficult to determine if women are in costume, especially in the winter when long coats conceal clothing.

Music during the procession alternated between three Catholic chants, chanted by the cantor walking before the coffin and some of the mourners walking behind (CD track 45), and muzyka Pod-hala played by the ensemble—never sung (CD track 46). The music played during the procession by the Górale ensemble consisted of *Janosikowe, wierchowe, Duchowe,* and *Sabałowe* (or *staroświeckie*) (see figs. 1.9 and 1.11, for examples of a *Sabałowa* and a *Duchowa* transcribed from my recording of this and another funeral, CD tracks 4 and 5). The unaccompanied chants were all part of the Catholic requiem, calling on God to have mercy and to accept the soul of the deceased into heaven (CD track 45). The chants, clerical robes, cross, and banner were both performed and material proclamations of the mourners' Christian beliefs. The muzyka Podhala together with traditional costumes identified the deceased, his family, and his community as Górale. Additional layers of meaning and identity specific to Józef Karpiel were created by the three men in military uniforms and the men in hunting outfits carrying guns. Thus Karpiel's body journeyed from home to church and then to grave surrounded with sonic and visual symbols of who he was in life: a Roman Catholic, a Górale, a sportsman, and one who served in the military.

The church service was a Catholic requiem mass, with music provided by the same cantor who led the chanting during the procession. The cantor accompanied himself on the church pipe organ, and the congregation sang with him on several hymns. I noted that women and men sang in different octave registers, in contrast to when men and women sing muzyka Podhala, which, with rare exception, is sung in the same register. It is interesting to note that the singing inside the church was the only vocal music during the funeral ritual accompanied by instruments. Chanting inside the home of the deceased (which I did not document at this funeral but did at other Górale funerals in Podhale) and during the processions was all unaccompanied. The Górale string band, on the other hand, was strictly instrumental with no singing, even though the band performed several ballads with relatively well-known texts. After the mass, the assembled processed to the cemetery beside the church while intoning a fourth religious chant.

The funeral service continued at the graveside, with additional chanting and prayers by the cantor or priest and mourners. At Józef Karpiel's funeral the Górale ensemble also contributed an additional nine tunes: more *wierchowe*, *Janosikowe*, *Sabałowe*, a few *Duchowe* (fig. 1.11, CD track 5), and the tune to a song called "Krywaniu." In the cemetery the ensemble was augmented by Jan Karpiel-Bułecka (*prym*), Andrzej Frączysty (*sekund*), and Janusz Zatorski-Sieczka (*basy*), swelling the ensemble to ten musicians, a sizable Górale orchestra. Before playing his violin, Jan Karpiel-Bułecka read a eulogy while the other musicians softly played the first two tunes. A second eulogy was spoken, and two rounds of gunshot were sounded while the ensemble played and the coffin was lowered into the earth. Finally, Jan led the band in a *wierchowa* and a *Sabałowa*, and the music stopped moments before the gravedigger resumed shoveling dirt into the grave (CD track 47). Of all the music I experienced in Poland, music played graveside at this and the three other Górale funerals I attended was the most beautiful and moving.

Funerals and the Musical Return to the Village

The music I have experienced at Górale funerals in Podhale can be divided into two distinct categories: music linked with the Roman Catholic Church and muzyka Podhala.[5] The Catholic Church music includes the chanting and singing in the house of the deceased around the casket, processional chants, and the chants, songs, organ music, and hymns in the church itself. The Catholic Church music may link Górale to the worldwide church and to an otherwordly life, but the muzyka Podhala, all played by a string band, is a strong statement about locality and self-conceptions linked firmly to the region of Podhale. A closer look at exactly which *nuty* were played at Józef Karpiel's funeral, however, suggests a need for meaningful qualifications.

I identify sixteen distinct *nuty* played by the Górale string band at this funeral during the procession and in the cemetery (one of the *nuty* is repeated). All the music was within the broader definition of muzyka Podhala as described in chapter 1, but it tended toward the genres in the border regions of the repertoire. For reasons that may be obvious, absent were *nuty* linked exclusively with the *góralski* and *zbójnicki* dance sequences. The *wierchowe* played, however, could be called *ozwodne* and could be used in a dance if played faster and with a more marked meter. In fact, four of the *wierchowe* played at the funeral are versions of *nuty* that Mierczyński calls *ozwodne* (music for dance) in his 1930 collection. Their use here for a funeral points out the flexible nature of the *wierchowa— ozwodna* continuum discussed in chapter 1 (see fig. 1.5). Absent also were any examples of sung Górale music—singing was exclusive to music related to the Church.[6] The *wierchowe* and the *Sabałowe* (also called *staroświeckie*) are unquestionably in the core repertoire of muzyka Podhala, but the *Janosikowe* and *Duchowe* extend the repertoire and show more overtly the influence of musical practices from neighboring regions. To review a discussion from chapter 1, *Janosikowe* are ballads associated with the legendary robber Janosik from Terchowa, Slovakia, and *Duchowe* are a unique and slightly controversial group of songs believed by some to have been composed by Andrzej Knapczyk-Duch in the first half of the twentieth century. Wrazen (1988, 107–109) places *Janosikowe* in her category of tunes of foreign origin, and Ćwiżewicz and Ćwiżewicz (1995) categorize them as "extended repertoire" of Górale. The unique rhythmic structures of *Duchowe* and their relatively fixed and immediately identifiable melodies put them in a separate category on the fringes of muzyka Podhala. Careful audition of the tracks for this chapter on the CD accompanying this book also reveals the use of double- and sometimes triple-*prym* style, a performance feature used for almost all the music played by the string band at the funeral. This multiple-*prym* style places even core repertoire *nuty* like *Sabałowe* on what some consider to be the stylistic fringes of conservative interpretations of muzyka Podhala. The first song played in the cemetery also stands alone: "Krywaniu" or "Hej, Krywaniu, Krywaniu" is a song setting of a poem by turn-of-the century poet and writer Kazimierz Tetmajer (1865–1940). Although not Górale, he was influential in popularizing and valorizing Górale culture in Poland during the early decades of the twentieth century. The song with its haunting melody is very popular among Górale today, but it can hardly be considered part of the old strata of traditional repertoire.

Of the sixteen individual *nuty* played by the Górale ensemble at this funeral, all were muzyka Podhala as I have defined the term. Yet fully eight were on the periphery of the repertoire according to some scholars and commentators. My interpretation of the repertoire, however, is that, at this most solemn rite, music most closely associated with the identity of the deceased and of his or her community is employed. Complementing the otherworldly Catholic chants is an earthly inscription with instrumental performance of a regional identity, grounded in Podhale with *Sabałowe* and *wierchowe*, but celebrating lived connections across malleable political and aesthetic borders with *Janosikowe* and *Duchowe*. This is the musical accompaniment Górale offer for a fellow Górale's passage from this world to the next. The music at that December funeral said who Józef Karpiel was and who his family and community are. In his case, it was Górale music for Górale.

Epilogue: Village Exhumed

"ZAKOPANE ODKOPANE?" (ZAKOPANE UNEARTHED?)
BY K. TREBUNIA-TUTKA

Refrain:
Hej, co inom śtyraj dona
Co tam panie w
Zakopanen?

Refrain:
Hej, co inom śtyraj dona [vocables]
So there, sir, what's up in
Zakopane?

Gąsienica, Bachleda
Siecka, Obrochta
Tatar, Marduła
Mateja, Sabała
Staszic, Goszczyński
Pol, Chałubiński
Stolarczyk, Witkiewicz
Dembowski, Sienkiewicz

Gąsienica, Bachleda
Siecka, Obrochta
Tatar, Marduła
Mateja, Sabała
Staszic, Goszczyński
Pol, Chałubiński
Stolarczyk, Witkiewicz
Dembowski, Sienkiewicz

Refrain

Refrain

Giewonty, Sobczaki
Stasecki, Walcoki

Giewonty, Sobczaki
Stasecki, Walcoki

Wale, Roje, Brzegi
Krzeptowscy, Wójcioki
Anczyc, Zamoyski
Gerson, Szymanowski
Eliasz, Modrzejewska
Hrabina, Raczyńska

Refrain

Zaruski, Karłowicz
Żeromski, Kasprowicz
Kossak, Paderewski
Orkan, Zborowski
Janiki, Cukry
Jarząbki, Krupy
Stopki, Suleje
Króle, Trzebunie

Wale, Roje, Brzegi
Krzeptowscy, Wójcioki
Anczyc, Zamoyski
Gerson, Szymanowski
Eliasz, Modrzejewska
Hrabina, Raczyńska

Refrain

Zaruski, Karłowicz
Żeromski, Kasprowicz
Kossak, Paderewski
Orkan, Zborowski
Janiki, Cukry
Jarząbki, Krupy
Stopki, Suleje
Króle, Trzebunie

The above is a song from *Etno-Techno*, one of the worldbeat fusion CDs considered in chapter 5. Like all the songs on that CD, Krzysztof Trebunia-Tutka's poem is set to music that emphasizes a techno dance beat but incorporates musical gestures and timbres suggestive of muzyka Podhala, including the same DD EE DD CC *basy* ostinato used for "Nie patrzcie przez lupy" (see fig. 5.14). This time, however, the ostinato is matched with a *krzesana* "po dwa" fiddle tune that would do well for a *góralski* dance in just about any Podhalan village. The refrain is sung by Krzysztof, who also recites or raps the litany of surnames that make up the entire content of the three verses.

"Zakopane odkopane?" summarizes in a song what I have tried to accomplish with a book. The title is a pun: although the origins and exact meaning of the town's name are obscure (Budak 1991), *zakopane* can literally mean "buried." The second word in the title, *odkopane*, means the opposite: unearthed, dug up, unburied. Thus the song title can be rendered "Zakopane un-kopaned?" "The buried unburied?" or perhaps "Zakopane undone?" The question mark is in the original and we are left to wonder exactly what the question is. Belying the agrarian roots of the term applied to the core methodology employed when researching this book, *field*work, I have done my share of digging around in Zakopane and in the region that this village-cum-town symbolizes. I have tried to unearth some truths, some understanding about what makes Podhale such a special place. I have even tried to undo some myths about what makes mountain music what it is and is not.

Part of what I unearthed in Podhale is the pervasive influence of individuals defined as "outsiders" or at least "non-Górale" since many of these individuals have been invited "inside." Yet the relationship remains uneasy, even as many of the individuals named in "Zakopane odkopane?" are generally held in high regard by Górale. This tension is captured in the refrain "Co tam, panie, w Zakopanen?" (So there, sir, what's up in Zakopane?), a reference to one of the most famous phrases in Polish literature, the opening line of Wyspiański's play *Wesele* (The wedding): "Cóż tam, panie, w polityce? Chińcyki trzymają się mocno!?" (So there, sir, in politics? The Chinese are going strong!?).[1] The play is ostensibly a representation of a wedding between a man of noble heritage and a peasant woman—a not uncommon trend during the Young Poland movement in the last half of the nineteenth century. The line "So there, sir . . ." is spoken by a peasant trying to strike up a conversation with a man who represents the inteligencja and who does not deign to take up the peasant's admittedly absurd question. This line, like the play itself, represents the tensions between village and city, uneducated and educated, peasant and inteligencja.

So, sir, exactly what is up, unburied, exhumed in Zakopane? in Podhale? Part of the answer is in the three verses of Krzysztof's song. Consisting entirely of surnames, the verses read like a who's who of Podhalan cultural history and contain many of the names that have figured prominently in this book. As in Wyspiański's *Wesele*, the characters that populate Krzysztof's song embody a class clash between Górale (stand-ins for Wyspiański's peasants) and non-Górale (equivalent to the elite urbanites in *Wesele*). Each verse is roughly divided into half Górale names and half non-Górale Polish names. The first two verses each begin with the names of notable Górale individuals and families: Gąsienica, one of the oldest names in Podhale and the maiden name of the mother of the house where I lived in 1994–95; Obrochta, as in Bartuś, the influential violinist from the late nineteenth and early twentieth centuries; Sabała, the iconic Górale from the end of the nineteenth century (in the introduction of this book); Giewont, the *przydomek* (by-name) of Tadeusz Gąsienica-Giewont, renowned senior violinist in the late twentieth century (quoted elsewhere in this book); and so on. The second half of both verses lists non-Górale who were nonetheless influential in Podhale: Staszic, one of the first

Poles to conduct scientific research in the Tatras (from 1802); Goszczyński, known as the first ethnographer in Podhale (see chapter 3); Chałubiński needs no further elaboration; Witkiewicz, the artist who designed the monument to Chałubiński and Sabała, and who redefined Zakopane-style architecture; Eljasz, the artist who created the image of early tourists reproduced as figure 0.2 in the introduction; Szymanowski, the great Polish composer who valorized the *zbójniki* legend with his ballet *Harnasie;* and so on. The list is notably tilted toward artists and musicians, and individuals who were instrumental in developing the image of Podhale and promoting tourism. The third verse is again a bipartite construction, only this time non-Górale are first, followed by the final four lines of Górale names, concluding with Trebunie. From Gąsienica to Trebunia, Górale get the first and last word in this poem. As other songs on the *Etno-Techno* CD remind us, relations between Górale and lowlanders are not always this convivial, but this poetic feast only hints at the sorts of fissures revealed in Wyspiański's *Wesele.*

I agree with Krzysztof Trebunia-Tutka. One discovers with a little digging that what is up in Zakopane is that Zakopane (and, by extension, Podhale) is all about the people who live there, make music there, create costumes, write poems, build houses, cook food in homes and in restaurants, hike the mountain trails, design monuments, and so forth. These are the people who make mountaineers and mountain music, and they are the people who decide who and what is included in those categories of "Górale" and "muzyka Podhala." The creation, negotiation, and maintenance of these ethnic and cultural categories require both those constructed as Górale and those interpreted as non-Górale. This is especially true of ethnicity, for without the politics of difference—without the notion of "indigenous" people contrasting with "outsiders"—there is no need to create the ethnic category "Górale" (or "Persian" or "Roma" or "Basque" or "Chicano," for that matter). And although Krzysztof's song is markedly national in that the names he lists are all Polish, the song's musical context reminds us that what is up in Zakopane is also globalization. The techno rhythmic foundation, as described in chapter 5, marks "Zakopane odkopane?" as generically worldbeat and only esoterically Górale. Finally, what is up in Zakopane is the status of Górale. While Krzysztof's poem retains a politic of difference (Górale and non-Górale meet but do not mix), it rejects the politics of inequality. In the twentieth century

Górale, at least locally, achieved a level of parity with the inteligencja grouped with them in this song. Many of the Górale family names featured in the song are known for their members who have achieved high levels of educational, business, and artistic success. If the monument discussed in the introduction (see fig. 0.1) were designed today, I would guess that the earthy Sabała would displace the urban physician Chałubiński from his privileged position.

I do not anticipate ever finding myself named in a Górale song, yet "Zakopane odkopane?" does renew the uncomfortable reflexive twitch that I mentioned in the introduction. I join the ethnographers and culture brokers evoked in Krzysztof's song who would interpret Górale cultural practices. How am I implicated in the imagining, negotiating, making, and maintaining of music from this particular range of mountains? How will my fieldwork, writing, lecturing, teaching, and music making affect the very cultural practices that I study and teach? On the one hand, I believe that my impact will be similar to the very sorts of cultural brokering that I critique in the preceding pages: I have defined a thing called muzyka Podhala, delimited musical practices that fall within that term, and more or less indicated who the people are who actively engage in these practices. For some readers, then, I have confirmed or reified a constructed category. Others will note that I recognized a well-defined style and repertoire as a cultural invention, a negotiated canon of music practice that is nonetheless challenged by Górale musicians deeply and personally invested in its meaning. They will note that I believe muzyka Podhala exists, but only as a cultural construct; that I believe it is beautiful and important, but not sacred and unchangeable.

Glossary

a   as in father, cot

ą   as in the French *bon*

e   as in get, let, pen

ę   like *in* in the French *matin*

i   as in meet, tree

o   as in ought, bought, and sometimes as in go

ó   as in boot (same as *u*)

u   as in boot

y   as in bid

b   as in book

c   like *ts* or *tz* as in blitz, but, when followed by *i*, like *ć*

ć   c followed by i or written as ć, like ch in church, cheek

ch   like the *ch* in the Scottish *loch*

cz   like the *ch* of chair, choice, choo-choo

d   as in dog

dz   as in adze

dź   like the *j* in jeep

dż   like the *dg* in bridge

f   as in fat

g   as in good

h   as in have

j   like *y* in yes

k   as in kind

l   as in late, but, when preceding *i*, as in value

ł   as in English *w*, wood

m   as in mud

n   as in no, but, when followed by *i*, like *ń*

ń   *n* followed by *i* or written as *ń*, as in the first *n* in onion

p   as in party, but with less aspiration

r   rolled *r*

rz   like the *j* in French *Jacques* or the *s* in pleasure (same as *ż*)

s   as in set, but, when followed by *i*, like *ś*

ś   *s* followed by *i* or written as *ś*, like sh in sheep

sz   as in push (darker and farther back in mouth than *ś*)

t   as in take

w   like *v* in verb

z   as in zone

ż   like *s* in pleasure, *j* in the French *Jacques* (same as *rz*)

ź   like *s* in Rhodesia (brighter than *rz*)

USAGE OF POLISH TERMS

Polish is a Slavic language written with a modified roman alphabet. Polish speakers and writers decline and conjugate words with abandon. In this book, however, Polish words are generally printed in their nominative form, declined only to agree with number (singular or plural) and gender (masculine, feminine, or neuter) but not further declined to indicate their grammatical function. For example, *drobna* (nominative, feminine, singular) refers to a certain genre of music, but the corresponding dance is called *drobny* (nominative, masculine, singular). The plural form for both dance and music genres is *drobne*. Polish and other non-English words are rendered in italics throughout, with some exceptions.

A number of key words are adopted as English terms, are not declined, and are rendered in roman type. Occasionally my usage here will seem strange to Polish readers, but my intention is to ease the reading process for English readers. Chief among such terms is "Górale," the Polish plural noun form of *Góral*, but used here as both noun and adjective, singular and plural (see Wrazen 1991, 175). "Podhale," the Tatra Mountain region that forms the geographical focus of this book, is similarly used, although I also use "Podhalan," an Anglicized adjectival form. "Muzyka Podhala" is a third term that I use in Polish nominative form throughout the text. All proper names are adapted in their native form, rendered in roman type, and generally not declined.

The idea of a particular song or tune (*nuta*) is problematic when writing about muzyka Podhala, but certain tune/ostinato and sometimes text combinations do constitute fairly fixed units or "pieces" of music. Such units are treated here as distinct songs or musical pieces and are placed in quotes. Genre names, on the other hand, are treated as Polish or Górale dialect words and are rendered in italics: *krzesana* "wiecno" or simply "wiecno," *krzesana* "trzy a roz," and "Hej Madziar Pije" are a few examples. Music and dance genres with familiarity beyond Podhale and Poland are presented as they are given in the *New Harvard Dictionary of Music*, for example, csárdás, mazurka, verbunkos.

altówka: three-string bowed lute about the size of a viola, with a flattened bridge allowing all three strings to be bowed simultaneously; associated with Hungarian and Slovak music; also called *kontra*

baca: head shepherd responsible for the sheep of many owners, and for the apprentice shepherds called *juhasi*

basy: three-stringed, cello-sized bowed lute tuned D, D an octave higher, and A pitched between the two Ds

ceper: derogatory term for non-Górale; lowlander

cepowiny: also called *oczepiny;* capping ritual in a wedding when the bride's head is covered with a scarf symbolizing matronhood; the scarf either covers the wedding wreath or the wreath is first removed. At the end of the *cepowiny* the groom's headcovering is also altered by removing the long eagle feather from his hat.

ciupaga: long-handled axe or tomahawk favored throughout the Carpathian mountains and used in the *zbójnicki* dance

csárdás: Hungarian dance and music in fast duple meter related to the *verbunkos;* spelled *czardasz* in Polish

Dom Podhalan: the "home" or cultural center of the highlanders; often operated by the local branch of the *Związek Podhalan*, the Górale fraternal organization

drobna: duple meter dance and music genre for *góralski* dance; similar to the *krzesana* but often with a more complex harmonic accompaniment

drużba: groomsman

Duchowa: adjective form of the surname Duch (literally, "spirit"); refers to a genre of *nuta* named after Andrzej Knapczyk-Duch (1866–1946)

düvö: probably from Romany *dui* or "twice"; a bowing technique for accompanying

Hungarian and Romany *verbunkos* and *csárdás* dance music that produces two pulses with each change in bow direction

gęśle: fiddle; folk violin (see *złóbcoki*)

góra: mountain

Górale: mountaineers, highlanders; used here to refer specifically to the old-family residents of the Polish Tatra Mountain region, *Skalny Podhale*

góralski: adjectival form of the noun *góra* (mountain); generally used in this book to refer to the regional couples dance

hala: mountain pasture, alp; can also be used to refer to mountains

inteligencja: intellectuals, generally with class connotations in nineteenth- and early-twentieth-century Poland

Janosikowa: adjectival form of the surname Janosik; refers to a genre of tune and ballad about the legendary highway robber from Terchowa, Slovakia, Juraj Jánošík, who lived from 1688 to 1713 when he was executed

juhas: apprentice shepherd, usually a boy or a young man

juhaski: male dance genre that uses the same music and dance steps as the *góralski* but without women's participation

karcma: (*karczma* in standard Polish) roadhouse, inn, restaurant with a bar

kolęda: carol; *kolędy* tend to be common throughout Poland, and those sung in Podhale are generally not specific to the region; traditionally sung during the Christmas season which extends into January

kołysanka: cradle-song, lullaby

kontra: alternative name for *altówka*, a three-stringed bowed lute about the size of a viola

kozak: literally Cossack, but also refers to a lively men's dance related to the *zbójnicki*

krakowiak: dance from the Kraków region in fast duple meter with syncopations similar to the more modern polka

krzesana: duple meter dance and music genre for the *góralski* dance marked by a quick tempo; many *nuty* are named for their harmonic/ostinato patterns

Liptów: Tatra Mountain region in Slovakia, southwest of Podhale

mazurka: triple-meter folk dance from the Mazowia region of Poland, near Warsaw

muzyka: music; used by Górale to refer to a band of musicians; an ensemble

muzyka Podhala: music of Podhale; generally refers to the core repertoire of music believed to be indigenous to *Skalne* Podhale

niezależność: independence

nuta: literally "note"; used by Górale musicians to refer to a melodic idea or tune family and sometimes a harmonic/ostinato pattern; here interchanged with the imperfect translations "tune" and "melody"

oberek: quick triple-meter Polish folk dance

Orawa: region to the west of Podhale that spans the Polish/Slovak border

ozwodna: duple meter dance within the *góralski*, usually featuring five-bar or ten-beat phrases; may share melodic material with *wierchowe* and *pasterskie;* typically the first dance of a *góralski* sequence is an *ozwodna;* also called *rozwodna*

pasterska: unaccompanied song, either unmetered or sung with great rhythmic freedom (rubato); when more than one person is singing, performed with harmony, but each verse ending in unison

po góralsku: in the Górale manner; dancing *góralski* or *zbójnicki* would be dancing *po góralsku*, for example; speaking in the Górale dialect is speaking *po góralsku*

pod: under, below, beneath

Podhalan: Anglicized adjectival form of Podhale

Podhale: piedmont; at mountain base; used here to refer to *Skalne* Podhale

polonaise: French term for a processional couples dance in triple meter with some links to sixteenth-century Polish folk dances

Polskie Towarzystwo Tatrzańskie (see *Towarzystwo Tatrzańskie*)

prym: lead violin part; also used to refer to the lead violinist or *prymista*

prymista: lead violinist

przydomek: by-name; name attached with a hyphen to surnames among Górale, some of which have taken on legal status and are handed down from father to children, for example, Gąsienica-*Giewont*, Karpiel-*Replon*, Karpiel-*Bułecka*

przyśpiewka: pre-song or couplet sung by the lead male dancer to request a particular dance

pytace: askers, announcers, criers; men engaged for their strong voices and their skill with horses who wear formal long brown coats adorned with ceremonial sashes and ride through the village announcing a wedding with formulaic song

rozwodna: music and dance genre in the *góralski* (see *ozwodna*)

ruch regionalny: regional movement; refers to a late-nineteenth- and early-twentieth-century movement related to nationalism that prized the folk traditions of Podhale

Sabałowa: adjectival form of the surname Sabała; refers to the legendary storyteller, musician, and mountain guide Jan Krzeptowski-Sabała (1809–1894); *Sabałowa* is a genre of tunes (*nuty*) considered an old-style representative of the nineteenth-century tunes of Sabała's time

Sądecka: Polish Carpathian Mountain region to the east of Podhale

Sejm: Polish congress

sekund: accompanying violin part; the *sekund* parts consist entirely of double-stops played on the beat

sekundzista: accompanying violinist; for muzyka Podhala, two *sekundysty* are most common, although there may be more

Skalne Podhale: literally "rocky piedmont"; refers to the region of Poland that includes the Tatra Mountains and the close-in foothills

skanking: style of dancing associated with reggae

Spisz: border region between Poland and Slovakia, primarily in Slovakia, east of the Tatra Mountains

stajeras: a fast triple-meter dance

staroświecki: old world, of the old world, old-fashioned; often used to describe a genre of muzyka Podhala tunes that extend down to a G requiring the use of the D-string by the *prym*

Towarzystwo Tatrzańskie: Tatra Society; organization founded in 1873 by non-Górale to develop, promote, and protect the Tatra region; later renamed *Polskie Towarzystwo Tatrzańskie*

verbunkos: Hungarian dance and music from the mid-eighteenth century used to recruit soldiers; usually in two parts, a slow introduction followed by a fast section, both duple meter; related to *csárdás*

wesele: wedding (usually implying the wedding celebration but not necessarily the church ceremony), related to the noun *wesołość*, meaning joy, mirth, hilarity

wiecno or *wiecna:* dialect form of Polish *wieczny*, meaning eternal, perpetual; a popular tune within the *krzesana* dance and music genre with two different phrases, each of which can be extended in length by the lead violinist

wierchowa: mountain peak song; genre of singing or instrumental music related to the *ozwodna* and *pasterska;* the most typical phrase structures are two phrases of five bars or ten beats each

wolność: freedom

Zakopiańczyk: resident of Zakopane, often implying that the resident is not Górale and is therefore a *ceper*

zbójnicki: mountain bandit's dance historically related to the Hungarian *verbunkos* military recruiting dance

zbójnik: bandit, brigand, highway robber; specifically legendary robbers who roamed the Tatras in the seventeenth and eighteenth centuries

zespół: troupe, team, unit; used here specifically to mean a folkloric song-and-dance troupe

zielona: literally "green," but in the context of muzyka Podhala, refers to specific tunes or *nuty* that signal the end of a *góralski* dance sequence

złóbcoki: fiddle; Górale dialect name for a narrow fiddle (see figs. 2.6 and 3.5)

Związek Podhalan: Podhalan Alliance; fraternal organization for Górale established in 1904

zwyrtanie: to turn or spin; dance steps when dancers embrace or when a group of dancers form a circle, turning first to the left and then to the right; used to initiate each dance within a *góralski* sequence and to end the last dance of the sequence

Notes

1. For an explanation of how I use Polish words and the Polish system of declensions and conjugations, see the glossary.

2. The monument was designed by Stanisław Witkiewicz (1851–1915), a Polish artist who also favored Sabała's company.

3. My use of the term "locality" is inspired by Appadurai but is not identical to his use (1996, 178 ff). I agree that locality is relational and contextual, but I do not downplay the spatial dimension of locality as he does. The Tatra Mountains are an important player in this book, although the meaning of these mountains is continually reinterpreted by those who encounter them.

4. I thank Philip V. Bohlman for helping me situate Podhale in Europe as a unique region in the folklorist's imagination.

I. PODHALE

1. The singular form of these genre names are *pasterska, wierchowa, ozwodna, Sabałowa, Janosikowa, krzesana, drobna, zbójnicki,* and *zielona. Cepowiny* is always plural.

2. For a more comprehensive discussion of Górale taxonomy and a detailed explanation of the categories of Górale music (with the exception of carols and wedding tunes), see Wrazen 1988, 72–104.

3. References such as ac19.vii.92.1 direct the reader toward fieldwork documentation housed at the University of California, Santa Barbara, and Muzeum Tatrzańskie, Zakopane. For an explanation of the numbering system, please see "Note on Citations of Fieldwork Media."

4. Except where another source is cited, all music examples/transcriptions in this study are mine.

5. These genre names are declined *drobna* when referring to music (feminine), *drobny* when referring to dance (masculine), and *drobne* when plural. Please refer to the explanation of Polish usage in the glossary.

6. On 11 April 2003 a group of students and I had occasion to perform "Marsz Madziarski" for the Hungarian ensemble Muzsikás. Márta Sebastyén recognized the tune as being related to a musical setting of a poem by Petöfi Sándor popular in the nineteenth century.

7. *Düvö* is probably from Romany *dui,* or "twice," and is common in Hungarian and Romany verbunkos and csárdás dance music. I have not noticed the term used by Górale musicians.

8. Dr. Tytus Chałubiński's special association to this tune is discussed in chapters 2 and 3.

2. MAKING HISTORY

1. Hucuł is a mountaineer group from the East Carpathians.

2. Wallachians are a distinct ethnic group with origins in the Balkans (Chirot 1976, 8–13). They are believed to have been nomadic shepherds.

3. Interview with the author, 9 March 1995, Zakopane (ac9.iii.95).

4. See, for example, Padraic Kenney's (1997) study of Wrocław, formerly German Breslau, where, after the war, there resided a volatile mix of Germans, Jews, Russians, and Poles from Poland's various regions, all of whom had different cultural practices. He explains that over the years in Wrocław, the myth of social integration was successfully promoted.

5. Interview with the author, 1 June 1995, Zakopane (ac1.vi.95).

6. Czechoslovakia split into two independent states on 1 January 1993: the Czech Republic and the Slovak Republic. Here I use the term "Slovakia" to refer to the historical region south of Podhale and "Slovak Republic" when writing specifically about the present-day nation-state.

7. Zakopane may have obtained a charter from King Stefan Batory already in 1578, but if such a charter ever existed it has been lost (Radwańska-Paryska and Paryski 1995, 1381).

8. Witold Paryski and especially Jan Gutt-Mostowy have both been very generous to me with their time and help.

9. This society was first called "Galicyjskie Towarzystwo Tatrzańskie" but changed its name to "Towarzystwo Tatrzańskie" in 1874 and was then called "Polskie Towarzystwo Tatrzańskie" from 1920 to when the organization joined with Polskie Towarzystwo Krajoznawcze in 1950, again changing its name to "Polskie Towarzystwo Turystyczno-Krajoznawcze," as it remains today.

10. Demographic information gained primarily from Gąsowski 1991.

11. I should note that women's costumes in Podhale have tended to change more dramatically since the late nineteenth century, as is illustrated by Stanisława Trebunia-Staszel (1995). Patriarchy being no weaker in Poland than elsewhere in Europe, Górale identity focuses first on males giving them greater iconic stature, leaving women with more freedom to manipulate symbolic presentation.

3. MAKING MOUNTAIN MUSIC

1. Interview, 16 May 1995, Zakopane (ac16.v.95).

2. I have found no record of a priest named Chybiński who collected music in the Tatras. Giewont may have been referring to the priest Eugeniusz Janota (1823–1878), who did collect songs later commented on by musicologist Adolf Chybiński (1961, 174–175).

3. Gorączkiewicz's collection was preceded by some fifty years by Franciszek Józef Sulzer's 1782 *Geschichte des Transalpinischen Danciens*, which contains in the third volume the tune "Walachische Tänze und Lieder," in which the first half is exactly like the first part of a *zbójnicki* tune still played in Podhale (see Chybiński 1961, 166–167). I do not include Sulzer's work in my survey, since he presumably collected the tune in Wallachia, not Podhale.

4. ". . . ma jedną figurę właściwą tylko goralom, kiedy goral zamknięty krążącém kołem taceczników, wyrabia na środku rozmaite skoki, a razem ciska raz poraz siekiérką w górę i chwyta ją w powietrzu ze zręcznością zadziwiającą. Nadaje to jakiś męski charakter tańcowi, przypomina wojenne tańce starożytnych" (Goszczyński 1853, 153).

5. Archaic spellings from the original source are retained in this quote.

6. In August 2000 I visited the Biblioteka Warszawskiego Towarzystwa Muzycznego where the manuscript was formerly housed and confirmed that it was lost during the bombing of Warsaw in the Second World War. Szurmiak-Bogucka and Bogucki (1961, 278–279), Szurmiak-Bogucka (1991, 709), and Chybiński (1961, 145, 170–171) mention the manuscript in their surveys of literature on music in Podhale, but they use only information that can be found in Hławiczka's 1936 article. It appears that Hławiczka may have been the only music scholar who worked with the actual manuscript.

7. The dialect texts in examples 3.7, 3.8, and 3.9 are reproduced as faithfully to the way they appear in Hławiczka's article as I can make them. In the article they are written by hand (not typeset) and are difficult to read. They do not reflect current trends in spelling Górale dialect.

8. Above I noted that Chybiński makes similar criticisms of Gorączkiewicz's 1829 transcriptions, suggesting that some augmented fourths had been changed to perfect fourths.

9. For information specifically on the regional movement and its links to ethnography and tourism, see Gromada 1982, Jazowska-Gumulska 1994, Wnuk and Kudasik 1993, and Zborowski 1930.

10. Zborowski, a linguist and ethnographer, was the director of the Muzeum Tatrzańskie in Zakopane from 1922 until his death in 1965.

11. As mentioned above, Józef Styrczula-Maśniak believed that the transcriptions made later by Kotoński were superior to Mierczyński's, noting that Kotoński took much more time to complete a transcription (fieldnotes 24.viii.1992); that is, his critique is linked to the different methods of the musical folklorists.

12. Perhaps influenced by Mierczyński, Szurmiak-Bogucka (1974, 97) also represented this same wedding song in ¾ time.

13. Interview, 3 August 1995, Kościelisko (ac3.viii.95).

14. Two additional major collections that do not focus on music, however, include Tylkowa (2000) and Dutkowa (1991).

15. The nineteenth-century literary movement included some interest in folk culture and music (see Stopka 1897, 1898, mentioned briefly above). The Górale literary tradition continued through the second half of the twentieth century with the work of Włodzimierz Wnuk (1981, 1985) in several books that deal with historical and contemporary issues among Górale.

4. VILLAGE ON STAGE

1. Earlier versions of portions of this chapter were published in the journals *The World of Music* (Cooley 1999a) and *Ethnologies* (Cooley 2001).

2. I believe that this devaluation of staged folklore is still common today, although significant steps are being made in folklore studies, ethnomusicology, and anthropology toward a revaluation (see, for example, Cantwell 1991, 1993; Bauman, Sawin, and Carpenter 1992; Price and Price 1994; Bendix 1997; Kirshenblatt-Gimblett 1998; DeWitt 1999; and Greenhill 2001). In earlier decades a few lonely voices called for more attention among social scientists and humanists to front-region tourist performances (MacCannell 1986 [1976]).

3. I thank Dorota Dutsch, a professor of classics at the University of California, Santa Barbara, and native of Poland, for pointing out that the specific connotations of *zespół* are related to Communist Party uses of song and dance troupes throughout Poland, and are not specific to Podhale.

4. "Jak ja prowadziłam ten festiwal, to ja się tak starałam, żeby górale nie

zapomnieli o tym, że są góralami" (interview with Krzystyna Słobodzińska, Zakopane [ac20.vii.95]).

5. For a description of the structure and use of alpine horns in Podhale, see
Chybiński 1961, 333–344.

6. An earlier and expanded version of this case study was published in *Polish
Music Journal* (Cooley 1998).

7. As a point of clarity, none of the individuals named in this case study
began learning muzyka Podhala in Skalni. They all come from families with
strong musical traditions.

8. The pairing of a "first fiddler" and a "first violinist" by Chybiński and
repeated by Władysław Trebunia-Tutka seems to refer to an archaic practice of
pairing a standard violin with a *złóbcoki* (see fig. 2.7).

5. GLOBAL VILLAGE

1. By the mid-twentieth century "folk music" was a complex and contested
concept. When Poles use the term in the context of the communist era, they
generally mean musical practices associated with village life produced by the peasant class (see Noll 1986), although it was just as likely to have been performed
by urban-based professional song and dance troupes. Contemporaneously in the
United States "folk music" was taking on new meanings (and new sounds) as a
genre of urban-based acoustic popular music, in some cases associated with the
political Left (Filene 2000; Garofalo 2002, 162–163).

2. Before a Twinkle Brothers performance in Santa Barbara, California, 30
August 2002, I spoke with Norman Grant about his collaboration with the
Trebunia-Tutka family.

3. Lech Wałęsa was a shipyard worker and strike leader from Gdańsk who
became president of Poland by popular election in 1990.

4. The family name is Trebunia-Tutka, which is declined as "Trebunie-
Tutki" or simply "Tutki" (nominative plural) when referring to their band.

5. Conceiving of the music as structured harmonically may be a relatively
new layer added to a presumably older conception of ostinato patterns among
Górale musicians. Although neither modern muzyka Podhala nor reggae adheres
to the rules of what in my American conservatory training was called "functional"
or "tonal" harmony, musicians in both traditions talk about chords as a basic item
of musical structure. I have not tested this hypothesis with the Górale and reggae
musicians considered here, but I imagine that they found some common ground
in the musically implied or actualized harmonic shifts with chord changes, and
this is what I mean by "harmonic structures."

6. I thank Harry Andrews, a former student of mine at Rhode Island College, for this insight.

7. Hankus Netsky pointed out the centrality of "the beat" to the overall
sound of the Tutki/Twinkle fusions. I am also indebted to ethnomusicologist Eve
McPherson for reminding me that I cannot be sure how others hear the music,
and that the reggae sound may be subverted to the Górale in the minds of some.

8. The survey questions were developed with the assistance of sociologist
Jon Cruz. They were included in a larger ethnographic survey at the generous
offer of Dr. Monika Golonka-Czajkowska of Kraków.

9. "Góralu, czy ci nie żal" is based on an 1864 poem by Michał Bałucki
called "Dla chleba" (For bread) (Radwańska-Paryska and Paryski 1995, 48).

10. Tutki released two additional fusion CDs in 2000, but both were re-
releases of previous material.

6. VILLAGE FOR HIRE

1. For a study of Górale music and classical music in Podhale, see Długołęcka and Pinkwart 1992.

2. Timothy Rice (1994) wrote about similar experiences "appropriating" Bulgarian music and dance, first far away from Bulgaria and then in Bulgaria.

7. BACK TO THE VILLAGE

1. The band receives such public tips throughout the wedding ceremony, leading to an inevitable more private moment. Imprinted on my memory is a scene in a Polish bar in Chicago where a Górale string band gathered after playing a wedding. As I entered the bar, the *basy* player was lying on his back on the floor in a pool of dollar bills, gentling shaking his *basy* above him with all four limbs to coax out any additional tips. It has been suggested to me that the practice of tipping musicians through the *basy*'s f-holes began when most monies were metal coins. One can imagine the satisfying sound of a heavy gold coin bouncing off the interior woods of a *basy*.

2. The alteration of the groom's headgear may reflect what some believe to be the relative parity of gendered roles in Podhale. Indeed, colleagues and research assistants in Poland have suggested to me in informal conversations that women in Podhale do experience a degree of equality with men. Wrazen (1988), in her dissertation, depicts women as having attenuated power.

3. On the evening before the funeral, family and friends gather in the home of the deceased to sing and to mourn. I have never attended this portion of a Górale funeral, but I have been informed that the music consists of "church" songs and not laments or muzyka Podhala.

4. I believe that the preponderance of Styrczula-Maśniaks in the band can be explained by their family relations by marriage to the deceased. At the time of this writing, two of the musicians who played at this funeral have since had funerals of their own: Józef Styrczula-Maśniak (1922–1998) and the young Marek Łabunowicz (1972–2001).

5. For transcriptions of all the music performed during the processions and by the string band graveside, see Cooley 1999b, 354–361.

6. The practice of not singing muzyka Podhala at funerals is not inviolable. At the funeral of Antonia Knapczyka-Ducha, the wife of the musician Andrzej Knapczyk-Duch, an elderly woman sang a song sometimes attributed to Andrzej Knapczyk-Duch—a *Duchowa*—at the graveside accompanied by two young musicians on violins (v7.iv.95).

EPILOGUE

1. I am deeply indebted to Dorota Dutsch for leading me to the puns and literary references in Krzyszof Trebunia-Tutka's poetry.

References Cited

Adorno, Theodor W. 1973. *Philosophy of Modern Music.* Translated by Anne G. Mitchell and Wesley V. Blomster. New York: Seabury Press.

Alexiou, Margaret. ca. 1974. *The Ritual Lament in Greek Tradition.* Cambridge: Cambridge University Press.

Anderson, Benedict. 1991 [1983]. *Imagined Communities: Reflections on the Origin and Spread of Nationalism.* Rev. ed. London: Verso.

Anonymous. 1963. "90 lat turystyki górskiej." *Wierchy: Rocznik Poświęcony Górom* 32:5–6.

Antoniewicz, Włodzimierz, ed. 1959–70. *Pasterstwo Tatr Polskich i Podhala.* 8 volumes. Wrocław: Zakład Narodowy im. Ossolinskich.

Antoniewicz, Włodzimierz, Kazimierz Dobrowolski, and Witold H. Paryski, eds. 1970. *Pasterstwo Tatr polskich i Podhala.* Vol. 8: *Studia Podhalańskie oraz bibliografia pasterstwa Tatr i Podhala.* Wrocław: Zakład Narodowy Imienia Ossolińskich, Wydawnictwo Polskiej Akademii Nauk.

Appadurai, Arjun. 1996. *Modernity at Large: Cultural Dimensions of Globalization.* Minneapolis: University of Minnesota Press.

Austerlitz, Paul. 2000. "Birch-Bark Horns and Jazz in the National Imagination: The Finnish Folk Music Vogue in Historical Perspective." *Ethnomusicology* 44(2):183–213.

Bachleda-Księdzularz, Franciszek. 1981. "Prawda i fałsz w tańcu góralskim." *Podhalanka* 1(6):35–41.

———. 1984. "Owieczki na halach." *Podhalanka* 1(9):4–7.

Barber, Karin, and Christopher Waterman. 1995. "Traversing the Global and the Local: Fújì Music and Praise Poetry in the Production of Contemporary Yorùbá Popular Culture." In *Worlds Apart: Modernity through the Prism of the Local,* ed. Daniel Miller, 240–262. New York: Routledge.

Barth, Fredrik. 1996 [1969]. "Ethnic Groups and Boundaries." In *Theories of Ethnicity: A Classical Reader,* ed. Werner Sollors, 294–324. New York: New York University Press.

Barz, Gregory F., and Timothy J. Cooley, eds. 1997. *Shadows in the Field: New Perspectives for Fieldwork in Ethnomusicology.* New York: Oxford University Press.

Bauman, Richard, Patricia Sawin, and Inta Gale Carpenter. 1992. *Reflections on the Folklife Festival: An Ethnography of Participant Experience.* Bloomington: Indiana University Special Publications of the Folklore Institute no. 2.

Baumann, Max Peter. 1996. "Folk Music Revival: Concepts between Regression and Emancipation." *The World of Music* 38(3):71–86.

———, ed. 2001. "Folk Music in Public Performance." Thematic issue of *The World of Music* 43(2+3).

Bendix, Regina. 1985. *Progress and Nostalgia.* Berkeley: University of California Press.

———. 1989. "Tourism and Cultural Displays: Inventing Traditions for Whom?" *Journal of American Folklore* 102:131–46.

———. 1997. *In Search of Authenticity: The Formation of Folklore Studies.* Madison: University of Wisconsin Press.

Benet, Sula. 1979 [1951]. *Song, Dance, and Customs of Peasant Poland.* With a preface by Margaret Mead. New York: Roy.

Bielawski, Ludwik. 1961. "Wstęp." In Adolf Chybiński, *O polskiej muzyce ludowej: Wybór prac etnograficznych*, ed. Ludwik Bielawski, 7–20. Kraków: Polskie Wydawnictwo Muzyczne.

Bohlman, Philip V. 2002a. *World Music: A Very Short Introduction.* Oxford: Oxford University Press.

———. 2002b. "World Music at the 'End of History.' " *Ethnomusicology* 46(1):1–32.

Borneman, John. 1996. "Until Death Do Us Part: Marriage/Death in Anthropological Discourse." *American Ethnologist* 23(2):215–238.

Boym, Svetlana. 2001. *The Future of Nostalgia.* New York: Basic Books.

Brożek, Andrzej. 1985. *Polish Americans: 1854–1939.* Warsaw: Interpress.

Brzozowicz, Grzegorz, and Maciej Chmiel. 1994. "Najlepsi w 1993 r." *Gazeta Stołeczna*, 7 January 1994, weekend section, 9.

Brzozowska, Teresa. 1965. "Zbójnictwo." In *Słownik Folkloru Polskiego*, ed. Juliana Krzyżanowskiego, 464–465. Warsaw: Wiedza Powszechna.

Budak, Józef. 1991. "Nazwa Zakopane i nazwy terenowe miasta Zakopanego." In *Zakopane: czterysta lat dziejów*, ed. Renata Dutkowa, 1:492–503. Kraków: Krajowa Agencja Wydawnicza.

Cantwell, Robert. 1984. *Bluegrass Breakdown: The Making of the Old Southern Sound.* Urbana: University of Illinois Press.

———. 1991. "Conjuring Culture: Ideology and Magic in the Festival of American Folklife." *Journal of American Folklore* 104(412):148–163.

———. 1993. *Ethnomimesis: Folklife and the Representation of Culture.* Chapel Hill: University of North Carolina Press.

Cebula, Ewa. 1992. "Działalność artystyczna i organizacyjna Studenckiego Zespołu Góralskiego 'Skalni' w zakresie popularyzacji folkloru" (Artistic and organizational activities of the student Górale troupe "Skalni" in the realm of the popularization of folklore). Master's thesis. Kraków: Akademia Wychowania Fizycznego.

Ceribašić, Naila. 1998. "Folklore Festivals in Croatia: Contemporary Controversies." *The World of Music* 40(3):25–49.

Chapman, Malcolm. 1993. "Social and Biological Aspects of Ethnicity." In *Social and Biological Aspects of Ethnicity*, ed. Malcolm Chapman, 1–46. Oxford: Oxford University Press.

Chirot, Daniel. 1976. *Social Change in a Peripheral Society: The Creation of a Balkan Colony.* New York: Academic Press.

Chodurska, Elżbieta. 1996. *Festiwal '96: XXVIII Międzynarodowy Festiwal Folkloru Ziem Górskich* (festival program book). Zakopane: Urząd Miasta.

Chybiński, Adolf. 1922. "Z dawnej pasterskiej poezji i muzyki górali podhalańskich." *Wierchy* 1:98–111.

———. 1961. *O polskiej muzyce ludowej: Wybór prac etnograficznych.* Edited by Ludwik Bielawski. Kraków: Polskie Wydawnictwo Muzyczne.

Čiurlionytė, Jadvyga. 1980. "Union of Soviet Socialist Republics, §VII, 2: Lithuania, folk music." In *The New Grove Dictionary of Music and Musicians*, ed. Stanley Sadie, 19:373–377. London: Macmillan.

Clinton, Hillary Rodham. 1996. *It Takes a Village: And Other Lessons Children Teach Us.* New York: Simon and Schuster.

Cohen, Erik. 1988. "Authenticity and Commoditization in Tourism." *Annals of Tourism Research* 15:371–386.

Cole, John W. 1984. "Reflections on the Political Economy of Ethnicity." In *Ethnic Challenge: The Politics of Ethnicity in Europe*, ed. Hans Vermeulen and Jeremy Boissevain, 84–99. Göttingen: Edition Herdot.

Comaroff, John L. 1987. "Of Totemism and Ethnicity: Consciousness, Practice, and the Signs of Inequality." *Ethnos* 52(3–4):301–323.

——. 1996. "Ethnicity, Nationalism, and the Politics of Difference in an Age of Revolution." In *The Politics of Difference: Ethnic Premises in a World of Power,* ed. Edwin N. Wilmsen and Patrick McAllister, 162–183. Chicago: University of Chicago Press.

Connerton, Paul. 1989. *How Societies Remember.* Cambridge: Cambridge University Press.

Cooley, Timothy J. 1997. "Casting Shadows in the Field: An Introduction." In *Shadows in the Field: New Perspectives for Fieldwork in Ethnomusicology,* ed. Gregory F. Barz and Timothy J. Cooley, 3–19. New York: Oxford University Press.

——. 1998. "Authentic Troupes and Inauthentic Tropes." *Polish Music Journal* 1(1). Los Angeles: University of Southern California. Online: www.usc.edu/dept/polish_music/PMJ/issues.html.

——. 1999a. "Folk Festival as Modern Ritual in the Polish Tatra Mountains." *The World of Music* 41(3):31–55.

——. 1999b. "Ethnography, Tourism, and Music-culture in the Tatra Mountains: Negotiated Representations of Polish Górale Ethnicity." Ph.D. dissertation, Brown University.

——. 2000. "Constructing an 'Authentic' Folk Music of the Polish Tatras." In *After Chopin: Essays in Polish Music,* ed. Maria Trochimczyk, 243–261. Polish Music History series, vol. 6. Los Angeles: Polish Music Center at University of Southern California.

——. 2001. "Repulsion to Ritual: Interpreting Folk Festivals in the Polish Tatras." *Ethnologies* 23(1):233–253.

——. 2003. "Theorizing Fieldwork Impact: Malinowski, Peasant-Love, and Friendship." *British Journal of Ethnomusicology* 12(1):1–17.

Cooley, Timothy J., and Dick Spottswood. 1997a. *Fire in the Mountains: Polish Mountain Fiddle Music.* Vol. 1: *The Karol Stoch Band.* Compact disc recording with notes. Newton, N.J.: Yazoo, a division of Shanachie Entertainment Corp.

——. 1997b. *Fire in the Mountains: Polish Mountain Fiddle Music.* Vol. 2: *The Great Highland Bands.* Compact disc recording with notes. Newton, N.J.: Yazoo, a division of Shanachie Entertainment Corp.

Cruz, Jon. 1999. *Culture on the Margins: The Black Spiritual and the Rise of American Cultural Interpretation.* Princeton, N.J.: Princeton University Press.

Ćwiżewicz, Krzysztof. 2001. "Musical Rites of Entertainment among Górale of the Polish Tatra Mountains." Ph.D. dissertation, University of London, Goldsmiths' College.

Ćwiżewicz, Krzysztof, and Barbara Ćwiżewicz. 1995. "Music of the Tatra Mountains: The Trebunia Family Band." Compact disc recording with notes. Monmouth: Nimbus Records.

Czekanowska, Anna. 1990. *Polish Folk Music: Slavonic Heritage, Polish Tradition, Contemporary Trends.* Cambridge: Cambridge University Press.

Dąbrowska, Grażyna. 1995. "Dance in the Transformations of the Harvest Customs in Poland." In *Dance, Ritual, and Music,* ed. Grażyna Dąbrowska and Ludwik Bielawski, 63–69. Warsaw: Instytut Sztuki PAN.

Dahlig, Ewa. 1991. "Traditional Musical Instruments and Tourism: The Case of Złóbcoki." In *Schladminger Gespräche zum Thema Musik und Tourismus,* ed. Wolfgang Suppan, 83–87. Tutzing: Hans Schneider.

Dawson, Andrew H. 1991. "Poland." In *Tourism and Economic Development in Eastern Europe and the Soviet Union,* ed. Derek R. Hall, 190–202. London: Belhaven.

DeWitt, Mark F., ed. 1999. "Music, Travel, and Tourism." Thematic issue of *The World of Music* 41(3).

Długołęcka, Lidia, and Maciej Pinkwart. 1992. *Muzyka i Tatry*. Warszawa: Wydawnictwo PTTK "Kraj."

Dobrowolski, Kazimierz. 1938. *Dwa studia nad powstaniem kultury ludowej w karpatach zachodnich*. Krakow: Drukarnia Uniwersytetu Jagiellońskiego.

Dorson, Richard. 1976. *Folklore and Fakelore: Essays toward a Discipline of Folk Studies*. Cambridge, Mass.: Harvard University Press.

Durkheim, Emile. 1915. *The Elementary Forms of the Religious Life*. Translated by J. W. Swain. London: Allen and Unwin.

Dutkowa, Renata, ed. 1991. *Zakopane: czterysta lat dziejów* (Zakopane: four hundred years of history). 2 vols. Kraków: Krajowa Agencja Wydawnicza.

Elschek, Óskár. 2001. "Folklore Festivals and Their Current Typology." *The World of Music* 43(2+3):153–169.

Elscheková, Alica, ed. 1981. *Stratigraphische Probleme der Volksmusik in den Karpaten und auf dem Balkan*. Bratislava: Verlag der Slowakischen Akademie der Wissenschaften.

Eriksen, Thomas Hylland. 1993. *Ethnicity and Nationalism: Anthropological Perspectives*. London: Pluto.

Erlmann, Veit. 1996. "The Aesthetics of the Global Imagination: Reflections on World Music in the 1990s." *Public Culture* 8(3):467–487.

————. 1999. *Music, Modernity, and the Global Imagination: South Africa and the West*. New York: Oxford University Press.

Errington, Frederick, and Deborah Gewertz. 1989. "Tourism and Anthropology in a Post-Modern World." *Oceania* 60(1):37–54.

Fabian, Johannes. 1983. *Time and the Other: How Anthropology Makes Its Object*. New York: Columbia University Press.

Feld, Steven. 2001. "A Sweet Lullaby for World Music." In *Globalization*, ed. Arjun Appadurai, 189–216. Durham, N.C.: Duke University Press.

Fenton, Steve. 1999. *Ethnicity: Racism, Class and Culture*. Lanham, Md.: Rowman and Little.

Filene, Benjamin. 2000. *Romancing the Folk: Public Memory and American Roots Music*. Chapel Hill: University of North Carolina Press.

————. 2004. *"O Brother,* What Next? Making Sense of the Folk Fad." *Southern Cultures* 10(2).

Frith, Simon. 1996. *Performing Rites: On the Value of Popular Music*. Cambridge, Mass.: Harvard University Press.

Garofalo, Reebee. 2002. *Rockin' Out: Popular Music in the USA*. 2nd ed. Upper Saddle River, N.J.: Prentice Hall.

Gąsowski, Tomasz. 1991. "Rozwój demograficzny Zakopanego w latach 1770–1978." In *Zakopane: czterysta lat dziejów*, ed Renata Dutkowa, 1:392–418. Kraków: Krajowa Agencja Wydawnicza.

Gewertz, Deborah, and Frederick Errington. 1991. "We Think, Therefore They Are? On Occidentalizing the World." *Anthropological Quarterly* 64(2):80–91.

Goffman, Erving. 1956. *The Presentation of Self in Everyday Life*. Edinburgh: University of Edinburgh Social Sciences Research Centre.

Gołaszcziński. 1851. "Śpiewy i tańce ludu góralskiego pod Karpatami w obwodzie Sandeckim ułożone na Pianoforte i Violin przez Gołaszcziński 851." Manuscript in the Bibliotece Warszawskiego Towarzystwa Muzycznego, #7695.

Gorączkiewicz, Wincenty. 1829. *Krakowiaki. Zebrane i ułożone na fortepiano*. Vienna: Dom Biasoni.

Goszczyński, Seweryn. 1853. *Dziennik podróży do Tatrów*. Petersburg: Nakładem B. M. Wolffa.

Greenhill, Pauline. 2001. "Festival." Thematic issue of *Ethnologies* 23(1).

Greenwood, Davydd J. 1977. "Culture by the Pound: An Anthropological Perspective on Tourism as Cultural Commoditization." In *Hosts and Guests: The Anthropology of Tourism*, ed. Valene L. Smith, 129–138. Philadelphia: University of Pennsylvania Press.

Gromada, Thaddeus V. 1975. "Zakopane's Golden Age." *Tatrzański Orzeł* 28(2): 6–8.

———. 1982. " 'Góral' Regionalism and Polish Immigration to America." In *Pastor of the Poles: Polish American Essays Presented to Right Reverend Monsignor John P. Wodarski in Honor of the Fiftieth Anniversary of His Ordination*, ed. Stanislaus A. Blejwas and Mieczysław B. Biskupski, 105–115. New Britain, Conn., Central Connecticut State College: Polish Studies Program Monographs.

Guilbault, Jocelyne. 1993. *Zouk: World Music in the West Indies*. With Gage Averill, Édouard Benoit, and Gregory Rabess. Chicago: University of Chicago Press.

Gut-Stapińska, Aniela. 1928. "Zwyczaje i zabobony ludu podhalańskiego w okresie świąt Bożego Narodzenia." *Kurier Literacko-Naukowy*, no. 53.

———. 1933a. "Wesele góralskie." *Kurier Literacko-Naukowy*, no. 5.

———. 1933b. "Burso, nieznany zabytek folklorystyczny na Podhalu." *Kurier Literacko-Naukowy*, no. 41.

———. 1938. "O strój i gwarę podhalańską." *Zagon*, no. 1.

Gutt-Mostowy, Jan. 1998. *Podhale: A Companion Guide to the Polish Highlands*. New York: Hippocrene.

Guy, Nancy. 1999. "Governing the Arts, Governing the State: Peking Opera and Political Authority in Taiwan." *Ethnomusicology* 43(3):508–526.

Hagedorn, Katherine. 2001. *Divine Utterances: The Transformation of Memory in Afro-Cuban Performance*. Washington, D.C.: Smithsonian.

Hall, Derek R., ed. 1991. *Tourism and Economic Development in Eastern Europe and the Soviet Union*. London: Belhaven.

Hebdige, Dick. 1979. *Subculture: The Meaning of Style*. London: Methuen.

Hławiczka, Karol. 1936. "Najstarszy zbiór melodyj pieśni i tańców podhalańskich." *Muzyka Polska* 3(4):253–263.

Hobsbawm, Eric, and Terence Ranger, eds. 1983. *The Invention of Tradition*. Cambridge: Cambridge University Press.

Holst-Warhaft, Gail. 1992. *Dangerous Voices: Women's Laments and Greek Literature*. London: Routledge.

Hood, Mantle. 1960. "The Challenge of 'Bi-Musicality.' " *Ethnomusicology* 4(1): 55–59.

———. 1982 [1971]. *The Ethnomusicologist*. New ed. Kent, Ohio: Kent State University Press.

Hornbostel, Erich M. von. 1975 [1905]. "The Problems of Comparative Musicology." Translated from the German by Richard Campbell, "Die Probleme der vergleichenden Musikwissenschaft." In *Hornbostel Opera Omnia*, ed. Klaus P. Wachsmann, Dieter Christensen, and Hans-Peter Reinecke, 247–270. The Hague: Martinus Nijhoff.

Jabłońska, Teresa, Anna Liscar, and Stefan Okołowicz. 2002. *Tatry*. Translations by Teresa Bałuk-Ulewiczowa. Lesko: BOSZ. Co-publisher: Zakopane: Muzeum Tatrzańskie im. dra Tytusa Chałubińskiego.

Jackowski, Antoni. 1991. "Rozwój funkcji turystycznej Zakopanego w okresie międzywojennym (1918–1939)" (The development of the function of tourism in Zakopane in the interwar period [1918–1939]). In *Zakopane: czterysta lat dziejów*, ed. Renata Dutkowa, 2:22–36. Kraków: Krajowa Agencja Wydawnicza.

Jameson, Fredric. 2000. *The Jameson Reader.* Edited by Michael Hardt and Kathi Weeks. Malden, Mass.: Blackwell.

Janota, Eugeniusz. n.d. Unpublished manuscript of seven cards. Formerly included in a larger folder entitled "Tecka po śp. Bronisławie Gustawiczu" (Portfolio after the late Bronisław Gustawicz) in the Ethnographic Museum of Kraków. Currently filed separately in a dual filing system: II/187 or I/236/ RKP. Handwritten title on the folio reads "Trębita—Rogoźnik. Obchód w śpiewie Sałasów Pod Karpackich z okolicy NowegoTargu" (Alpine horn— Rogoźnik. Celebration in song of the huts beneath the Carpathians around Nowy Targ).

Jazowska-Gumulska, Maria. 1994. "Tradycja i współczesność regionalizmu podhalańskiego." *Pomerania*, no. 10:31–34.

Kaeppler, Adrienne, and Olive Lewin, eds. 1988. *Come Mek Me Hol' Yu Han': The Impact of Tourism on Traditional Music.* Papers presented at the Fourth International Colloquium of the International Council for Traditional Music held in Kingston and Newcastle, Jamaica. 10–14 July 1986. Kingston: Jamaica Memory Bank.

Kantor, Józef. 1907. "Czarny Dunajec, Monografia etnograficzna." *Materiały Antropologiczno-Archeologiczne i Etnograficzne* 9:116–141.

———. 1920. "Pieśń i muzyka ludowa Orawy, Podhala i Spisza." *Pamiętnik Towarzystwa Tatrzańskiego* 37:178–204.

Kaufman, Nikolai. 1988. *Pogrebalni i drugi oplakvaniia v Bulgariia* (Funerals and laments in Bulgaria). Sofia: Izdvona Bulgarskata akademiia na naukite.

Keil, Charles, and Angeliki V. Keil. 1992. *Polka Happiness.* With photographs by Dick Blau. Philadelphia: Temple University Press.

Kenney, Padraic. 1997. "Polish Workers and the Stalinist Transformation." In *The Establishment of Communist Regimes in Eastern Europe, 1944–1949*, ed. Norman Maimark and Leonid Gibianskii, 139–166. Boulder: Westview.

Kirshenblatt-Gimblett, Barbara. 1988. "Authenticity and Authority in the Representation of Culture: The Poetics and Politics of Tourist Production." In *Kulturkontakt, Kulturkonflikt: Zur Erfahrung des Fremden*, ed. Ina-Maria Greverus, Konrad Köstlin, and Heinz Schilling, 59–69. Frankfurt am Main: Institut für Kulturanthropologie und Europäische Ethnologie, Universität Frankfurt am Main.

———. 1995. "Theorizing Heritage." *Ethnomusicology* 39(3):367–379.

———. 1998. *Destination Culture: Tourism, Museums, and Heritage.* Berkeley: University of California Press.

Kirshenblatt-Gimblett, Barbara, and Edward M. Bruner. 1992. "Tourism." In *Folklore, Cultural Performances, and Popular Entertainments: A Communications-centered Handbook*, ed. Richard Bauman, 300–307. New York: Oxford University Press.

Kleczyński, Jan. 1883. "Pieśń zakopiańska." *Echo Muzyczne i Teatralne*, no. 1:9–10.

———. 1884a. "Zakopane i jego pieśni." *Echo Muzyczne i Teatralne*, no. 41:419– 421, no. 42:429–430, no. 44:447–448, no. 46:468–470.

———. 1884b. "Wycieczka po melodie." *Echo Muzyczne i Teatralne*, no. 56:567– 569, no. 58:588–590, no. 60:610–611, no. 62:631–632, no. 64:653.

———. 1888. "Melodye zakopiańskie i podhalańskie." *Pamiętnik Towarzystwa Tatrzańskiego* 12:3–66. Krakow: Nakład Towarzystwa Tatrzańskiego.

Kleszcz, Jerzy, and Włodzimierz Kleszcz. 1992. J-card notes in *Twinkle Inna Polish Stylee: Higher Heights.* Warsaw: S1 Polish Radio and Kama, ca. 1992. Cassette.

Kleszcz, Włodzimierz. 1994. "Trebunie—Tutki wołają: 'Comeback Twinkle to

Trebunia Family.' " Promotional information passed out at a Polish Radio studio concert, Warsaw, 10 November.

Kligman, Gail. 1988. *The Wedding of the Dead: Ritual, Poetics, and Popular Culture in Transylvania*. Berkeley: University of California Press.

Kolberg, Oskar. 1968a. "Góry i Podgórze," part 1: *Dzieła Wszystkie*. Vol. 44. Wrocław: Polskie Towarzystwo Ludoznawcze.

———. 1968b. "Góry i Podgórze," part 2: *Dzieła Wszystkie*. Vol. 45. Wrocław: Polskie Towarzystwo Ludoznawcze.

Kolbuszewski, Jacek. 1982. *Tatry w literaturze polskiej*. Kraków: Wydawnictwo Literackie.

Konaszkiewicz, Zofia. 1987. *Funkcje wychowawcze dziecięcych i młodzieżowych zespołów muzycznych*. Warsaw: Centralny Ośrodek Metodyki Upowszechniania Kultury.

Kotoński, Włodzimierz. 1953a. "Uwagi o muzyce ludowej Podhala cz. I: O 'nutach' góralskich." *Muzyka* 4(5–6):3–25.

———. 1953b. "Uwagi o muzyce ludowej Podhala cz. II: O Materiał dzwiękowy, skale, harmonika." *Muzyka* 4(7–8):43–58.

———. 1953c. "Uwagi o muzyce ludowej Podhala cz. III: O twórczym sposobie wykonania." *Muzyka* 4(11–12):26–45.

———. 1954. "Uwagi o muzyce ludowej Podhala cz. IV: dokończenie." *Muzyka* 5(1–2):14–27.

———. 1955. *Piosenki z Podhala*. Kraków: Polkie Wydawnictwo Muzyczne.

———. 1956. *Góralski i zbójnicki: Tańce górali podhalańskich*. Kraków: Polskie Wydawnictwo Muzyczne.

Kubik, Josef. 1985. "Die Instrumentale Volksmusik in Podhale." *Jahrbuch für musikalische Volks-und Völkerkunde* 12:81–104.

Kulczycki, Zbigniew. 1970. *Zarys historii turystyki w Polsce*. Warszawa: Sport i Turystyka.

Kuropas, Myron B. 1986. Foreword to *Ethnicity and National Identity: Demographic and Socioeconomic Characteristics of Persons with Ukrainian Mother Tongue in the United States*, ed. Oleh Wolowyna, ix–xii. Cambridge, Mass.: Harvard Ukrainian Research Institute.

Larsen, Terri, ed. 1991. "The Year in Europe." *Reggae Report* 9(1):37.

Lehr, Urszula, and Danuta Tylkowa. 2000. "Wiadomości o regionie" (About the region). In *Podhale: Tradycja we współczesnej kulturze wsi*, ed. Danuta Tylkowa, 11–83. Kraków: Biblioteka Etnografii Polskiej, no. 55.

Lenk, Carsten. 1999. " 'Cultivated' Folk Music: More Invention Than Discovery? Appropriation and Mediation of Songs in East Bavaria." *The World of Music* 41(2):63–97.

Lewandowska, Bożena. 1982. "Stan badań kultury muzycznej Górali Polskich Karpat." *Etnografia Polska* 26(1):167–194.

Little, Kenneth. 1991. "On Safari: The Visual Politics of a Tourist Representation." In *The Varieties of Sensory Experience: A Sourcebook in the Anthropology of the Senses*, ed. David Howes, 148–163. Toronto: University of Toronto Press.

Lloyd, A. L. 1980. "Europe, §II: Eastern." In *The New Grove Dictionary of Music and Musicians*, ed. Stanley Sadie, 6:301–312. London: Macmillan.

Lomax, Alan. 1968. *Folk Song Style and Culture*. New Brunswick, N.J.: Transaction.

Lukes, Steven. 1975. "Political Ritual and Social Integration." *Sociology* 9:289–308.

MacAloon, John J., ed. 1984. *Rite, Drama, Festival, Spectacle: Rehearsals toward a*

Theory of Cultural Performance. Philadelphia: Institute for the Study of Human Issues.

MacCannell, Dean. 1989 [1976]. *The Tourist: A New Theory of the Leisure Class.* New York: Schocken.

Maciata-Lassak, Halina. 1993. " 'Piscołka,' 'fujarka,' 'końcowka': Podhalański instrument ludowy dawniej i dzisiaj." Master's thesis, Uniwersytet Jagielloński, Kraków.

Magocsi, Paul R. 1975. *An Historiographical Guide to Subcarpathian Rus'.* Cambridge, Mass.: Harvard Ukrainian Research Institute, Harvard University. Offprint series no. 1.

―――. 1994. *Our People: Carpatho-Rusyns and Their Descendants in North America.* Ontario: Multicultural History Society of Ontario.

Majda, Jan. 1991. "Środowisko literackie Zakopanego (do roku 1918)." In *Zakopane: czterysta lat dziejów,* ed. Renata Dutkowa, 2:288–338. Kraków: Krajowa Agencja Wydawnicza.

Malczak, Antoni. 1992. "Święto Dzieci Gór." Interview in newsletter *Latawice* (July–August). Nowy Sącz: Wojewódzki Ośrodek Kultury.

Marošević, Grozdana. 1998. "The Encounter between Folklore Studies and Anthropology in Croatian Ethnomusicology." *The World of Music* 40(3): 51–81.

Matlakowski, Władysław. 1901. *Zdobienie i sprzęt ludu polskiego na Podhalu.* Warsaw: Skład Główny w Księgarni E. Wendego i S-ki.

Merriam, Alan P. 1960. "Ethnomusicology, Discussion and Definition of the Field." *Ethnomusicology* 4:107–114.

―――. 1964. *The Anthropology of Music.* Evanston, Ill.: Northwestern University Press.

Mierczyński, Stanisław. 1930. *Muzyka Podhala.* Lwów: Książnica—Atlas.

―――. 1935. *Pieśni Podhala na 2 i 3 równe głosy.* Warszawa: Wydawnictwo Związku Nauczycielstwa Polskiego.

Miller, Elżbieta, Agata Skrukwa, and Medard Tarko. 1973. *Dzieła wszystkie Oskara Kolberga: Katalog wystawy* (Catalog to the complete works of Oskar Kolberg). Translated by James Sehnert. Warsaw: Ludowa Spółdzielnia Wydawnicza.

Moore, Robin. 1997. *Nationalizing Blackness: Afrocubanismo and Artistic Revolution in Havana, 1920–1940.* Pittsburgh: University of Pittsburgh Press.

Morris, Leon. 1990. "Lech, I'm only Gdansk-ing!" *Echoes* (January 13): 18.

Nagengast, Carole. 1991. *Reluctant Socialists, Rural Entrepreneurs: Class, Culture, and the Polish State.* Boulder: Westview.

Naglak, Anna. 1981. "Kulturotwórcze i wychowawcze funkcje studenckiego zespołu góralskiego 'Skalni' " (Kultural and educational function of the student Górale troupe "Skalni"). Master's thesis. Kraków: Instytut Pedagogiki Uniwersytet Jagielloński.

Nevskaia, Lidiia Georgievna. 1993. Balto-slavianskoe prichitanie: rekonstruktsiia semanticheskoi struktury (Laments). Moskva: Nauka.

Noll, William H. 1986. "Peasant Music Ensembles in Poland: A Culture History." Ph.D. dissertation, University of Washington.

―――. 1991. "Economics of Music Patronage among Polish and Ukrainian Peasants to 1939." *Ethnomusicology* 35(3):349–379.

Nuñez, T. A. 1963. "Tourism, Tradition, and Acculturation: Weekendismo in a Mexican Village." *Ethnology* 2(3):347–352.

Okamoto, Sachiko. 2001. "Polish Highlander Music in Chicago: Górale Identity and Musical Tradition." Master's thesis, Indiana University, Bloomington.

Paryski, Witold H. 1991. "Powstanie zakopiańskiego ośrodka turystycznego (do 1914 r.)" (Origins of Zakopane as a tourist center [to 1914]). In *Zakopane: cztery-*

sta lat dziejów, ed. Renata Dutkowa, 2:7–21. Kraków: Krajowa Agencja Wydawnicza.

Pekacz, Jolanta. 1992. "On Some Dilemmas of Polish Post-Communism Rock Culture." *Popular Music* 11(2):205–208.

Pertierra, Raul. 1987. "Ritual and the Constitution of Social Structure." *Mankind* 17(3):199–211.

Peterson, Richard A. 1997. *Creating Country Music: Fabricating Authenticity*. Chicago: University of Chicago Press.

Pieterse, Jan Nederveen. 1996. "Varieties of Ethnic Politics and Ethnicity Discourse." In *The Politics of Difference: Ethnic Premises in a World of Power*, ed. Edwin N. Wilmsen and Patrick McAllister, 25–44. Chicago: University of Chicago Press.

Piotrowski, Marcin. 1986. *Zespół Folklorystyczny w życiu Kulturalnym wsi współczesnej: Studium wybranych zespołów Polski centralnej* (Folklore troupes in the cultural life of contemporary villages: Study of select troupes in central Poland). Warszawa: Centralny Ośrodek Metodyki Upowszechniania Kultury.

Price, Richard, and Sally Price. 1994. *On the Mall: Presenting Maroon Tradition-Bearers at the 1992 FAF*. Bloomington: Indiana University, Special Publications of the Folklore Institute, no. 4.

Przerembski, Zbigniew Jerzy. 1981. "Z badań nad preferencjami muzycznymi górali podhalańskich." *Muzyka* 3–4:85–112.

———. 1986. "Regionalne zróżnicowanie kulminacji melodycznej w polskich pieśniach ludowych." *Muzyka* 2:33–43.

———. 1987. "Do interpretacji skali góralskiej." *Muzyka* 2:39–54.

———. 1989. "O niektórych archaicznych cechach śpiewów górali podhalańskich." *Muzyka* 4:31–49.

Radwańska-Paryska, Zofia, and Witold Henryk Paryski. 1995. *Wielka encyklopedia Tatrzańska*. Poronin: Wydawnictwo Górskie.

Reinfuss, Roman. 1971. *Jesień Tatrzańska: Migawki festiwalowe*. Kraków: Polskie Wydawnictwo Muzyczne.

Remes, Pieter. 1999. "Global Popular Musics and Changing Awareness of Urban Tanzanian Youth." *Yearbook for Traditional Music* 31:1–26.

Rice, Timothy. 1994. *May It Fill Your Soul: Experiencing Bulgarian Music*. Chicago: University of Chicago Press.

———. 1997. "Toward a Mediation of Field Methods and Field Experience in Ethnomusicology." In *Shadows in the Field: New Perspectives for Fieldwork in Ethnomusicology*, ed. Gregory F. Barz and Timothy J. Cooley, 101–120. New York: Oxford University Press.

Robertson, Roland. 1992. *Globalization: Social Theory and Global Culture*. London: Sage.

Ronström, Owe. 1996. "Revival Reconsidered." *The World of Music* 38(3):5–20.

Rosaldo, Renato. 1989. *Culture and Truth: The Remaking of Social Analysis*. Boston: Beacon.

Ryback, Timothy. 1990. *Rock around the Bloc: A History of Rock Music in Eastern Europe*. New York: Oxford University Press.

Sadownik, Jan, ed. 1971 [1957]. *Pieśni Podhala: Antologia*. Kraków: Polskie Wydawnictwo Muzyczne.

Said, Edward. 1978. *Orientalism*. New York: Pantheon.

Sarkissian, Margaret. 2000. *D'Albuquerque's Children: Performing Tradition in Malaysia's Portuguese Settlement*. Chicago: University of Chicago Press.

Schechner, Richard. 1982. "Collective Reflexivity: Restoration of Behavior." In *A Crack in the Mirror: Reflexive Perspectives in Anthropology*, ed. Barbara Myerhoff and Jay Ruby, 39–81. Philadelphia: University of Pennsylvania Press.

———. 1983. *Performative Circumstances: From the Avant Garde to Ramila*. Calcutta: Seagull.

Scruggs, T. M. 1999. " 'Let's Enjoy as Nicaraguan': The Use of Music in the Construction of a Nicaraguan National Consciousness." *Ethnomusicology* 43(2):297–321.

Sharp, Cecil J. 1954. *English Folk Song: Some Conclusions*. 3rd ed. Revised by Maud Karpeles with an appreciation by Ralph Vaughan Williams. London: Methuen.

Shelemay, Kay Kaufman. 1997. "The Ethnomusicologist, Ethnographic Method, and the Transmission of Tradition." In *Shadows in the Field: New Perspectives for Fieldwork in Ethnomusicology*, ed. Gregory F. Barz and Timothy J. Cooley, 189–204. New York: Oxford University Press.

Slobin, Mark, ed. and trans. 1982. *Old Jewish Folk Music: The Collections and Writings of Moshe Beregowski*. Philadelphia: University of Pennsylvania Press.

———. 1984. "*Klezmer* Music: An American Ethnic Genre." *Yearbook for Traditional Music*. 16:34–41.

———. 1992. "Micromusics of the West: A Comparative Approach." *Ethnomusicology* 36(1):1–87.

———. 1996a. "Bosnia and Central/Southeast Europe: Musics and Musicians in Transition." In *Worlds of Music: An Introduction to the Music of the World's Peoples*, ed. Jeff Todd Titon, 3rd ed., 211–251. New York: Schirmer.

———, ed. 1996b. *Retuning Culture: Musical Changes in Central and Eastern Europe*. Durham, N.C.: Duke University Press.

Smith, Valene L., ed. 1977. *Hosts and Guests: The Anthropology of Tourism*. Philadelphia: University of Pennsylvania Press.

Sollers, Werner, ed. 1996. *Theories of Ethnicity: A Classical Reader*. New York: New York University Press.

Spafford, Aaron. 2002. "Tuning Analysis of Polish Fiddle Music in the Gorale Region." Senior Project, University of California, Santa Barbara.

Stęszewski, Jan. 1970. "Polish Folk Music." *Polish Music/Polnische Musik* 5(2):5–11.

———. 1980. "Poland, II: Folk Music." In *The New Grove Dictionary of Music and Musicians*, ed. Stanley Sadie, 15:29–39. London: Macmillan.

Stokes, Martin, ed. 1994. *Ethnicity, Identity, and Music: The Musical Construction of Place*. Oxford: Berg.

Stopka, Andrzej. 1897. *Sabała*. Kraków: L. Zwoliński i Spółka.

———. 1898. "Materyały do etnografii Podhala (Zakopane, Kościelisko, Poronin, Czarny Dunajec)." *Materyały Antropologiczno-Archeologiczne i Etnograficzne* 3: 73–166.

Styrczula-Maśniak, Edward. 1991. "Muzykanci spod Giewontu: Kapela Maśniaków z Kościeliska" (Musicians beneath Giewont: The Maśniak Music Group from Kościelisko). Master's thesis, Uniwersytet Jagielloński, Kraków.

Sugarman, Jane C. 1997. *Engendering Song: Singing and Subjectivity at Prespa Albanian Weddings*. Chicago: University of Chicago Press.

———. 1999. "Imagining the Homeland: Poetry, Songs, and the Discourses of Albanian Nationalism." *Ethnomusicology* 43(3):419–458.

Suliteanu, Ghisela. 1971. "The Traditional System of Melodic Prose of the Funeral Songs Recited by the Jewish Women of the Socialist Republic of Rumania." In *Folklore Research Center Studies*, ed. D. Noy, 3:291–349. Jerusalem: Hebrew University.

Sulzer, Franciszek Józef. 1782. "Walachische Tänze und Lieder." *Geschichte des Transalpinischen Daciens*, vol. 3.

Suppan, Wolfgang. 1976. "Research on Folk Music in Austria since 1800." *Yearbook of the International Folk Music Council* 8:117–129.

———, ed. 1991. *Schladminger Gespräche zum Thema Musik und Tourismus.* Tutzing: Hans Schneider.

Szurmiak-Bogucka, Aleksandra. 1959. *Górole, górole, góralko muzýka: Śpiewki Podhala.* Kraków: Polskie Wydawnictwo Muzyczne.

———. 1974. *Wesele góralskie.* Kraków: Polskie Wydawnictwo Muzyczne.

———. 1991. "Muzyka i taniec ludowy." In *Zakopane: czterysta lat dziejów,* ed. Renata Dutkowa, 1:694–711. Kraków: Krajowa Agencja Wydawnicza.

Szurmiak-Bogucka, Aleksandra, and Kazimierz Bogucki. 1961. "Stan badań nad folklorem muzycznym i tanecznym na terenie Polskich Karpat." *Etnografia Polska* 5:277–287.

Szymanowski, Karol. 1999. *Szymanowski on Music: Selected Writings of Karol Szymanowski.* Edited and translated by Alistair Wightman. London: Toccata.

Taylor, Timothy D. 1997. *Global Pop: World Musics, World Markets.* New York: Routledge.

Theurer, Johannes. 1993–94. "World Music Charts Europe." Compiled on behalf of the World Music Workshop of the European Broadcasting Union. Radio B2, Berlin.

Titon, Jeff Todd. 1985. "Stance, Role, and Identity in Fieldwork among Folk Baptists and Pentacostals in the United States." *American Music* 3:16–24.

———. 1997. "Knowing Fieldwork." In *Shadows in the Field: New Perspectives for Fieldwork in Ethnomusicology,* ed. Gregory F. Barz and Timothy J. Cooley, 87–100. New York: Oxford University Press.

———, ed. 1996. *Worlds of Music: An Introduction to the Music of the World's Peoples.* 3rd ed. New York: Schirmer.

Tolbert, Elizabeth Dawn. 1988. "The Musical Means of Sorrow: The Karelian Lament Tradition." Ph.D. dissertation, University of California, Los Angeles.

Trebunia-Staszel, Stanisława. 1995. "Znaczenie i funkcje stroju podhalańskiego we współczesnym życiu mieszkańców Podhala." *Wierchy* 61:125–142.

———. 1997. " 'Góralem nie wystarczy się czuć, góralem trzeba być . . . ' o świadomości regionalnej młodzieży podhalańskiej." *Krakowskie Studie Molopolskie* 1(2):23–38.

———. 2000. "Rola podhalańskiego ruchu regionalnego w kształtowaniu kultury regionu." Ph.D. dissertation, Jagiellonian University, Kraków.

Turino, Thomas. 2000. *Nationalists, Cosmopolitans, and Popular Music in Zimbabwe.* Chicago: University of Chicago Press.

Turner, Victor. 1973. "Symbols in African Ritual." *Science* 179(4078):1100–1105.

———. 1984. "Liminality and the Performative Genres." In *Rite, Drama, Festival, Spectacle: Rehearsals toward a Theory of Cultural Performance,* ed. John J. MacAloon, 19–41. Philadelphia: Institute for the Study of Human Issues.

Tylkowa, Danuta, ed. 2000. *Podhale: Tradycja we współczesnej kulturze wsi.* Kraków: Biblioteka Etnografii Polskiej, No. 55.

Vermeulen, Hans. 1984. Introduction to *Ethnic Challenge: The Politics of Ethnicity in Europe,* ed. Hans Vermeulen and Jeremy Boissevain, 7–13. Göttingen: Edition herdot.

Wade, Peter. 2000. *Music, Race, and Nation: Música Tropical in Colombia.* Chicago: University of Chicago Press.

Walser, Robert. 1995. "Rhythm, Rhyme, and Rhetoric in the Music of Public Enemy." *Ethnomusicology* 39(2):193–217.

Warner, Elizabeth A. 1990. "The Russian Folk Song and Village Life." In *Russian*

Traditional Folk Song, ed. Elizabeth A. Warner and Evgenii Kustowskii, 18–67. Hull, England: Hull University Press.

Warszyńska, Jadwiga. 1991. "Ruch turystyczny w Zakopanem po drugie wojnie światowej." In *Zakopane: czterysta lat dziejów*, ed. Renata Dutkowa, 2:37–52. Kraków: Krajowa Agencja Wydawnicza.

Wedel, Janine R., ed. 1992. *The Unplanned Society: Poland during and after Communism*. New York: Columbia University Press.

Whisnant, David E. 1983. *All That Is Native and Fine: The Politics of Culture in an American Region*. Chapel Hill: University of North Carolina Press.

Wilmsen, Edwin N. 1996. "Introduction: Premises of Power in Ethnic Politics." In *The Politics of Difference: Ethnic Premises in a World of Power*, ed. Edwin N. Wilmsen and Patrick McAllister, 1–23. Chicago: University of Chicago Press.

Wnuk, Włodzimierz. 1981. *Na góralską nutę*. Warszawa: Instytut Wydawniczy Pax.

———. 1985. *Górale za wielką wodą*. Warsaw: Ludowa Spółdzielnia Wydawnicza.

Wnuk, Włodzimierz, and Andrzej Kudasik. 1993. *Podhalański Ruch Regionalny*. Kraków: Oficyna Podhalańska.

Wolf, Erik R. 1994. "Perilous Ideas: Race, Culture, People." *Current Anthropology* 35(1):1–12.

Wrazen, Louise. 1988. "The *Góralski* of the Polish Highlanders: Old World Musical Traditions from a New World Perspective." Ph.D. dissertation, University of Toronto.

———. 1991. "Traditional Music Performance among Górale in Canada." *Ethnomusicology* 35(2):173–193.

Wytrwal, Joseph A. 1977. *Behold: The Polish-Americans*. Detroit: Endurance.

Zborowski, Juliusz. 1930. "Regionalizm podhalański za oceanem." *Ziemia* 15(23): 486–488.

———. 1972 [1930]. "Moda i wieś góralska." In *Pisma Podhalańskie*, ed. Janusz Berghauzen, 1:329–346. Kraków, Wydawnictwo Literackie.

Zejszner, Ludwik. 1845. *Pieśni ludu Podhalan, czyli górali tatrowych polskich*. Warsaw: Drukarnia pod Fir. J. Kaczanowskiego.

Illustrations

Audio Examples

Except where otherwise indicated, the recordings on the CD accompanying this book were made by Cooley. The CD was mastered by Kevin Kelly at the University of California, Santa Barbara. Special thanks to the following record companies for permissions to reproduce their recordings: Yazoo (tracks 10 and 13), Gamma (track 33), Twinkle Music (tracks 32 and 34), Kamahuk (tracks 32, 34, and 35), and Folk (track 36).

1. *Pasterska*, performed by the troupe *Skalni* at a festival in Zakopane (ac19.viii.92.4) (fig. 1.6).
2. *Wierchowa*, performed by *Góralska Kapela* from Chicago, at the University of California, Santa Barbara. Bogusława Łowisz, Zdzisław Miernicki, voices; Jan Rózalowski, *prym*; Stanisław Zatłoka, *sekund*; Andrzej Tokarz, *basy*. Recorded by Diana Lantz, 25.iv.2003 (fig. 1.7).
3. *Ozwodna*, performed by the troupe *Skalni* at a festival in Zakopane (ac19.viii.92.4) (fig. 1.8).
4. *Sabałowa*, instrumental. Performed in a funeral procession for Józef Karpiel, in Kościelisko. Stanisław Michałczek, first *prym*; Marek (Maja) Łabunowicz, second *prym*; Bronisław Styrczula-Maśniak, Józef Styrczula-Maśniak, and Zdzisław Styrczula-Maśniak, *sekund*; and Tadeusz Styrczula-Maśniak, *basy* (v1.xii.94) (fig. 1.9).
5. *Duchowa*, instrumental. Performed graveside at the funeral for Stanisława Styrczula-Maśniak in Kościelisko. Also audible are the sounds of rain and the gravedigger shoveling dirt into the grave. Musicians included Jan Karpiel-Bułecka, *prym*; Stanisław Michałczek, *prym*; Stanisław Styrczula-Maśniak, *sekund*; Andrzej Frączysty, *sekund*; and Janusz Zatorski-Sieczka, *basy* (v30.v.95) (fig. 1.11).
6. *Krzesana* "wiecno." Marion Styrczula-Maśniak, *prym*; Władysław Styrczula-Maśniak, *sekund*; Stanisław Styrczula-Maśniak, *basy* (dv10.i.2003) (fig. 1.13).
7. *Krzesana* "po dwa" (in two). Marion Styrczula-Maśniak, *prym*; Władysław Styrczula-Maśniak, *sekund*; Stanisław Styrczula-Maśniak, *basy* (dv10.i.2003) (fig. 1.14).
8. *Krzesana* "po śtyry" (in four). Marion Styrczula-Maśniak, *prym*; Władysław Styrczula-Maśniak, *sekund*; Stanisław Styrczula-Maśniak, *basy* (dv10.i.2003) (fig. 1.15).
9. *Krzesana* "trzy a roz" (three and one), as played by Paweł Staszel, *prym*, with *Skalni* at a festival in Zakopane. Women can be heard singing a *pasterska* in the background (ac19.viii.92.4) (fig. 1.16).
10. "Marsz Madziarski"/"Hej Madziar Pije," with different text ("Marsz Góralski"). Performed in 1929, in Chicago, by Stanisław Bachłeda, voice; Karol Stoch, *prym*; Józef Nowobielski and Franciszek Chowaniec, *sekund*; and Stanisław Tatar, *basy* (re-released on Yazoo 7012 in 1997; reproduced with permission) (fig. 1.17).
11. "Marsz Chałubińskiego," performed by Krzysztof Trebunia-Tutka, demonstrating voice with *sekund*, followed by *prym* and then *sekund* alone (dv9.i.2003) (fig. 1.18).

12. *Cepowiny*, at the wedding of Halina Maciata and Tomasz Lassak in Chicago (ac25.ix.93.2) (fig. 1.20).
13. "Zielona" *nuta* 1. Performed in 1929, in Chicago, by Stanisław Bachłeda, voice; Karol Stoch, *prym*; Józef Nowobielski and Francisek Chowaniec, *sekund*; and Stanisław Tatar, *basy* (re-released on Yazoo 7012 in 1997; reproduced with permission) (fig. 1.24).
14. "Zielona" *nuta* 2. Performed by *Skalni* at a festival in Zakopane (ac19.viii.92.4) (fig. 1.25).
15. *Wierchowa*, probably Władysław Trebunia-Tutka on *prym* (ac19.vii.92.1) (fig. 1.28).
16. *Sabałowa*. Stanisława Szostak, *prym*; Władysław Trebunia-Tutka, second *prym* and *sekund* (ac19.vii.92.1) (fig. 1.29).
17. "Mój Janicku nie bij ze mnie," Stanisława Szostak, lead singer and *prym* (ac19.vii.92.1) (fig. 1.30).
18. "Slovak tune (waltz)," Stanisława Szostak, *prym* (ac19.vii.92.1) (fig. 1.31).
19. *Pasterska*, Stanisława Szostak, lead singer (ac19.vii.92.1) (fig. 1.32).
20. "Hej ta helpa" (csárdás), probably Stanisława Szostak on *prym* (ac19.vii.92.1) (fig. 1.33).
21. *Pasterska*, singing led by Stanisława Szostak, followed by an instrumental repeat, and then a *wierchowa*, Władysław Trebunia-Tutka, *prym*, and Stanisława Szostak, *sekund* (ac19.vii.92.1) (fig. 1.3).
22. Early recording of Bartuś Obrochta, probably made in 1914 by Juliusz Zborowski. Courtesy of the Muzeum Tatrzańskie (fig. 1.13). This suite contains a *Sabałowa*, a *krzesana* or *drobna*, and a *zielona*. Like the other known recordings of Obrochta, the original wax cylinder recording was reportedly worn out by Adolph Chybinski who used them when making his transcriptions of Obrochta's *nuty* (see Chybinski 1961, 508–528). Although the sound quality is poor, the masterful violin playing comes through.
23. *Wierchowa*, Krzysztof Trebunia-Tutka and Paweł Staszel, double-*prym* style (ac19.viii.92.1) (fig. 4.8).
24. Demonstration. *Wierchowa* interrupted by Władysław Trebunia-Tutka, who begins an explanation of the different violin parts (continued through track 31).
25. Demonstration. Władysław Trebunia-Tutka, second-*prym* part (v22.vii.95) (fig. 4.9).
26. Demonstration. Władysław Trebunia-Tutka, first-*prym* part (v22.vii.95) (fig. 4.10).
27. Demonstration. Władysław Trebunia-Tutka, second-*prym* part, continued (v22.vii.95) (fig. 4.11).
28. Demonstration. Władysław Trebunia-Tutka, first *sekund* part (v22.vii.95) (fig. 4.12).
29. Demonstration. Władysław Trebunia-Tutka, second *sekund* part (v22.vii.95) (fig. 4.13).
30. Demonstration. Władysław Trebunia-Tutka's historical explanation of style.
31. Demonstration. Władysław Trebunia-Tutka, first *sekund* part (v22.vii.95) (fig. 4.14).
32. "Skanking on the Grass," by Norman Grant and Władysław Trebunia-Tutka based on traditional music and text, Twinkle Brothers and Tutki: *Twinkle Inna Polish Stylee: Higher Heights* (Kama and Twinkle Music 1992; re-released in 1997 on CD by Twinkle Music and Kamahuk; reproduced with permission) (fig. 5.3).
33. "Pod Jaworkem," Kapela Krzysztofa Trebuni-Tutki: *Żywot Janicka Zbójnika* (Gamma 1992; reproduced with permission) (fig. 5.5).

34. "Husband the Outlaw," by Norman Grant and Władysław Trebunia-Tutka based on traditional music and text, Twinkle Brothers and Tutki: *Twinkle Inna Polish Stylee: Higher Heights* (Kama and Twinkle Music 1992; re-released in 1997 on CD by Twinkle Music and Kamahuk; reproduced with permission) (fig. 5.6).

35. "Nasze Reggae (Pamięci Boba)," a tribute to Bob Marley based on a song by Victor Ford, arranged by Krzysztof Trebunia-Tutka with new words by Włodzimierz Kleszcz and Trebunie-Tutki: *Trebunie-Tutki w Sherwood* (Kamahuk 1996; reproduced with permission) (see pp. 195–196).

36. "Nie patrzcie przez lupy," words by Izabela Zając with music by Włodzimierz Kiniorski, Michał Pastuszka, Krzysztof Trebunia-Tutka, and Andrzej Rajski, Trebunie-Tutki and Kinior Future Sound: *Etno-Techno* (Folk 2000; reproduced with permission) (figs. 5.13 and 5.14).

37. Last verse of a hymn followed by a *pytace* song (fig. 7.4), and "wybodną." Singing led by Andrzej Słodyczka and Stanisław Lasak (v14.i.95.1).

38. *Cepowiny: pytace* song beginning the *cepowiny* (v14.i.95.2) (fig. 7.5).

39. *Cepowiny: pytace* Andrzej Słodyczka and Stanisław Lasak singing to the hostesses, using the *nuta* in figure 7.5 (v14.i.95.2) (see pp. 230 and 232).

40. *Cepowiny:* hostesses Anna Gąsienica-Roj, and Helios and Maria Stopka, singing to the *pytace* (v14.i.95.2) (fig. 7.6) (see pp. 232 and 234).

41. *Cepowiny: pytace* singing to the hostesses (v14.i.95.2) (fig. 7.7) (see pp. 232 and 235).

42. *Cepowiny: pytace* continue singing to the hostesses, using the *nuta* in figure 7.6 (v14.i.95.2) (see pp. 233–234).

43. *Cepowiny:* hostesses respond to *pytace,* using a variation of the *nuta* in figure 1.20 (v14.i.95.2) (see pp. 40 and 233).

44. *Cepowiny: pytace* singing to hostesses using the *nuta* in figure 7.7 (v14.i.95.2) (see pp. 233 and 235).

45. Funeral procession for Józef Karpiel, Kościelisko. Chants related to the Requiem Mass procession (Ave Maria) (v1.xii.94). The casket was carried on a horse-drawn carriage, which is also audible on this track (see p. 242).

46. Wierchowa played during funeral procession for Józef Karpiel in Kościelisko. Stanisław Michałczek, first *prym;* Marek (Maja) Łabunowicz, second *prym;* Bronisław Styrczula-Maśniak, Stanisław Styrczula-Maśniak, Józef Styrczula-Maśniak, and Zdzisław Styrczula-Maśniak, *sekund;* and Tadeusz Styrczula-Maśniak, *basy* (v1.xii.94). Also audible is the barking of dogs as the procession moves past their yards, and the sound of church bells as the procession approaches the church (see p. 242).

47. Wierchowa and Sabałowa played graveside at the funeral for Józef Karpiel, Kościelisko. Jan Karpiel-Bułecka, *prym;* Andrzej Frączysty, *sekund;* Stanisław Michałczek, Marek (Maja) Łabunowicz, Bronisław Styrczula-Maśniak, Stanisław Styrczula-Maśniak, Józef Styrczula-Maśniak, and Zdzisław Styrczula-Maśniak, *sekund;* and Tadeusz Styrczula-Maśniak and Janusz Zatorski-Sieczka, *basy* (v1.xii.94). The sound of dirt being tossed into the grave is audible at the very end of the track (see p. 243).

Index

TIMOTHY J. COOLEY is Assistant Professor of Music at the University of California, Santa Barbara, and co-editor (with Gregory F. Barz) of *Shadows in the Field: New Perspectives for Fieldwork in Ethnomusicology*.